HUMBOLDT'S
MEXICO

HUMBOLDT'S MEXICO

In the Footsteps of the Illustrious
German Scientific Traveller

Myron Echenberg

McGill-Queen's University Press
Montreal & Kingston • London • Chicago

© McGill-Queen's University Press 2017

ISBN 978-0-7735-4940-1 (cloth)
ISBN 978-0-7735-4941-8 (ePDF)
ISBN 978-0-7735-4942-5 (ePUB)

Legal deposit second quarter 2017
Bibliothèque nationale du Québec

Printed in Canada on acid-free paper

McGill-Queen's University Press acknowledges the support
of the Canada Council for the Arts for our publishing
program. We also acknowledge the financial support of the
Government of Canada through the Canada Book Fund
for our publishing activities.

Library and Archives Canada Cataloguing in Publication

Echenberg, Myron J., author
Humboldt's Mexico : in the footsteps of the illustrious
German scientific traveller / Myron Echenberg.

Includes bibliographical references and index.
Issued in print and electronic formats.
ISBN 978-0-7735-4940-1 (cloth).
– ISBN 978-0-7735-4941-8 (ePDF).
– ISBN 978-0-7735-4942-5 (ePUB)

1. Humboldt, Alexander von, 1769–1859 – Travel – Mexico.
2. Germans – Travel – Mexico. 3. Scientists – Travel –
Mexico. 4. Mexico – History. 5. Mexico – Description
and travel. I. Title.

Q143.H9E35 2017   509.2   C2017-900560-X
                                        C2017-900561-8

Contents

Illustration Sources and Abbreviations · vii

Figures, Map, and Tables · ix

Chronology and Map of Humboldt's Itinerary in New Spain, 1803–1804 · xi

Mesoamerican Chronology · xiii

Preface · xv

Acknowledgments · xix

Introduction: Humboldt's Achievements · xxi

Prologue: Humboldt's Mexican Adventure in Historical Context · xxxiii

PART ONE
Arrival in Mexico, 23 March to 12 April 1803: From Acapulco to Mexico City

1 Acapulco: The Place of Broken Reeds · 3

2 Diego Rivera's Imagery · 11

3 Chilpancingo and Guerrero State: A Gruelling Climb through the Rugged Sierra Madre del Sur Mountain Range · 19

4 Humboldt and Colonial Governance in New Spain · 25

5 Taxco: The Baroque Legacy of the First Great Colonial Silver Mine · 34

6 William Spratling and Silver Jewellery Design in Taxco · 39

7 Cuernavaca: A Brief Stay in the Valley of Eternal Spring · 53

8 Ecological and Economic History in the Mexican Tableland Valleys of Anáhuac (Toluca, Mexico, and Puebla) · 61

9 Mexico City: Humboldt's Stay in the City of Palaces · 74

10 Culture and Higher Learning in Humboldt's Mexico · 84

PART TWO
Visits to the Mexican Heartland, 14 May to 10 October 1803:
Silver Mines and Active Volcanoes

11   Pachuca, Land of Mines, and Mining Haciendas · 101
12   Cornishmen and Women Settle in the Pachuca Region · 109
13   Guanajuato: An Exhausting Month at New Spain's Richest
       Silver Mine · 116
14   Humboldt the Mining Inspector and Mexican Silver Mining · 123
15   Morelia (Colonial Valladolid): Colonial Crafts and the Ascent
       of a Live Volcano · 135
16   The Principal Volcanoes of the Mexican Highlands · 142

PART THREE
Homeward Bound, 30 January to 7 March 1804:
Demography, Disease, and Departure from Veracruz

17   Puebla: Churches, Libraries, and Beautiful Pottery · 157
18   Humboldt to the Fore Again: Water Issues and Mexican
       Demographic History · 164
19   Xalapa: A Brief Stay in the City of Flowers · 169
20   The Ruins of Zempoala in the Gulf Lowlands · 174
21   Veracruz: Journey's End · 182
22   The Impact of Smallpox and Yellow Fever on Mexico · 190

Conclusion: Humboldt's Legacy · 198
A Guide to Publications by or about Alexander von Humboldt
   in Mexico · 209
A Guide to Readings on Humboldt · 213
Citations · 215
Bibliography · 219
Index · 227

Illustration Sources and Abbreviations

I gratefully acknowledge the following persons and institutions – identified by acronyms in the text – for the photographs and illustrations in this book.

ADM   "Los dos volcanes, Popocatepetl e Iztaccihuatl." *Artes de Mexico*, no. 73 (2005).

AKR   Kettenmann, Andrea. *Rivera*. Cologne: Taschen, 2006.

APV   *Atlas del patrimonio natural, histórico y cultural de Veracruz, II*. Veracruz: Gobierno de Estado, 2010.

ATG   *Atlas geográfico y físico del Reino de la Nueva España*, edited by Charles Minguet and Jaime Labastida. Mexico City: Siglo XXI, 2003.

CEH   Fundación, Carlos Slim. *Centro historico, 10 anos de revitalización*. Mexico City: n.d.

HCU   Labastida, Jaime, ed. *Humboldt, ciudadano universal*. Mexico City: Siglo XXI, 1999.

LUW   Klencke, Herman. *Alexander von Humboldt's leben und wirken, reisen und wissen*. Leipzig: Verlag von Otto Spamer, 1870.

UNV   Holl, Frank, ed., *Los viajes de Humboldt: Una nueva visión del mundo, Antiguo Colegio de San Ildefonso, 25 Sept. 2003–25 Jan. 2004*. Mexico: 2003–04.

VDC   *Vues des Cordillères et monuments des peuples indigènes de l'Amerique*. Paris: Schoell, 1810.

Figures, Map, and Tables

FIGURES

2.1 Diego Rivera, *The Creation*, 1922–23 • 13
2.2 Diego Rivera, *Nude with Calla Lilies*, 1944 • 15
6.1 The Spratling logo • 45
9.1 Central Square and Tolsá's El Caballito statue, cast in 1803 • 79
9.2 Humboldt's house, 3 Calle de San Agostín, today, 80 Calle de Uruguay • 81
9.3 Statue of Humboldt, donated by Emperor Wilhelm II and erected in 1910 on the grounds of the Convent of San Agustín • 82
10.1 Humboldt's sketch of volcanoes of Puebla • 85
10.2 Humboldt's sketch of the peak of Orizaba • 85
10.3 Velatri codex hieroglyphs in Borgia Museum, Velatri • 86
10.4 Sun Stone, popularly called the "Calendar Stone," unearthed in 1790 • 89
10.5 Coatlicue (Serpent Skirt) • 90
11.1 San Miguel Regla Hacienda • 104
11.2 Basalt formations and falls • 108
15.1 Humboldt and his companions near El Jorullo Volcano, after a sketch by Alexander von Humboldt • 138
16.1 Gerardo Murillo (Dr Atl), *Popocatépetl*, 1908 • 153
16.2 Luis Nishizawa, *El Regresso* • 154
17.1 Cholula pyramid, after a sketch by Alexander von Humboldt • 158
20.1 Ruins of Zempoala • 175
21.1 The port of Veracruz in 1804 • 183

MAP

Humboldt's route through New Spain, 1803–04 • x

TABLES

8.1 Rainfall in seven cities of Anáhuac, 1976 • 64
16.1 Principal volcanoes of the Mexican highlands • 143

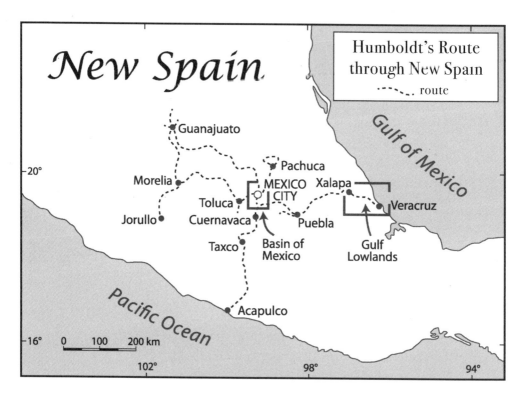

Humboldt's route through New Spain, 1803–04

Chronology and Map of Humboldt's Itinerary in New Spain, 1803–1804

1803

23 March – arrives in Acapulco.

29 March – departure for Mexico City.

31 March – reaches Papagayo River.

1 April – reaches pine forests and cooler air.

2 April – arrives in Chilpancingo.

3 April – reaches Zumpango, Zopilote, and Mezcala.

5 April – from Tepecoacuilco to Taxco and departure
   via Tehuilotepec.

6 April – arrives in Iguala, Cocula, and Tlacotepec.

9 April – arrives in Puente de Ixtla.

10 April – arrives in Cuernavaca and Huitzilac.

12 April – arrives in Mexico City, excursions around the city for
   rest of month.

14 May – trip to Pachuca.

15 May – arrives in Pachuca.

17 May – climbs El Cerro de Zumate.

19 May – to Minas de la Regla, of Conde de Regla, Sr Terreros.

20 May – visits Hacienda de Regla.

21 May – travels to Atotonilco el Grande.

22 May – travels near Puente de la Madre de Dios and sleeps in los
   Baños de Atotonilco, next to village of Magdalena.

23 May – travels to Actopan.

24 May – travels in Actopan region.

25 May – from Actopan to Carpio.

26 May – arrives in morning in Mexico City.

1 August – departure for Guanajuato. Sleeps that evening in town
   of Huehuetoca.

2 August – in Arroyo Zarco, staying at travellers' inn.

3 August – in San Juan del Río.

4 August – arrives in Querétaro and spends night at Celaya.

7 August – arrives in Guanajuato.

10 September – trip to El Jorullo, through Bajío, via Irapuato and the Yuririapúndaro lagoon. Sleeps that night in Salamanca.

14 September – arrives in Morelia on his birthday.

17 September – arrives in Pátzcuaro.

19 September – climbs El Jorullo.

21 September – returns to Pátzcuaro.

22 September – in Morelia.

24 September – in Zinapécuaro.

28 September – travels through Maravatío and Ixtlahuaca to Toluca.

29 September – spends entire day on Nevado de Toluca.

30 September – departure for Mexico City.

October–December – Humboldt's diary does not provide dates for the last three months of 1803, spent in Mexico City. Presumably the time was devoted to research and to packing the travellers' considerable goods as they prepared for the return trip to Europe via Veracruz.

1804

9–12 January – visit to Huehuetoca with the viceroy.

20 January – to Chalco, Río Frio, Texmelucan; arrives in Puebla.

22 January – Puebla.

24 January – visits pyramid at Cholula.

26 January – to Cofre de Perote.

7 February – collects plant and rock samples on slopes of Perote volcano and repeats exercise on Pico de Orizaba a few days later.

10 February – arrives in Xalapa.

15 February – leaves for Veracruz.

19 February – arrives in Veracruz.

7 March – sails for Havana, although had hoped to leave on 23 February.

29 April – leaves Havana for US.

22 May – enters Delaware River bound for Philadelphia.

9 July – departs for Bordeaux.

1 August – arrives at mouth of Garonne River, in front of Bordeaux.

Mesoamerican Chronology *

PRECLASSIC

Early	San Lorenzo	1200–1000 BCE
Middle	La Venta, Monte Albán	1000–300 BCE
Late	Teotihuacán	300 BCE–300 CE

CLASSIC

Early	Tikal, Copán	300–600 CE
Late	El Tajín, Uxmal	600–900 CE

POSTCLASSIC

Early	Tula, Mitla	900–1200 CE
Late	Tenochtitlán	1200–1500 CE

*Adapted from Malmstrom, *Cycles of the Sun, Mysteries of the Moon*, Chapter 2.

Preface

Alexander von Humboldt was born into the minor Prussian nobility at Tagel, the family estate, near Berlin, on 14 September 1769, three years after the birth of his elder brother, the distinguished linguist and philosopher Wilhelm, and two months after that of Napoleon Bonaparte, whose path Alexander would cross on several occasions. He died on 6 May 1859, and his state funeral in Berlin four days later drew thousands of admirers, ranging from the Prussian royal family to ordinary citizens.

Much has been written about Humboldt in virtually every European language. He himself wrote in French, Spanish, and German, and left over thirty volumes of publications, a few diaries, and literally thousands of letters. Yet, while Humboldt's name sounds so familiar, few informed readers associate him with Mexican science, travel, and what today might be called tourism. In her recent and outstanding *The Invention of Nature*, Andrea Wulf has given English-speaking readers the best biography to date of the intrepid German scientist. Nevertheless, she devoted only a page or two to Humboldt's year-long Mexican adventures but an entire chapter to his interaction with Thomas Jefferson. Even scholars specializing in Mexico have in most cases only read excerpts of Humboldt's writings, culling his work for their own purposes and interests, such as whether, for example, to describe the colonial economy and especially silver mining as resulting from Mexico's demographic situation around the year 1800 or to search for clues to Aztec archaeology and art history.

The main reasons for such selective reading stem from the scattered and opaque nature of Humboldt's writings on Mexico, which are found in several works, many editions, and in multiple languages. Two works do stand out. By far the most comprehensive and important is his *Political Essay on the Kingdom of New Spain* (PE), whether in its original four volumes or in its abridged single volume in English, Spanish, or French. The first English edition appeared in 1811, the same year the original French edition was published in Paris by Schoell. The work went through nine editions in the second and third decades of the nineteenth century, four in English, two in French, two in Spanish, and one in German. It was a publishing record for the time and did much to destroy the old myths and ancient prejudices about Spanish America while attracting admiring attention to New Spain among northern European readers. The Mexican historian Vivó Escoto has called the *Political Essay* "the first modern description of our nation. Thanks to it, Mexico could become widely known in the European world." He adds that the work covered virtually everything, "mines, land, sky, water, plants, animals, people," and that it was the "first great synthesis of our nation."

The second major source is what is known as Humboldt's *Tage-bücher*, or confidential diaries and notebooks. This material has been edited, reorganized, and translated by German scholars in Berlin, led by Ulrike Leitner and Margot Faak. Of special note are Leitner's *Alexander von Humboldt: Von Mexiko-Stadt nach Veracruz, Tagebuch*, and Faak's *Alexander von Humboldt: Reise auf dem Río Magdalena, durch die Anden und Mexico.*

Humboldt's diaries belong to the von Heinz family, descendants of elder brother Wilhelm, and can be found in the manuscript department of the Berlin State Library at Schloss Tegel in Berlin. Because they record the voluminous scientific observations and measurements of Humboldt, they run to over nine volumes, but they also note his private views on a variety of political and social issues. They bolster his analysis, especially as they contain sometimes angry criticism of Spanish colonialism that he did not want to appear in his formal published works, lest he offend his royal host Charles IV. The efforts of Leitner and Faak have made it possible for scholars to consult this material both in its original French and in translated portions in German, English, or Spanish. The diaries are especially useful for the latter part of Humboldt's Mexican voyage, from Puebla to Veracruz in 1804, where the *Political Essay* is either cursory or silent.

Humboldt's Mexico is divided into three parts, with odd-numbered chapters describing the cities and regions Humboldt visited in the order corresponding to his itinerary in Mexico, beginning with Chapter 1 on Acapulco and ending with Chapter 21 on Veracruz. The even-numbered chapters, beginning with Chapter 2 on Diego Rivera's imagery and ending with Chapter 22 on the impact of smallpox and yellow fever on Mexico, are parallel chapters reflecting on aspects of Humboldt's passage and meditating on his journey within the broader context of Mexican history and culture. Part 1 contains the first ten chapters, from Humboldt's arrival in Acapulco on 23 March to his stay in Mexico City beginning on 12 April 1803. Part 2, chapters 11 through 16, consists of visits to the Mexican heartland as far north as Guanajuato from 14 May to 10 October 1803. Lastly, Part 3, chapters 17 to 22, covers Humboldt and his companions from their departure from Mexico City on 30 January through to their sailing from Veracruz on 7 March 1804.

Humboldt's name is venerated in his native Germany and in Latin America, but virtually forgotten in the English-speaking world, save for the naming of natural phenomena after him. Best known is the Humboldt Current, the cold water flow off the coast of Chile and Peru that acquired his name in 1840. Maps of the world reveal towns, rivers, mountains, and lakes bearing his name, few of which he ever visited. He travelled extensively in what is now Cuba, Venezuela, Colombia, Bolivia, Peru, and Mexico during his remarkable five-year voyage from 1799 to 1804. His stopover in the United States on his way back to Europe was very brief, confined to Philadelphia and Washington, DC, but this has not prevented hyperbolic but ahistorical efforts to appropriate his name. For example, an excerpt in the town history of Humboldt, South Dakota, declares boldly that the town "was named in honor of the great German naturalist-botanist-scientist, the Baron Alexander von Humboldt, who was known to have accompanied the railroad builders on their way west to the land of the buffalo and the Indian"!

Acknowledgments

While I cannot recall when I first heard of Alexander von Humboldt, this project has been a wonderful voyage of discovery for me. Humboldt had so fallen out of favour in the world of science by the mid-twentieth century that I probably never heard him mentioned during my otherwise excellent formative education in the public school system of English-speaking Quebec. I likely first heard his name mentioned in 1965 when I visited Peru, where my wife, Eva, was born. For her, growing up in Lima, Humboldt was famous for the ocean current that was named after him and that so affected the climate and sea life around the Equator.

This project has enabled me to explore fascinating subjects, among them late eighteenth-century German Enlightenment liberalism, Mexican art history, and the history of science. I have learned much, and while I have emerged with great admiration for this intellectual giant, I hope not to have stumbled into the biographer's trap of blindness over the subject's shortcomings. Humboldt's view of the universe as a unified whole governed by both social and scientific laws is very attractive to me. Before I ever encountered Humboldt, his philosophy of the unity of knowledge and nature echoed strongly in my teaching of the history of health and disease in the Third World, where my medical science students were exposed to social elements of health and my social science and humanities students to necessary principles about the behaviour of pathogens.

I am greatly indebted to many who have accompanied me on this journey. My two friends and Latin American historians at McGill, Catherine LeGrand and Daviken Studnicki-Gizbert, put up with my many questions about Mexican history, and Catherine graciously read an earlier draft of the text. Their counsel has helped me avoid some of the pitfalls awaiting historians working outside their established fields, but my stubbornness has no doubt illustrated the penalties of ignoring their advice. I am also grateful to three McGill friends and colleagues, Rosalind Boyd, Margaret Lock, and Brian Young, whose advice and encouragement sustained my confidence in this project. Fieldwork in Mexico involved travelling in Humboldt's footsteps, and my companions were, in addition to my wife, good friends and good sports Ruth and Tony Shine, Claudia and Will Graham, and Mary and Tom Sosnowski. Their patience held firm as they put up with wild goose chases, while I endured puns such as whether my project on Humboldt was "still current." Tony Shine also gave valuable suggestions on the book cover and layout of the artwork. Eva believed in my sometimes eclectic project and encouraged me at every step. To her I owe the greatest debt.

The same devotion was present among my extended family. My son-in-law, Juan Hernández Cordero, is an applied scientist at the Universidad Nacional Autónoma de México, and he facilitated my contact with like-minded Mexicans. His appreciation of my interests grew gradually but steadily. My daughter Margo's knowledge of Mexican history and culture completed the other side of the intellectual equation. Katya, Siena, and Lía usually tolerated their grandfather's obsession, though occasionally they chorused, "Not Humboldt again!"

At McGill-Queen's University Press, executive director Philip Cercone and associate managing editor Kathleen Fraser gave unfailing enthusiasm and support. I am grateful to Judith Turnbull for her thorough and patient editing. The two anonymous peer-reviewers used by the press offered valuable suggestions, and graphic artist Isabelle Champoux produced the map of Humboldt's travels in Mexico.

ƒ

Humboldt's Achievements

It is impossible to resist superlatives in accounting for Humboldt's accomplishments. His entire Mexican adventure was a remarkable achievement, requiring a scientific understanding and the physical stamina few individuals could have claimed then or now.

Humboldt and his two travelling companions, the French botanist Aimé Bonpland and the Ecuadorean adventurer Charles Montúfar, spent 350 days in Mexico. They first touched down at the Pacific port of Acapulco on 23 March 1803 after a long and harrowing voyage from Guayaquil, Ecuador, and they departed from Veracruz on 7 March 1804. Acapulco, once the terminal of Spain's illustrious Manila Galleon trade from East Asia, had become a somewhat seedy port by the time Humboldt visited, but he was still able to describe the coast as *one of the most picturesque we ever saw.** Heading for the colonial capital of New Spain, Humboldt next traversed what Mexicans still call *la tierra caliente*, the torrid lands of the tortuous Sierra Madre del Sur range, where dusty granite rocks helped the daytime temperatures exceed 33°C. These difficult conditions in what is now the State of Guerrero failed to deter Humboldt and his party from taking their meticulous geological readings and noting the tropical vegetation. As always, Humboldt was equipped with no less than thirty-six of the

.

*I have chosen to italicize all direct quotes from Humboldt.

most modern instruments modern science could provide. In addition to standard sextants and barometers, these included such specialized equipment as a cyanometer to gauge the blueness of the sky and an inclinometer to measure the horizontal component of the intensity of the Earth's magnetism.

After a brief respite at Chilpancingo, now the state capital of Guerrero, Humboldt entered cooler pine forests en route for Taxco, the first of three great silver-mining towns on Humboldt's itinerary. Taxco made a poor impression on him during his overnight stay. He found that the famous silver lode was almost played out and the town's lavish baroque architecture not to his more austere taste. Next, the travellers entered the fertile Cuernavaca valley, home to what Humboldt dubbed "the city of eternal spring" in reference to the benign climate that had attracted generations of rulers to Cuernavaca, dating back to Aztec times.

Only three weeks from landing in Acapulco, on 12 April 1803, Humboldt entered *the city of palaces*, his nickname for Mexico City, after struggling through changing temperatures, high altitude, and difficult roads. The capital, where he would live for seven months (not counting brief excursions to the surrounding towns), took his breath away. *There is no city in all of Europe*, he gushed, *which in general appears more beautiful than Mexico.* He adored the urban layout, the handsome architecture, and the colourful markets. The snow-capped volcanoes of Popocatépetl and Iztaccíhuatl provided a majestic vista, while the archives and libraries of the city, to which he was afforded unprecedented access, gave him unique insights into the political economy of Spain's remarkable colony. What is often overlooked by observers is that Humboldt was attracted also to the Mesoamerican past, and he dedicated long hours to the study of pre-Hispanic art and culture.

Because he valued the human element in nature, Humboldt did not neglect disciplines such as history, anthropology, political economy, or what today are called "area studies." He was not a historian, but his influence on the writing of Mexican and Latin American history was substantial. His approach to the history of the continent was novel for his day. He was the first, for example, to see the continuity of pre-Columbian history and to include major polities like the Aztecs and the Incas not as exotic entities, but as major contributors to what he regarded as the narrative of the past. Columbus, Cortés, and the other *conquistadores* were important, of course, but they did not make all that preceded them irrelevant. Humboldt's penchant for the big narrative attracted others, not the least of whom was William H. Prescott, the scholarly American historian of the Spanish-speaking world in the mid-nineteenth century. Like Humboldt, Prescott believed in telling his story in narrative detail, and he attracted a huge general as well as scholarly readership. He wrote to Humboldt in 1843 to acknowledge how he had been guided by Humboldt's research.

Humboldt's writings on political economy are somewhat ambivalent. On the surface, he endorsed his sponsor, the Spanish Crown, by praising its creation in New Spain of a prosperous, reform-minded society. But a more careful reading reveals a deeper criticism, that centuries of Spanish rule had turned modern descendants of the ancient Aztecs into wretched victims and that the *odious monopoly* of Iberian commercial interests, together with financial mismanagement, had deprived New Spain of its glorious human and commercial potential. Writing in 1808, a time of great political upheavals in Europe in general and in the Iberian world in particular, Humboldt was cautious. His liberal, democratic sentiments and his passion for justice for the disinherited classes pointed him in the direction of supporting creole uprisings in Spanish America. But his hope that an enlightened Crown might still achieve some of his vision prevented him from overtly endorsing the rebellions in the colonies. In the view of the Mexican historian Enrique Krauze, Humboldt was "a mid-wife of Mexican consciousness" in that he helped support Mexico's transition to modernity.

Humboldt championed the study of the humanities in Mexico and was as proud of the achievements of the classical cultures of pre-Hispanic Mexico as he was of those maintained and developed by contemporaries in the late colonial period. He personally demonstrated a sustained research interest in the subject and saw his role to be that of godfather of this dazzling but little-known or appreciated cultural tradition in the wider European world. He basked in the

architectural pleasures of Mexico City and delighted in its importance as a centre of education and learning. Finally, he discussed the
social structure of Mexican society, arriving at harsh judgments over
the treatment of Indians.

Remarkably for a man trained in science, Humboldt made a
prodigious contribution to the emerging field of pre-Columbian, and
especially Aztec, art. Combining first-hand observation with a profound knowledge of documentary sources and an intense research
curiosity, he put forward evidence and comparative hypotheses of
great utility to later generations of art historians and anthropologists
interested in classical Mexican monuments.

Humboldt was the first non-state official to be granted access to
the colonial archives, and he made the most of this privilege. In
addition to conducting research on culture, he pored over raw economic and geographic information that he would publish in his later
writings. Among the unpublished documents were those pertaining
to the far north of America, from California to Nootka Sound.
He studied the voyages of Malaspina and Quadra, their maps and
diaries. He described beautiful colonial paintings that would fetch
a fortune on the London market, and a treasure trove of Indian
paintings done at the time of Cortés on subjects ranging from
genealogical trees to important battles. He was, however, disappointed by the lack of documents on Cortés's administration and
on the sixteenth century in general.

Humboldt was greatly impressed with the quality of higher education and training in Mexico City. His account of the state of arts
and science and of the men who taught these subjects is brimming
with superlatives. *No city of the new continent, without even excepting
those of the United States, can display such great and solid scientific
establishments as the capital of Mexico.*

One significant two-week excursion was a trip to a second silver-
mining region, Pachuca and Real del Monte, 100 kilometres north of
Mexico City. Humboldt not only documented the significant silver
production of the region but predicted that the mines would yield
still more wealth if Mexican or foreign mining capital were to invest
in technological improvements. Humboldt also praised the beauty

of the surrounding landscapes in the Huasca River valley, which offered some of the most spectacular sights in all of Mexico.

Next, in August, came a month's stay in Guanajuato, the third and wealthiest silver-mining city he visited, where the fabulous Valenciana mine ran in a straight line southeast and northwest of the town. The indefatigable Humboldt inspected every silver mine and climbed every mountain in the immediate region. He made three descents to the bottom of the Valenciana and was forced to rest for a week after enduring a nasty fall in one of the mines.

Well before he had undertaken his American voyages, Humboldt demonstrated both his scientific and his humanitarian skills in the applied field of mining and metallurgy. He was assigned by the Prussian administration as chief mining officer in remote northeastern Germany in 1792, when he was only twenty-three, and his inspection of mines showed his concern not only to increase production but also to bring about the social betterment of miners. He invented safety devices for miners, established a pension fund for them, and provided some applied education when, in 1794, on his own penny, he opened the Free Royal Mining School at Steben.

Mining was clearly one of Humboldt's principal areas of expertise and a significant reason for the Spanish Crown's decision to give him a free hand in visiting Mexico. The subject of Mexican silver mining, its technical aspects, its labour and sanitary conditions, its economic importance to New Spain, and its future prospects occupy a considerable portion of the *Political Essay*. The interest in mining helps explain the popularity of the book when it first appeared, especially among potential English investors, and its enduring value some 200 years later. David Brading, who has written the definitive study of mining and merchants in late colonial Mexico, lavishes high praise on the *Political Essay*, describing its "overwhelming excellence ... [as] a first-hand description of the industry that has never been superseded. Since then all students of Mexico's eighteenth-century economy have to some degree paraphrased Humboldt."

A major consequence of Humboldt's *Political Essay* was the attention it drew in northern Europe to the immense mineral resources of Mexico. Humboldt spoke so glowingly of silver mining and how it could be expanded to yield even greater profits if properly exploited that almost inevitably the result was a frenzy of investing in Paris and especially in London. After 1821, when Mexico had become independent, Humboldt was approached by European and Mexican financiers to participate in various mining ventures, but he would have none of it, pleading a *disinclination for public affairs* in a letter to his brother Wilhelm. Although some of these mining ventures were successful, speculation and unscrupulous operators created a bubble that burst in 1830, ruined many, and brought undeserved discredit to Humboldt's reputation among disgruntled investors. Having acted in good faith, Humboldt deeply resented the charge in the English press that he had led on investors with his exaggerated view of Mexico's mining potential. He defended himself by insisting that he had never offered investment advice nor sought to profit from his knowledge.

In September 1803, Humboldt and his party left Guanajuato to visit Michoacán, the province inhabited by Tarascan Indians who had been evangelized by the enlightened Spanish bishop Vasco de Quiroga. Humboldt praised the craft skills and industriousness of the Tarascans living around Lake Pátzcuaro, but what attracted him most was the newly formed live volcano, El Jorullo, located in the southern part of the province. His ascent of El Jorullo and the scientific observations he conducted there would represent a major scientific contribution to volcanology. Along with mines, mountains too were his passion, and on his return trip to Mexico City, Humboldt took the time to climb the snow-capped Nevado de Toluca, some 15,500 feet above sea level.

Humboldt was deeply interested in terrestrial magnetism, specifically the study of the Earth's geomagnetic field, and he contributed significantly to the progress of this new science. He carried out measurements of temporary disturbances of the Earth's magnetosphere, coining the term "magnetic storm" for this component of space weather. In the fields of comparative climatology, meteorology, and isoline cartography, Humboldt was a pioneer. He invented weather maps showing isotherms and isobars, which are still used today, typically on TV weather programs. Isotherms were lines connecting points with the same mean temperature, while isobars were lines connecting points with the same barometric pressure for a given time or period. Humboldt was alert to the presence of Mexican microclimates, such as the coastal dunes at Veracruz, problems of heat radiation in the forests of Guerrero, and the insulation properties of black-sand soils in the volcanic region of Michoacán. Humboldt was the first to observe reverse polarity and to discover a decrease in the planet's magnetic force from the poles to the Equator. He propagated the notion of seismic waves, and he coined the term "Jurassic" for the geological era of almost 200 million years ago.

Back in Mexico City in October 1803, Humboldt began preparations for his return to Europe. Conducting further research and filling trunks with new botanical and geological specimens, as well as with Indian codices and sculptures, occupied him and his team until late January 1804, when the group set off for Veracruz and the Gulf of Mexico. The journey would take them through two more important provincial towns, Puebla and Xalapa. Puebla, the second-largest city in New Spain, was endowed with beautiful colonial architecture and breathtaking views of the mountains and volcanoes of the Trans-Mexican Volcanic Belt, which surrounded the city in every direction. In his inimical fashion Humboldt could not resist visiting two of these slopes, the Cofre de Perote and the Pico de Orizaba. He and his companions collected numerous samples of rocks and plants on the slopes and admired the enterprise of Indians who carried ice from the snowy fields all the way to the coast at Veracruz to supply sherbet makers there. Like many before and after him, Humboldt was awed by the floral beauty of Xalapa, dubbing it the *city of flowers*. He recognized its microclimate, where warmth and moisture produced a natural greenhouse effect, earning the town a reputation as a floral wonder.

Many of Humboldt's interests involved the plants and animals that inhabited the planet. During their travels in South America and Mexico, Humboldt and Bonpland were the first to tabulate plant life in connection with meteorology and geography. Not only did they build a vast collection of new plants, they rejected the hierarchical

and racist views of Georges-Louis Leclerc, Comte de Buffon, and
many others who argued that all things American, whether plants,
animals, or humans, were "weaker" than or "immature" compared to
Europeans. Humboldt would return to this point in his master work
Cosmos, in which he would reject entirely *the depressing assumption
of inferior and of superior races of men*. Humboldt was also the first
to enumerate plants native to America before the Spanish conquest:
manioc, yucca, maize, potato, sweet potato, tomato, peanut, vanilla,
avocado, and cocoa. Humboldt and his companion were also the first
to send *curare* poison and *guano* back to Europe for analysis, which
led, in the case of *guano*, to a fertilizer boom on the Pacific coast of
South America.

From Xalapa, Humboldt and his party began the treacherous
descent to the coast, taking only three days to reach Veracruz on 19
February, where they hoped to embark quickly on a vessel to Cuba
and then on to Europe. There they cooled their heels until 7 March,
no doubt near exhaustion after their arduous adventures. Humboldt
spent his time completing his maps and observing living conditions
in Veracruz, then a port city infamous for being a major site of the
deadly yellow fever. Humboldt agreed the city was overcrowded and
unsanitary, but he refused to see the city only in negative terms. While
like other scientists he did not grasp the complex etiology of a viral
disease like yellow fever, which was transmitted by a mosquito vector,
Humboldt correctly recommended that sanitary improvements, such
as supplying the inhabitants with potable water and draining the
town's marshes, would dramatically improve the quality of public
health in the port.

ADMIRERS AND DETRACTORS

Most observers have nothing but admiration for Humboldt's
tremendous achievements. While some have resorted to hyperbole
in their praise, a minority have been detractors. The most influential critic is Mary Louise Pratt in her *Imperial Eyes: Travel Writing
and Transculturation*. She argues that Humboldt imposed a Western

rationalist model on Indigenous American peoples and cultures that deprived them of their originality and autonomy. In Mexico, a popular historian, José Iturriaga de la Fuente, is among the most severe of those nationalists who have decided that Humboldt's loyalties lay with opponents of Mexican liberalism and progress. A more sophisticated critic is Juan A. Ortega y Medina, a historian at the Universidad Nacional Autónoma de México (UNAM) who in 1960 published *Humboldt desde México*. He concludes that whether advertently or not, Humboldt's writings paved the way for expansionists in the United States who coveted Mexican land and resources. These arguments will be taken up in the appropriate place in this book, but they lack merit.

Far more substantial is the list of Humboldt's admirers ranging over time and space. Enrique Krauze has defended Humboldt against ahistorical nationalist criticisms and regards him as a friend of both the United States and the promising and progressive new state of Mexico. During his long life, Humboldt received praise from Mexican liberals and conservatives alike. Benito Juárez, the courageous liberal president who had rallied the country against the French invasion, honoured Humboldt after his death in 1859 with the title "Benefactor of the Nation" and commissioned a marble statue from Italy in memory of a man so committed to Mexican liberalism and progress. President Santa Anna conferred on Humboldt the Grand Cross of the Order of Guadaloupe in 1854 and even suggested a town be named in his honour, though this did not happen. Thanking him, the now elderly Humboldt wrote Santa Anna from Berlin on 22 December 1854 that he still believed in Mexico's potential for a prosperous future, *provided it was linked to progress in the arts and sciences.* Streets in several Mexican cities are named after him, and statues of him adorn prominent public places throughout the republic. Mexico's leading conservative politician and historian, Lucas Alamán y Escalada, shared an interest in mining engineering and politics with Humboldt, and the two men, sometimes agreeing to disagree, corresponded for over thirty years. In the early years of independence, in 1824, Alamán, as minister of interior and exterior relations, declared that "the entire nation is full of gratitude for your work" and invited him to pay a return visit. For a variety of reasons, however, Humboldt would never revisit the Americas.

Elsewhere in Latin America, Humboldt inspired a variety of figures. One was Simon Bolívar, who consciously sought to emulate the German traveller by climbing Mount Chimborazo in 1821. It was Humboldt's mysticism rather than his science that attracted the erratic liberator of the Americas. Writers as diverse as the Cuban Alejo Carpentier and the Colombian Gabriel García Márquez have also found inspiration in Humboldt. In his *Tientos y diferencias* (Tints and Differences), Carpentier sees Humboldt as a point of departure for creole American aesthetics. Similarly, in *One Hundred Years of Solitude*, García Márquez has the dying Melquíades speak in tongues in which the only thing clear is "equinox, equinox, equinox" and the name of Alexander von Humboldt, suggesting he is there at the dawn of modern history when a new collective memory begins. Among other men of letters, the Argentinian Domingo Faustino Sarmiento in his *Civilization and Barbarism* praised Humboldt for having "portrayed America most truthfully."

In the English-speaking world, Humboldt's admirers covered both sides of the Atlantic. Most influential in spreading his fame was William Macgillivray, a leading Scottish ornithologist and professor of natural history at the University of Aberdeen. In 1832, he published *The Travels and Researches of Alexander von Humboldt*, with an enlarged edition in 1852. Intended for the informed public, the work abridged and paraphrased all of Humboldt's travel writing that had appeared in French over the course of the early nineteenth century. Macgillivray's preface makes clear his admiration for the learned German naturalist: "The celebrity which Baron Humboldt enjoys, and which he has earned by a life of laborious investigation and perilous enterprise, renders his name familiar to every person whose attention has been drawn to political statistics or natural philosophy. In the estimation of the learned no author of the present day occupies a higher place among those who have enlarged the boundaries of human knowledge." Two giants of English science, Charles Lyell, who revolutionized geology, and Charles Darwin, shared Macgillivray's admiration. When he first stepped ashore in South America, Darwin wrote: "The mind is a chaos of delight, out of which a world of future and more quiet pleasure will arise. I am at present fit only to read Humboldt; he like another sun illumines everything I behold." In the United States, Humboldt was an inspiration for the landscape painter Frederic Edwin Church. Church's most spectacular works followed his numerous visits to Mexico and to South America, where he sought out sites Humboldt had written about. His paintings of the two Ecuadorean volcanoes, Chimborazo and Cotopaxi, with their accurate details and botanical depictions in the foreground, evoke Humboldt's original renderings in his *Vues des Cordillères et monuments des peuples indigènes de l'Amérque* (vc).

Humboldt's Mexican Adventure
in Historical Context

HIS EARLY YEARS

The grandfather of Wilhelm and Alexander von Humboldt was a captain in the Prussian army who had been rewarded with a patent of nobility in 1738. The boys' father, Major Alexander Georg von Humboldt, campaigned with Frederick the Great. A gregarious soldier, he later became the Prussian sovereign's royal chamberlain, but he died in 1779, leaving the boys' mother to raise them. She was born Marie-Elizabeth Colomb, from a French mercantile Huguenot family with some Scottish ancestry as well. The Humboldt family's property and wealth derived from a glass factory at Neustadt an der Dosse in the Potsdam district. Ambitious for her sons but aloof, Marie-Elizabeth was a strict Calvinist who provided her sons with competent tutors but little affection.

Alexander was an indifferent and dreamy student unlike his brilliant older brother. Wilhelm later became a diplomat, Prussian minister of education, founder of the University of Berlin (called "Humboldt University" in East Berlin after 1949), and an outstanding classicist, comparative linguist, and liberal philosopher. If Wilhelm was the prodigy, young Alexander was sickly and remote, happy only when collecting plants and insects. He later called their home at Tegel *the Castle of boredom*.

In their early years, both Humboldt brothers were exposed to ideas of the Enlightenment and Romanticism. Joachim Heinrich Campe, an early and influential tutor of the boys, was a devoted admirer of Jean-Jacques Rousseau. The brothers joined in the German Romantic reaction to rationalism espoused by their friends and mentors Schiller and Goethe, whose influential *The Sorrows of the Young Werther*, published in 1774, led them to question rationalism.

Young Alexander enjoyed travel and adventure literature. He had read Daniel Defoe's *Robinson Crusoe* and most notably George Forster's *A Voyage Round the World*, published in English in 1777 and translated into German a year later. The book was a popular illustrated natural history of Forster's travels with his father, Reinhold, who had replaced Banks as naturalist aboard Captain James Cook's second voyage of discovery from 1772 to 1775. George Forster would later become a mentor, friend, and travelling companion to Alexander. One affiliation not often noticed was Alexander's membership in the African Association around 1794. He was one of the hundred members of this geographical body that sponsored Mungo Park's expedition to West Africa.

Alexander pursued his higher education in a variety of German institutions. He went first to Frankfort on the Oder in 1786 to study political economy. Next, he followed Wilhelm to Göttingen, the leading Enlightenment university in Germany, where he studied natural science. Preparing for a civil servant's career in keeping with his mother's wishes, Alexander also studied in Hamburg, doing bookkeeping, statistics, and fiscal policy; finally he attended the Freiberg Academy of Mines, to which the geologist A.G. Werner drew students from all over Europe. Whether formally or not, Alexander was extraordinarily well read, having studied such diverse fields as botany, literature, archaeology, electricity, mineralogy, and the natural sciences. He worked as a mining inspector in the Prussian administration until his mother's death in 1796 left him an inheritance large enough for him to live independently and to travel.

One example of the broad liberalism of the Humboldt brothers was their firm support of Jewish emancipation. The young brothers were frequent participants in the Berlin salon associated with the

Kantian philosopher and physician Marcus Herz and his beautiful wife, Henriette, née de Lemos. She was a descendant of the Lemos family, a Portuguese Jewish family that had first settled in Germany at the beginning of the sixteenth century and still maintained commercial ties with international trade, offering young Alexander yet another exposure to the New World. Marcus Herz had been a friend of Moses Mendelssohn, grandfather of the composer Felix, and Moses's Berlin bank facilitated Humboldt's American travels by extending a letter of credit to him after another Berlin banking house withdrew credit just as Alexander was about to sail for America. Henriette taught Alexander Hebrew, and as a teenager, he wrote her long wistful letters in that language. The Herz family home in Berlin was a veritable club for intellectuals. Young Alexander observed innovative experiments in electricity by Benjamin Franklin and Count Volta. All took part in discussions of Kant and the poetry of Schiller, Goethe, and Lessing. Here, for the first time in history, prominent Germans and Jews could meet socially on almost equal footing. Later in life, Humboldt fought for Jewish emancipation, having seen the injustice of cultural prejudice first-hand.

YEARS OF PREPARATION

Throughout their five years in the Americas, the French botanist Aimé Bonpland was Alexander's devoted companion and a fellow scientist who helped strengthen Humboldt's empirical understanding of botany. Upon their return to Paris in 1805, Bonpland followed Linneaus's example and became keeper of a royal garden of the creole empress Josephine at her retreat near Paris. Bonpland became her beloved confidant after her divorce from Napoleon, and he was with her when she died. In distress, he returned to South America, where he took up residence in Paraguay and was eventually imprisoned for several years by the notorious dictator Dr Francia. Humboldt, who for years had seen to it that Bonpland's pension was forwarded to him, appealed to Simón Bolívar on Bonpland's behalf and helped secure his release. Bonpland died in Paraguay in 1858.

Humboldt's interest in geology and mining developed early. While only twenty-one and still a student in 1790, he published his first book, on the basalt rock of the Rhine Valley. In 1792, Humboldt was appointed first as assessor in the Department of Mines and then as superintendent of mines at Bayreuth, part of a newly acquired territory of the Prussian kingdom. For several years he worked in this remote area near the Polish border where gold and copper were mined, travelling from mine to mine, many of them half abandoned. Humboldt rose rapidly in Prussian government service. In 1795, however, dissatisfied with this life, he turned down a promotion as director general of mining in Silesia. Happier roaming the hills studying local geology and botany and carrying out experiments, he visited Vienna that same year to study more botany.

ALTERNATIVE DESTINATIONS

Fortune truly smiled on Humboldt's American voyages. After his mother's death in 1796, when his inheritance permitted him to resign from the Prussian civil service, he slowly began to formulate in his mind a project inspired by what the Forsters had achieved with Captain Cook. Using his own funds, he would offer his services as a scientist aboard an expedition of scientific exploration, but in which direction? He seemed to have no preference other than to tag along with one of two French enterprises. One possibility was Bonaparte's grand French military and scientific expedition to Egypt, and the other was to join up with whichever voyage Captain Nicholas Baudin was able to persuade the French republic to sponsor. Although an independent journey with Bonpland under Spanish sponsorship became the third option and, as it happened, the successful project, it proved to be more serendipitous than planned. To compound the uncertainty, all three plans were contingent on peace, a rare prospect during the turbulent years of the later French republic from 1798 to 1801.

Much of the uncertainty centred on the lofty ambitions of Napoleon Bonaparte. Wanting to further French interests and his own while dealing a blow to British trade access to India and to establish a scientific enterprise in the region of "the Orient," Napoleon persuaded the Directory of the French Republic to launch a large Egyptian campaign, preceded by extensive naval engagements in the Mediterranean. Despite many decisive victories on land and an initially successful military occupation of Egypt, French naval defeat at the Battle of the Nile in 1798 left Napoleon's Armée d'Orient land bound and ultimately forced to retreat to France by 1801.

Napoleon's overweening ambition was to emulate Alexander the Great and dominate the Middle East, but the project's scientific dimension spoke to his personal conviction that he was a child of the Enlightenment. When he sailed from Toulon on 19 May 1798, Bonaparte counted a huge fleet of 13 ships of the line, 14 frigates, and 400 transport ships, accompanied by some 40,000 soldiers, 10,000 sailors, and a large contingent of 167 scientists and savants. The scholars included the naturalist Étienne Geoffroy Saint-Hilaire, the chemist Claude Louis Berthollet, and many other leading lights. The cataloguing of their findings was not completed until the 1820s, and it had a profound influence on the future of Egypt.

Humboldt and Bonpland had hoped to join the Egyptian expedition sailing from Toulon, but the British blockade thwarted their plans. In early 1799, perhaps not aware of what had become a precarious adventure, they travelled to Marseilles, hoping to join a camel caravan in Tunis and meet up with the French scientists.

As for the second option, Captain Nicholas Baudin had developed a reputation as an accomplished botanical voyager. In 1796, to much public acclaim, he delivered a large collection of flora and fauna from the West Indies to Paris for deposit in the Natural History Museum. There, he earned the backing of Professor Antoine-Laurent Jussieu for another scientific expedition in 1800 to the western coast of New Holland, as Australia was then called. After some delay, he finally received Bonaparte's backing for a scaled-down version. Baudin wanted eight scholars aboard each of his two ships but ended up with a bloated team of twenty-three, consisting of astronomers, landscape and portrait artists, geographers, mineralogists, botanists, zoologists, gardeners, naval surgeons, and a pharmacist. Scientific travel was becoming fashionable, and many distinguished families sought to count their immediate relatives among the young gentlemen included on Baudin's ships, *Le Géographe* and *Le Naturaliste*. Like the British expedition under Matthew Flinders that sailed at about the same time, Baudin set out to determine whether Australia was one land mass and to make scientific observations. On 19 October 1800, Baudin left Le Havre in his two ships bound for the limits of the southern Pacific via the Indian Ocean. When they called at Île de France (Mauritius), 2,400 kilometres southeast of the African coast, ten savants and several officers abandoned the journey, citing ill health and differences with Baudin. Only seven scientists saw the whole journey through. Bad weather and ill health dogged Baudin throughout, but he did reach all the way south to Van Diemen's Land (Tasmania) by January 1802 and ran into Flinders at Encounter Bay in April 1802. Baudin himself died of tuberculosis in September 1803 at Mauritius on the homeward voyage to France. Baudin never could publish his version of events, which fell to Louis de Freycinet and François Péron. All things considered, Humboldt and Bonpland were very fortunate not to have joined this voyage.

Unable to join the Egyptian expedition and too early for Baudin, Humboldt and Bonpland continued to look for a launching pad for international travel. In February 1799, they reached Murcia on Spain's Mediterranean coast, hoping for any safe passage to North Africa, but without success. Finally, however, their luck changed. They arrived in Madrid in late March where good connections and the willingness of the Spanish Crown to sponsor them enabled a mission to fall into place rather quickly. They garnered support from the Spanish prime minister, Mariano de Urquijo, for a journey to the Spanish colonies in America. Urquijo and the Saxon ambassador to Spain, the mineralogist Baron Philippe de Forrell, facilitated Humboldt's visit to the court of Charles IV at Aranjuez. The Spanish were impressed with Humboldt's mining background and especially by his willingness to fund his visit to the Spanish colonies in America entirely out of his own pocket. Their hope was that Humboldt would provide confidential information enabling the Crown to gain firmer control over the restless colonies and to encourage better development of colonial mineral resources. The Bourbons were reeling under external threats from France and internal mismanagement, and they hoped the young German's background in mining and mapping would be profitable to them.

Humboldt's correspondence with his brother Wilhelm and others expressed his surprise and joy at having gained permission for this American journey. While waiting for departure, he spent his time in Spain taking measurements in the Iberian Peninsula and meeting with Spanish and creole scientists for briefings. One of these was the historian Juan Bautista Muñoz, who would publish only one volume of his planned history of America. In early May, Humboldt and Bonpland arrived in La Coruña only to find the port blockaded by the British navy, which was intercepting ships carrying correspondence to and from America. Not until 15 June 1799 were the two travellers able to sneak out of the harbour at La Coruña, boarding the *Pizarro* on what was to be the journey of their lifetime.

During his four years abroad, Humboldt lacked precise news of war and peace in Europe or of the comings and goings of the Baudin mission. At various times, he still clung to the hope that he could join up with Baudin in the Pacific once he had finished his Spanish American travels. While in Peru, he had hoped to encounter Baudin on the Pacific coast, which would have caused him to abandon his Mexican journey. Similarly, when he first touched down in Acapulco, he thought about boarding a returning ship of the Manila Galleon to reach Baudin in the Pacific. In reality, Baudin never sailed around Cape Horn and up the Pacific coast. By the time Humboldt reached Mexico, Baudin was already beginning his ill-fated homeward voyage from Australia; his death at Mauritius in September 1803 was roughly around the time Humboldt was visiting Morelia.

In June of 1803, Humboldt wrote the National Institute of France that he was rethinking his plans. *The damaged state of our instruments … the impossibility of meeting with Captain Baudin, for whom we had waited in vain upon the shores of the Pacific, the reluctance we felt to traverse a boundless ocean in a merchant ship which could furnish no facilities for touching any of those lovely islands so interesting to the naturalist, but above all, the rapid advancement of science and the necessity of gaining acquaintance with the new discoveries which unquestionably have taken place during an interval of four or five years … these are the motives which have led us to abandon the projected plan of returning by the Philippines and through the Red Sea to Egypt.*

A month later, he wrote his friend Delambre about his disappointment at having to abandon plans to return to Europe via the Philippines. While seriously underestimating, by over twenty years, the time it would take him to complete the publication of his American findings, Humboldt *was only giving up temporarily, for I have many projects in view with regard to the East Indies, but I am anxious first to publish the results of this expedition. I hope to be with you early next year; the writing up of our observations will occupy us for two or three years.*

Alexander von Humboldt was an immensely talented scientist who fully deserved the acclaim he received for his many accomplishments. He was also fortunate, and in two respects: first, neither Egypt nor Australia, which he might have visited instead of the Americas, would have been likely to have produced such spectacular results; and second, science in the Spanish Empire, though poorly known to northern Europeans, had made great strides in the eighteenth century, and Humboldt profited from the knowledge acquired by his precursors.

SCIENTIFIC PRECURSORS

Humboldt's eclectic education and privileged social standing provided him with outstanding training and contacts. He further benefited from having grown up in the late eighteenth century, a time when feats of scientific travel captured the imagination of many who experienced what has been known as the second European era of exploration and discovery. British, French, and Spanish adventurers led the way. Captain Cook's feats were part of his childhood reading, and he was particularly drawn to French scientific accomplishments. The mathematician and navigator Louis Antoine de Bougainville had completed the first French circumnavigation of the Earth in 1769, the

year of Humboldt's birth. Earlier, French mathematician and naturalist Charles-Marie de la Condamine sailed to South America in 1735
on behalf of the Académie Royale des Sciences to test Newton's hy-
pothesis that the Earth was spherical. La Condamine reached the
Equator in the Andes, and from Quito, he descended down the Ama-
zon on a two-month canoe trip. This blend of science and adventure
Humboldt would later emulate.

Scientific inspiration from eighteenth-century Spain is not usually
associated either with the Enlightenment or with exploration and
travel. But this is a legacy of an old northern European bias, called
"the black legend," that held that the cruel Spanish colonial empire
could never be the source of enlightenment and progress. Also contributing to Spain's bad press outside the Iberian Peninsula was the
secrecy Spain maintained about its colonial empire; a major political
crisis that befell Spain during the reign of Charles IV (1788–1808),
whose government foundered among the court intrigues of Manuel
Godoy; international disputes; and, particularly, the Napoleonic invasion in 1808. The long French occupation of Iberia led to the exile
of numerous scientists and the disappearance of many of their
manuscripts. The reactionary nature of nineteenth-century Spain,
together with its impoverishment after the loss of most of its overseas
empire, precluded publication of scientific papers, and many documents were buried in archives, not to be rediscovered (but only sometimes published) until well into the twentieth century.

What should not be overlooked is how the enlightened Bourbon
ruler Charles III had earlier enthusiastically endorsed and funded
Spanish scientific research. In fact, botany had long been an interest
of the Spanish kings, dating back to the first Bourbon, Philip V, who
had requested all state officials in Spain and the Empire to be on the
lookout for unusual specimens of plants, animals, and minerals, and
to send them to Madrid. He had also insisted that two Spaniards, Jorge
Juan and Antonio de Ulloa, accompany la Condamine's expedition in
1735. Charles III facilitated research through Madrid institutions such
as the new Royal Botanical Garden, the Museum of Natural Science,
the Royal Academy of Medicine, and an astronomical observatory.
These bodies became centres of training for Spaniards as well as for

colonial subjects and for expeditions throughout the lands controlled by the Spanish Crown.

When Humboldt visited the Royal Botanical Garden in Madrid before setting out on his journey in 1799, he was fortunate to be briefed on botany in the Americas by two able Spanish botanists, Hipólito Ruiz and José Antonio Pavón. They had travelled to the Americas in 1777 on a royal expedition seeking specimens, bringing them back to Madrid on their return in 1788. Unfortunately, plagued by financial difficulties and with Charles IV in control, the two men encountered long delays in publishing their results. The first three volumes appeared in 1798–1802, but volume 4, though ready for the printer, and volume 5, though nearly so, did not appear until the mid-twentieth century. Even more pertinent to Humboldt's later accomplishments was the Royal Scientific Expedition (RSE) to New Spain. Plans were drawn up in 1785, and in 1787 the expedition was given a six-year term under the direction of the Aragonese physician Martín de Sessé, who was born in 1751 and had begun his career in Madrid in 1775. The RSE achieved relatively permanent status in Mexico City and was a focal point for probes all over New Spain in the last decade of the eighteenth century. The RSE also founded the Royal Botanical Garden of Mexico, which gave professional courses in botany, studies closely allied to medicine and especially pharmacology.

In 1790, Charles IV, at the urging of his naval minister, Antonio Valdés, ordered Alejandro Malaspina, an Italian in Spanish employ, already sailing off the coast of South America, to head north as far as Alaska to map the coastline in detail and to search for the long-desired passage from the Atlantic to the Pacific. The Malaspina Expedition resulted in significant scientific activity. The enlightened viceroy of New Spain, the Second Count of Revillagigedo, convinced that scientific knowledge would lead to economic benefits, encouraged young researchers, whether Spanish or Mexican born, to participate in the explorations. One such was José Mariano Moziño, who accompanied the Malaspina to the Pacific northwest, California, and the West Indies. Born to poor Spanish parents in the pueblo of Temascaltépec, state of Mexico, in 1757, he taught for a time in Oaxaca, studied medicine and botany in Mexico City, and was recruited there by Sessé for the RSE. Moziño carried out botanical surveys all over central and northern Mexico. Also recruited for the RSE was a young creole artist who studied at the Royal Art Academy of San Carlos in Mexico, Atanásio Echeverría. Humboldt mentioned both by name in his *Political Essay*, describing Moziño as a *distinguished doctor*, and *Señor Echeverría ... [as a] painter of plants and animals whose works can compete with the most perfect which Europe has produced of this class [of artist] ... [B]oth were born in New Spain and both occupy a very distinguished ... place among learned persons and artists without having left their native country.*

New Spain was not the only colony with able scientists. In Bogotá in 1801, Humboldt and Bonpland were delighted to meet one of the great botanists of the age, José Celestino Mutis, then seventy years old. Born in Cádiz and trained as a physician and botanist, Mutis received royal sanction to investigate regional flora and fauna in the rich Magdalena Valley of Colombia, which he explored on several occasions. Preferring to live in Bogotá as the personal physician to the viceroy, Mutis accumulated 20,000 types of plants and 7,000 animal species. After his death in 1808, his collections were transferred to the Royal Botanical Garden in Madrid. Unfortunately, his prints, many in colour, remained in the archives and were never published.

Another point of contact with like-minded scientists for Humboldt was his training in Europe. As a young man in the School of Mines in Freiberg, Saxony, he met fellow student Andrés del Río, born in Madrid in 1764. Río was later the distinguished discoverer of a new element, vanadium. Another student in Freiberg who preceded Humboldt was Fausto de Elhuyar, who later discovered the element tungsten. Both men had been sent by the Spanish Crown to Freiberg on scholarship, and both later lived in the American colonies as mining specialists.

Humboldt, late in his life and with typical modesty, understated his scientific accomplishments. His world view, expressed in his popular five-volume *Kosmos*, was that a universal whole consisted of two integrated halves, the physical universe and the human mind. He saw his role as having been to inspire others by establishing a variety of paths to pursue: *I have never been able to hoodwink myself as I have always been surrounded by people who were superior to me. My life has been useful to science less through the little I have contributed myself than through my efforts to let others profit of the advantages of my position. I have always had a just appreciation of the merits of others. I have even shown some acumen in the discovery of new talent. I like to think that, while I was at fault to tackle from intellectual curiosity too great a variety of scientific interests, I have left on my route some trace of my passing.*

TRAVELS IN THE AMERICAS, 1799–1804

Humboldt and his companion Bonpland experienced extraordinary adventures on their strenuous and often dangerous travels in the Americas between 1799 and 1804. They could not have realized they would be away from Europe for four years and ten months, would log about 65,000 kilometres, and would return with over thirty trunks of original data, ranging from monkeys to exotic plants and dried seeds. Nor could they have then imagined that it would take over three decades of dedicated research and writing, mostly by Humboldt, to publish the findings, in thirty volumes. Among their many adventures, whether on horseback or on foot, by boat or dugout canoe, Humboldt and Bonpland penetrated the tropical forests of the Orinoco River, traversed the great plains of Venezuela, and scaled the Andes. On the Orinoco, they travelled in a forty-foot boat filled with guides, instruments, plant samples, and monkey cages, to list only some of the items. In Quito, they added a third companion, Charles Montúfar, a young Ecuadorean who would, much later, die a hero during the War of Independence. Humboldt, Bonpland, and Montúfar climbed almost to the summit of Mount Chimborazo in Ecuador, then believed to be the tallest mountain in the world, without oxygen supplies or alpine equipment and wearing frock coats and button boots. They reached 19,300 feet before soft snow and altitude nausea stopped them short of the summit of 20,700 feet.

After exploring the Andes in Ecuador and Peru, the three young adventurers headed for Mexico, arriving in Acapulco in March 1803. Over the better part of a year, they travelled over much of the Mexican high plateau, and for good measure, they also stopped briefly in the United States before returning to Europe in August 1804. While absent from Europe, Humboldt wrote many letters and reports, and received sporadic news from home. His circles in Germany, France, Spain, and England knew only a fraction of his adventures, and rumours of his disappearance or death frequently appeared in various places. In the summer of 1803 in Paris, reports spread that he had been killed by Natives in North America. A year later, newspapers alarmed the public with the story that he had perished from yellow fever in Acapulco. Not only was Humboldt on his way back to Europe by then, yellow fever had never reached the Pacific side of Mexico. Humboldt was at pains to inform his friends of his good fortune, and he wrote several letters while his ship was observing normal quarantine in the mouth of the Garonne River, outside Bordeaux, in early August 1804. To his friend Karl Freiesleben, he expressed his *exhilaration that, after an absence of five years I am once more upon European soil. We made the entrance of the Garonne two hours ago. We have been most highly favored in our voyage, accomplishing the passage from Philadelphia in twenty-seven days ... My expedition in both hemispheres, extending over a distance of 40,000 miles, has been favored to an almost unprecedented degree. I was never once ill, and I am now in better health, stronger in body, more industrious, and gayer in spirits than ever. I return laden with thirty cases of treasures of all kinds, botanical, geological and astronomical, and it will take me years to bring out my great work.*

PARIS, 1804–1827

Only thirty-four years old when he returned, Humboldt had indeed accomplished a great deal. His detailed studies of flora and fauna, his careful measurements, maps, and illustrations of the land and the atmosphere he observed, his study of everything ranging from mines, to sugar plantations, to the properties of *guano* – all this was a revelation to his thousands of readers. At the same time, his American adventures rewarded him enormously, contributing to the fame that was to endure throughout his life and beyond.

Now a celebrity on his return, Humboldt established his residence in Paris on the Rue des Augustins, Faubourg Saint-Germain, for the next two decades. Frederick William III of Prussia had appointed him royal chamberlain in 1805; he did visit the court in Berlin periodically and accompanied the king to diplomatic congresses. Unlike his brother Wilhelm, who had become minister of education, Alexander was reluctant to exchange the glitter of Paris for the dull life of provincial Berlin, and he did not settle there until 1827, when diminishing funds obliged him to acquiesce to royal pleading to return.

In Germany, his influence expanded with his successful publications, and Goethe called him "our conqueror of the world." Earlier believing Alexander to have been unfocused and flighty, Goethe had come by 1826 to see his genius in a positive light: "Alexander von Humboldt has been with me for some hours this morning; what an extraordinary man he is! Though I have known him so long, I am always newly amazed by him. Humboldt possesses a versatility of genius which I have never seen equaled. Whatever may be the subject broached, he seems quite at home with it, and showers upon us treasures in profusion from his stores of knowledge."

Humboldt's base in Paris suited him perfectly, as the city was then the global centre of science, culture, and art, even if its politics were occasionally volatile. Humboldt cautiously continued to support liberal reform, but as a prominent figure in the Parisian scientific world for almost three decades, he spent most of his time working constantly, writing, editing, and publishing at his own expense the voluminous record of his travels and discoveries. His acquaintances and friends included the chemist and physicist Joseph Louis Gay-Lussac and the physicist and astronomer François Arago. Humboldt lived modestly in the Latin Quarter, his funds steadily depleted by his publications and his generosity to young scientists. He helped such men as the German chemist Justus von Liebig and the Swiss-born zoologist Louis Agassiz launch their careers.

THE PRIVATE LIVES OF ALEXANDER
AND WILHELM

A word needs to be said about issues of privacy and sexuality as they applied to the Humboldt brothers. Wilhelm, the father of three and happily married, was openly promiscuous, patronized prostitutes, and had a series of extramarital attachments throughout his life. His correspondence with his wife indicates that they had a warm relationship and were content with what would today be called an open marriage. Alexander, on the other hand, although exceptionally private about his personal life, showed a clear preference for the company of males and never married. Among his intimates was François Arago, with whom he met almost every day for fifteen years during his time in Paris. The British critic and translator Jason Wilson puts it this way: "Science was a male world; it was natural for Humboldt to surround himself with other male scientists in austere working conditions."

The absence of a smoking gun has not prevented speculation. As Wilson shows, many of his commentators treated the question as a dirty secret or exaggerated his clearly platonic relationships with women in Europe and the Americas. As might be expected, speculation in fiction cannot be restrained, and authors have of course addressed the subject. In Gabriel García Márquez's novel *The General in His Labyrinth*, Simón Bolívar and his entourage rescue a disreputable German traveller who sneers indecently about Humboldt's "shameless pederasty." Bolívar retorts indignantly to his aide-de camp: "That motherfucker isn't worth a single hair on Humboldt's head."

Even gay historians such as Robert Aldrich, who devotes a chapter entitled "Humboldt and His Friends" in his *Colonialism and Homosexuality*, admits that incontrovertible evidence of physical intercourse does not exist. But he does make the sound argument that Humboldt not only made close, long-term relationships with men but also denigrated marriage, writing that he was *convinced that the man who agrees to the yoke of marriage is a fool, and I would even say, a sinner. A fool because he gives up his own freedom without gaining any corresponding compensation. A sinner because he then gives Life to children without being able to give them the certainty of happiness.*

Alexander went to great lengths to keep prying eyes away from his personal letters and destroyed a significant number of these. In his publications, he deliberately avoided detail on such personal issues as his health, bodily discomforts, and fears. Perhaps the rare exception was his frequent mention of the annoyance of mosquitoes and other insects, understandable for a visitor to the steamy tropical rainforests of South America. He took the view that personal anecdotes distracted readers from grasping the purpose of science. Nevertheless, he did seem to be on a constant adrenalin rush throughout his adventures. Whereas Bonpland had nasty bouts of malaria and other fevers in the South American phase of their travels, Humboldt seemed to thrive in a disease environment so challenging for others. He wrote to his friend Wildenow: *I work a lot and sleep little, and while making my astronomical observations, am often exposed to the sun for up to five or six hours without a hat.*

The best way of situating Alexander in European letters after 1805 is to note his special relationship with his almost equally dazzling brother Wilhelm. The brothers remained close throughout their lives. Wilhelm's achievements as a liberal politician and philosopher are well documented. When his diplomatic career was cut short in Prussia, he retired and devoted himself to linguistics. His theory of language acquisition fell out of favour but was rescued by Noam Chomsky in the 1950s as an important precursor to current linguistic theory. Wilhelm proposed a law or force that promoted linguistic development close to what is now called the generative principle in the evolution of language. Wilhelm published little, but after his death in 1835 at the age of sixty-eight, Alexander took possession of Wilhelm's papers and published his letters as the *Briefe an eine Freundin* in two volumes in 1847. Based on Wilhelm's correspondence with his lover Charlotte Hildebrandt, the work became an international bestseller, with nineteen editions published in just a few years and with several English translations and abridgements. Another posthumous work was translated into English as *The Sphere and Duties of Government*. This work put forward Wilhelm's notion of individuality and was acknowledged by John Stuart Mill in his important liberal essay, *On*

Liberty. The two brothers certainly shared a belief in the ideal of a more open and humane society, but Alexander as a young adult came to distance himself from Wilhelm's philosophical idealism and secular religiosity. Alexander's materialism and atheism contrasted with Wilhelm's views, but these differences could not weaken their mutual admiration for each other. Wilhelm, the child prodigy, proved unsure of his ideas and reluctant to publish his writings. On the other hand, even before Alexander's post-American intellectual triumphs, he had become a very productive scholar. Only twenty-eight years of age when he resigned from Prussian state service in 1797, Alexander had produced the extraordinary total of thirty-five scientific books and papers. Clearly the most famous scientist in Germany by the 1830s, Alexander was a jealous guardian of Wilhelm's reputation and did much to secure his older brother's intellectual legacy.

THE BERLIN YEARS

From 1827 until his death in 1859, Humboldt lived in the Prussian capital of Berlin. He served the monarchy as chamberlain and councillor of state and maintained the same duties with the new king, Friedrich Wilhelm IV, who ascended to the throne in 1840. In addition, his presence at court required him to tutor the crown prince. He was able to make science popular by starting with the royals and extending his influence to the Privy Council, of which he was a member. He also taught physical geography to professors and students of all faculties at the University of Berlin, founded by his brother Wilhelm. He was hailed as the greatest figure in German science, with thousands attending his public lectures. His fame attracted scientists from all over Europe, as in 1828, when he presided over a gathering of 600 natural scientists.

He continued to travel frequently, visiting Vesuvius in Italy and making annual pilgrimages to Paris to maintain his scientific and personal friendships. He visited with Arago every day during his stays in the French capital. Humboldt hoped to return to Latin America, but this was never to happen. Perhaps he was waiting for financing and a formal invitation from the Mexican republic, but political and economic instability conspired against a second voyage. He had rejected any affiliation with mining ventures, and in 1822 he wrote to Wilhelm from Italy about his dream of living out the rest of his life as a savant in Mexico: *I have a big plan for a large Central Institute of Natural Science that would serve all of the liberated portion of America in Mexico. The viceroy will be replaced there by a republican government, and I have got it in my head to end my life in the most agreeable and, for science, most useful manner. I could live in a part of the world where I enjoy great prestige, and where everything is so conducive to my leading a happy existence ... The zoology of Mexico is largely unknown, and one could introduce the cultivation of many Mexican plants in our forests. You may laugh at my Mexican project, but owning neither family nor children, one should plan ahead on how to make one's old age as pleasant as possible.*

Nevertheless, one more great journey beckoned. In 1829, at the age of sixty, Humboldt embarked upon an eight-month expedition to the Urals and Siberia, publishing his account in French in 1843. Funded and sponsored by the tsarist government, which was keen to acquire information about potential mineral deposits, the journey was far more luxurious than the American one. Humboldt crossed the vast Asian steppe in a horse-drawn carriage, accompanied by two German scientists, a Russian mining expert, a cook, a valet, and various Russian minders. Though unhappy at this tight surveillance and despite his perceived obligation not to raise the thorny issue of serfdom, Humboldt did manage to extend the itinerary beyond the original agreement.

In 1834, Humboldt began his most ambitious project, a comprehensive survey of creation, which he called *Cosmos* (*Kosmos* in the original German). The fifth and final volume appeared posthumously in 1862, three years after his death, and was translated into almost every European language. He was buried beside Wilhelm in the family vault of the Tegel estate, revered as one of the great scientific travellers of the nineteenth century. His state funeral was memorable, as were the widespread commemorations among many nations on the centenary of his birth on 14 September 1869. In New York, a statue was unveiled in his honour, and in Dubuque, Iowa, which did not exist until Humboldt was sixty-three, the population doubled to 25,000 to mark Humboldt's centenary with hundreds of floats.

PART ONE

Arrival in Mexico, 23 March to 12 April 1803:
From Acapulco to Mexico City

CHAPTER I

Acapulco: The Place of Broken Reeds

Acapulco must truly have been a sight for the sore eyes and stiff bodies of Humboldt, Bonpland, and Montúfar when they touched down there on 23 March 1803. Not only had their last month been turbulent as the *Atlante* fought major squalls off the Pacific coast after leaving the Ecuadorean port of Guayaquil, but the travellers had also spent the first six weeks of 1803 aboard a creaky trade vessel, the *Causino*, on its 1,100-kilometre voyage northward from Lima's port of Callao to Guayaquil.

Mexico's chief port on the Pacific left a spectacular impression on the intrepid travellers. Humboldt gushed about how Acapulco ("the Place of Broken Reeds" in Nahuatl) constituted *one of the finest natural harbors in the known world. It forms an immense basin cut in granite rocks open towards the south-south-west, and with a breadth of more than 6 kilometers from east to west. I have seen few situations in either hemisphere with a more savage aspect, more dismal and yet more romantic at the same time. This rocky coast is so steep that a vessel of the line may almost touch it without running the smallest danger, because there are 10 to 12 fathoms of water everywhere. The landing is very dangerous during the rainy season, which lasts from May until December along the entire western coast of America. Great hurricanes are experienced in the month of June and September, and we then find on the coasts of Acapulco and San Blas a rough and angry sea. The rains destroy the fruits of the earth while the south-west wind tears up the largest trees.*

As the three men reached its coast, they found it *one of the most picturesque we ever saw, the sandy beach of Coyuca gilded by the sun's reflections, and framed by a densely grown banana plantation, coconut palm trees, and, behind all that, three mountain ranges, very high and partially wooded. An impressive view.*

Once they had landed, the three travellers found the town of Acapulco disappointing. Insects, especially cockroaches, were abundant, and caused them much discomfort. The nights were remarkably cold for the tropics, with temperatures dipping to 17°C before skyrocketing ten minutes after dawn, so that the rest of the day was marked by unpleasant heat. Unusually, since he rarely raised personal health issues, Humboldt complained of constipation and *bilious aches.* More of an annoyance than a concern were the nighttime noises made by geckos, nicknamed by Humboldt *the canaries of Acapulco.* Their five-day stay in the languid port was uneventful. They visited the small port of Marqués, southeast of Punta de la Bruja, but apart from thoughts about sailing the Pacific aboard the Manila Galleon to join up with the elusive Captain Baudin, they had little to say.

THE MANILA GALLEON TRADE

By the time of the scientists' visit, the glory days of the magnificent Manila Galleon trade were long since past. Acapulco had long been the destination of the trade-laden galleons sailing from Manila in the Spanish Philippines annually. The Manila Galleon trade had been Spain's answer to the Portuguese trade monopoly with Asia via the Indian Ocean and the South Atlantic. Spanish navigators had discovered that they could use trade winds in the Pacific much as they had in the Atlantic, where they made a wide swing or *volta* to the west to bring them home from Madeira. In Asia, the ships leaving Manila sailed north before turning east, and hit the west coast of the Americas in Baja California before turning along the coast south to San Blas and Acapulco. The monopoly power of the Seville trading houses petitioned the Crown not to allow three or more ships annually on this route, so that in 1593 a Spanish decree limited the trade to two ships sailing each year from either port, with one kept in reserve in Acapulco and one in Manila. To overcome the restriction on numbers, the ships were huge, averaging from 1,700 to 2,000 tons and capable of carrying 1,000 passengers. Most were as long as 150 feet. Built of Philippine hardwoods, they were the largest class of ships to be found anywhere in the sixteenth century, but as awkward merchant ships, they required an armed escort or *armada* to protect their valuable cargo of spices, porcelain, ivory, lacquer ware, and processed silk gathered from East Asia. On the other hand, East Asia valued silver, and Mexican silver financed the trade. The Asian goods were sold in Mexico, the rest in Spanish America, and, after land transport to Veracruz, in Europe as well. Every July or August, large galleons would leave Manila and arrive in November or December laden with rich goods of the East.

Humboldt observed the famous Manila Galleon trade only seventeen years before Mexico's success in achieving independence brought it to an end in 1821: *The oldest and most important branch of commerce of Acapulco is the exchange of merchandise of the East Indies and China for the precious metals of Mexico. The commerce limited to a single galleon is extremely simple; and though I have been on the spot where the most renowned fair of the world is held, I can add little information to that which has already been given before by others. The galleon, which is generally from twelve to 1,500 tons and commanded by an officer of the royal navy, sails from Manila in the middle of July or beginning of August when the south-west monsoon is already completely established. Its cargo consists of muslins, printed calicoes, coarse cotton shirts, raw silks, China silk stockings, jewelleries from Canton or Manila crafted by Chinese artists, spices and aromatics. The voyage formerly lasted from five to six months, but since the art of navigation has been improved, the passage from Manila to Acapulco is only three or four months.*

The galleon generally departs in the month of February or March, and it goes with ballast, for the lading in the journey from Acapulco to Manila in general only consists of silver, a very small quantity of cochineal [a red dye produced from crushed insects], cocoa from Guayaquil, Caracas wine, oil, and Spanish wool ... The number of passengers in general

*is very considerable, and augmented from time to time by colonies of
monks sent by Spain and Mexico to the Philippine Islands. The galleon
of 1804 carried out seventy-five monks.*

When Humboldt visited in 1803, Acapulco counted only 4,000
souls, many of whom were reputedly escaped convicts or slaves. He
described how the news of the fleet's annual arrival caused excite-
ment in Mexico City some 300 kilometres away, and how all sorts of
travellers hurried to meet the ships in Acapulco. Their hopes of significant profit were usually dashed, however, because most of the
goods had already been sold by previous arrangement to the great
mercantile houses of Mexico City, which distributed the goods all
over New Spain and beyond.

Humboldt noticed in 1803 that Acapulco had clearly seen better
days. Not only had the Manila trade declined, but only a dozen or so
small ships arrived annually from Central and South America: *The
trade of Acapulco with the ports of Guayaquil and Lima is far from active; the principal objects are copper, oil, some Chilean wine, a very small
quantity of sugar, quinine bark from Peru, and the cocoa of Guayaquil
destined either for the interior consumption of New Spain, for Havana
and the Philippine Islands, or in time of war, for Europe. The loading of
the vessels which return to Guayaquil and Lima is very trifling, and is
confined to a few woollens from Querétaro, a small quantity of cochineal,
and contraband East India goods. The length and the extreme difficulty
of the navigation from Acapulco to Lima are the greatest obstacles to
trade between the inhabitants of Peru and Mexico. The distance from
Guayaquil to Callao is only 210 marine leagues, yet very often more time
is required for this short passage from north to south than from Acapulco to Manila.*

ACAPULCO BEFORE AND AFTER HUMBOLDT'S VISIT

Though it was never a centre of empire, the Acapulco region had been
associated with Mexico's pre-Columbian cultures and empires, including the Olmec and the Aztecs, who brought the coast under loose
control for the first time in 1486. Aztec rule was brief and inconse-

quential. Spanish domination soon followed and led to significant expansion. Hernán Cortés began construction of a port in Acapulco in 1523. Ten years later, a major road from Mexico City was begun, and a major wharf installed. Manila Galleons began arriving annually after 1565, and the Crown ordered Spanish families to live in the region in order to preside over the monopolistic trade with the Philippines. Because Acapulco was the only Spanish city in the Western Hemisphere permitted to trade with Asia, its wealthy trade made it a tempting target for English and Dutch pirates.

Privateers like Sir Francis Drake, Henry Morgan, and Thomas Cavendish were active in the waters off New Spain's Pacific coast. One of Drake's techniques was to lie off Acapulco Bay near Puerto Marqués and swoop down on the rich prey just as it was about to reach safe harbour. To defend against these marauders, the Spanish Crown built the Fort of San Diego, but this did not prevent a Dutch fleet from attacking in 1615, destroying much of the fort and town before being driven off. San Diego was again destroyed, this time by the terrible earthquake of 1776; it was rebuilt yet again in 1783. Charles IV had hoped to revive the town around 1800 by naming Acapulco an official city, but he did little else. In the War of Independence begun in 1810, José Maria Morelos y Pavón, after defeating Royalist commander Francisco Parés at the Battle of Tres Palos, razed Acapulco. The last Manila Galleons called in 1821, the year of Mexican independence. For the next century, Acapulco was reduced to a sleepy fishing village, with only a small recovery occurring during the mid-nineteenth-century California gold rush.

ACAPULCO'S MODERN-DAY TRANSFORMATION

When Acapulco revived, it did so by building a reputation for glorious beaches and dazzling night life among foreign and national celebrities. First came the Prince of Wales and future king Edward VIII in 1920, who recommended Acapulco's harbour and unspoiled beauty to the European sailing elite. They and a few Americans began investing in hotels and marinas in Old Acapulco.

The Mexican government built port warehouses and a commercial wharf in the mid-1940s, and in the early 1950s, President Miguel
Alemán Valdés upgraded the port infrastructure, installing electrical
lines, drainage systems, roads, and the first highway to connect Acapulco with Mexico City. At this time, Acapulco became prominent as
a getaway for Hollywood movie stars and a port of call for shipping
and cruise lines. Elizabeth Taylor, Frank Sinatra, Eddie Fisher, and
Brigitte Bardot were among the brightest stars to shine in Acapulco.
Johnny Weissmuller and John Wayne invested in hotels in the northern end of the bay. From a population of 5,000 in the 1940s, the numbers increased tenfold to 50,000 in the early 1960s.

Celebrated and wealthy Mexicans also began to enjoy the Pacific
playground. Luis Miguel, Plácido Domingo, Dolores Olmedo, and
Diego Rivera were only the best known among hundreds more who
flocked to the resort. New hotels were continuously added, the more
luxurious in the south of the town, while middle-class Mexicans
began to visit Old Acapulco in the north and centre of the city. Southern beaches included the fashionable Punta Diamante and Puerto
Marqués. The 1970s saw more port expansion, and the 1990s the
building of the Ruta del Sol, an expressway from Mexico City that
reduced the journey between the two cities to under four hours, enabling affluent Mexicans to travel to Acapulco for weekends, where
they enjoyed condos and villas they built themselves. By 1996, the
port was further expanded so that cars assembled in Mexico could
be exported to the Pacific. Cruise ships and luxury liners began to
include Acapulco as a highlight of their Pacific routes from November to April.

It was not all good news. In 1997, Hurricane Pauline devastated
the city, leaving over 100 dead. In the next decade, the drug war in
Mexico reached Acapulco as cartels fought to control the route from
South America to the United States. A pitched battle between the
Mexican military and a drug cartel in the summer of 2009 took the
lives of eighteen gunmen and two soldiers. A year later, in March 2010,
at least fifteen died in drug-related gang violence, causing the US government to issue a travel advisory directed mainly at American col-

lege students in the habit of enjoying their spring break on the beaches and in the clubs of Acapulco.

Although its reputation has been surpassed by newer and more attractive resorts nearby, such as Ixtapa and Zihuatanejo, Acapulco continues to attract many visitors. Its natural beauty, extolled by Humboldt and others, can still be observed and enjoyed, despite the tacky overlay that some sections of the area reflect. Its consistent and unvarying climate makes it a reliable destination for sun worshippers. Average monthly temperatures have a remarkably stable range, from 31°C to 33°C throughout the year. Tropical storms can threaten from May to November, but a dry season persists for the rest of the year.

Easily reached from Mexico City some 300 kilometres northeast, Acapulco in 2005 had a population of 700,000, making it by far the largest city in the state of Guerrero. Today it offers a number of attractions consistent with Humboldt's interests.

First, a variety of cruises to Roqueta Island in the middle of Acapulco Bay depart from Caletilla Beach. There are places to snorkel, have lunch, visit a small zoo, and see a lighthouse. With imagination and looking only at the vegetation, the visitor can observe a coastline similar to the one Humboldt saw two centuries ago.

Second, the San Diego Fort and Historical Museum of Acapulco is located to the east of the main square. Unchanged from its rebuilding in 1783 except for renovations in 2000, the site preserves parts of the original moats as well as the five bulwarks and the battlements.

Third, northwest of Acapulco Bay and of Pie de la Cuesta lies a sweet water lake called "Coyuca de Benítez." Mangroves spread throughout the lagoon, as in Humboldt's time, and boat tours are available.

Fourth, murals by Diego Rivera can be seen at the home of Dolores Olmedo located in the traditional downtown area of Acapulco, at 6 Calle Cerro de la Pinzona, a few blocks beyond the Casablanca Hotel. The outside wall of the house is decorated with a Rivera mural composed of mosaic tiles, shells, and stones. Rivera lived here for the last two years of his life, completing the work in 1956. The home is privately owned, and no access is available to interior mural work Rivera carried out, but the exterior masterpiece is certainly worth seeing.

CHAPTER 2

Diego Rivera's Imagery

The corpulent giant Diego Rivera, over six feet tall and weighing more than 300 pounds, an exceptionally talented but extravagant muralist painter with an equally oversized sexual appetite and ego, would not appear to have much in common with the diminutive, sexually discreet, and formal German nobleman Alexander von Humboldt. But appearances can be deceiving. Beneath their images, both men shared a revolutionary ideology, and both clung to the romantic image of how noble Indigenous people led an inspired but tragically doomed resistance to Spanish conquest.

Each man valued the artistic gifts of pre-Columbian peoples and admired their love of colour and display. In their professional lives, both Rivera and Humboldt achieved great things, driven by extraordinary energy and conviction, as well as by a belief in scientific techniques and their own mastery of skills. For Humboldt, his scientific hunger was innate, as was Rivera's conviction that he was the leader of the Mexican muralists and that he towered above the other two *grandes*, José Oroszco and David Siqueiros, when it came to creating new techniques for frescoes and murals. Finally, both were concerned with their legacy and invested heavily in assuring they would not be forgotten. Humboldt depleted his fortune by self-publishing his enormous corpus of writings, while Rivera spent a good deal of money in building his personal museum in Coyoacán to house his vast collection of artefacts.

REVOLUTIONARY IDEOLOGY

Diego Rivera's political commitment moved slowly but steadily towards the left as the Mexican Revolution evolved after 1910. He participated briefly in the fighting, but unlike Siqueiros, he spent most of the turbulent years away in Europe. When he returned to Mexico in 1921, his art and politics had converged. Rivera benefited from the support of José Vasconcelos, who had been appointed as director of UNAM and secretary of public education in 1921 under President Álvaro Obregón. Vasconcelos, a lawyer, philosopher, revolutionary politician, and founder of the *indigenismo* ideology, believed in the young muralists Rivera and Siqueiros and granted them permission to work on public spaces. He gave Rivera a wall to cover at the National Preparatory School of the University of Mexico. In this fine baroque building of the early eighteenth century, Rivera produced *La Creación*, a mural of allegorical figures representing Mexico's racial history. The lower panels show how bloods had mixed; on a slightly higher plane, a rising group of figures represent Prudence, Strength, Justice, and Continence, with Science the topmost figure. Rivera now believed that mural painting represented a new art to which all people, educated or not, would have access, as it could be used to decorate public buildings ranging from post offices to schools, theatres, and ministries. The mural had taken him over a year to complete, but Rivera soon afterwards expressed concern that the work was too abstract and metaphorical to reach the masses. He would make amends in his subsequent work.

Humboldt too had expressed his support for the disadvantaged in society, even though it was from the more lofty heights of the Prussian nobility. In 1794, as a young man employed as inspector of mines in Steben, Germany, he had personally funded the Free Royal Mining School for mine workers.

In 1923, Rivera's second mural, for the courtyard of the Mexican Education Building, was much more explicit about his politics. One section, called the "Court of Labor," showed the toil of Mexicans in various forms. In the stairway was a trio of masked workers: one de-

Figure 2.1
Diego Rivera, *The Creation*, 1922–23, in the Museum of San Ildefonso,
Mexico City. (Photo courtesy of Rafael Doniz)

picted Rivera himself as an architect, another a stonecutter, and the
third a painter. Rivera included a revolutionary poem by Gutiérrez
Cruz urging miners to seize the mine for themselves. Under pressure
from Vasconcelos, Rivera removed the poem, but he insisted on keeping an adjacent panel depicting a peasant and a worker embracing
each other. During the four years he worked on the project, Rivera
was an active member of the new Mexican Communist Party (MCPP),
formed in the early 1920s. He and his painter friends Xavier Guerrero

and David Siqueiros – they had not yet had their falling out – served as co-editors for *El Machete*, the official newspaper of the MCPP. He took a short break from the mural job to visit Russia for the first of several trips there. Whereas Rivera's trips to Russia were ideological, Humboldt's voyages had always been scientific in purpose.

In mid-1927, Rivera completed his work in the chapel of the Agricultural College of Chapingo, with frescoes overflowing into the halls and stairway of the school. Perhaps his strongest statement was his depiction of the Earth enslaved by three symbolic oppressors: Clericalism, Militarism, and Capitalism. One figure wore the black garb of a priest, one a helmet and gas mask – with sword drawn – and the third, a fat man with a bulbous nose and protruding belly sitting beside Earth's head, held a bulging bag of money.

In 1929, Rivera was expelled from the MCPP. The charge was that he was a Trotskyist, but as Rivera himself admitted, he would not accept party discipline and disliked Stalinist rigidity. Rivera continued to see himself as a communist and applied for reinstatement three times, but he was only readmitted in 1955, after Stalin's death.

ROMANTIC LOVE OF PRE-HISPANIC ART, COLOUR, AND DISPLAY

In his autobiography, Rivera reveals that his lifelong love of pre-conquest Mexican art began in grade school. As a young art student in Spain and France before the First World War, he was completely absorbed in the European artistic tradition. What was lacking in his early work, he felt, was that he had not yet taken up Mexican themes. As he would remark later, "the secret of my best work is that it is Mexican." Rivera's murals, whether early or late, emphasized the love of colour and display he so admired in Indian culture. He used dominant tones – violet, green, red, and orange – to convey his passion. An iconic example is his *Nude with Calla Lilies*, done in 1944 in oil on hardboard.

Figure 2.2
Diego Rivera, *Nude with Calla Lilies*, 1944, in AKR.
(Photo courtesy of Rafael Doniz)

MASTERY OF INNOVATIVE SKILLS AND OF
SCIENTIFIC TECHNOLOGY

Like Humboldt, Rivera felt a contradictory admiration for the
United States. Each man was appalled by, in Humboldt's time, that
country's reliance on slave labour and slavery, and for Rivera, its
abuse of labouring people. Just as Humboldt believed that American
scientific and technological progress would accompany a new society built upon popular will, Rivera could never outgrow his passion
for American technological know-how and its brilliant innovators.
In his project for the Arts Institute in Detroit, Rivera set aside his
ideological opposition to capitalism, and because he admired Henry
Ford and his son Edsel, he was determined to leave Americans with
a mural that showed the power for good, and for bad, of industrialization and invention while illustrating the new world of the masses,
dominated by machines and naked mechanical power. Some twenty-
seven panels were divided into roughly three levels at the base. The
main level showed machines in motion, while the upper level portrayed the physiography of the region, its soil, minerals and fossils,
lake and river transport. Lastly, under the building's rafters, civilian
and military aviation and the races of man were depicted. Conveyor
belts, tubes, and piping all appeared as waves. In a pharmacological
panel, Rivera showed his admiration for science in the service of
humanity. He placed a child – in the arms of a nurse – being vaccinated by a white-gowned physician. A horse, a cow, and some sheep
stood in front of them, representing donors from which the vaccines
had been prepared.

One of the most controversial works Rivera produced in the
United States was the mural he prepared for the Rockefeller Center in
New York in 1933. Grandiosely entitled *Man at the Crossroads Looking
with Hope and High Vision to the Choosing of a New and Better Future*,
the mural would stress the power of technology but also the existen-
tial struggle between capital and labour for domination. Nelson Rockefeller objected to the flattering portrait of Lenin and wanted it
removed. He finally agreed to pay Rivera his entire fee but ordered the
mural destroyed. Rivera was furious and his large ego offended. He

expressed his indignation but also his enormous arrogance by asking whether an American millionaire who bought the Sistine Chapel would have the right to destroy Michelangelo's work. Several years later, Rivera reconstructed most of the Rockefeller mural. He and Oroszco had been commissioned by the Mexican government to do two large panels in the Palace of Fine Arts. Rivera angrily added an unflattering portrait of John D. Rockefeller to his oeuvre, placing his head only a short distance from the venereal disease germs pictured in the ellipse of the microscope.

Rivera brought science and technology into play frequently in his later murals. In San Francisco, he expressed his admiration for American inventors Henry Ford, Samuel Morse, and Robert Fulton, all of whom he considered artists as well as inventors. In Mexico during the Second World War, he created two large frescoes in the new Cardiology Institute. The east wall represented ancient cardiological knowledge, while the west wall displayed modern developments. Both frescoes included ancient Greek, African, Chinese, Aztec medicine, and a projection of future aspects of cardiology.

ASSURING HIS LEGACY: THE ANAHUACALLI MUSEUM IN COYOACÁN

Rivera and his wife, Frida Kahlo, were prolific collectors of pre-Colombian art and expressed fine taste in their selection of pieces. Together, they collected over 50,000 pieces and, beginning in the 1930s, planned the Anahuacalli Museum to house their collection. Rivera devoted a considerable portion of his personal fortune to the project, which began in 1955, and grew upset when the state dragged its heels about appropriating additional funds to complete its construction. Rivera died of cancer in 1957, and only the generosity of Rivera's rich benefactor, Dolores Olmedo, saw the project through to completion in 1964, when the museum opened. Rivera personally supervised the initial construction, but the building was completed after his death by architects Juan O'Gorman and Heriberto Pagelson and his own daughter, Ruth.

A century and a half earlier, Alexander von Humboldt had been similarly anxious to ensure that his life's work would remain before the public. Although it was not unusual to secure the publication of a work at the author's own expense in the early nineteenth century, Humboldt extravagantly exhausted his personal fortune in printing over thirty volumes of expensive books depicting his explorations. The biographer Charles Minguet estimates that of the fortune of 90,000 thaler that Humboldt inherited from his mother in 1796, he dispensed 40,000 on his five-year trip to the Americas and 100,000 on publishing, roughly 40,000 dollars in today's money.

Rivera conceived of Anahuacalli as an integrated "City of Arts," a space for architecture, painting, dance, and music. He contacted Frank Lloyd Wright and exchanged ideas with him. The central plaza was to serve as a fresh-air theatre and an open ecological space with a spectacular view of the city below. Anahuacalli means "house of water" in Nahuatl and reflects Mayan and Aztec influences. It is built of black basalt and takes the form of a pyramid. Rivera and Kahlo hoped that concerts, workshops, and festivals would take place at the site, but little of this has occurred and only limited numbers of visitors explore the site. Visitors must take guided tours. They enter the museum at its lowest level and work their way up through themes and cultures. Rivera stated in his autobiography that he organized the pieces in chronological order, but no anthropological labels are present. The site attracts far fewer visitors than the popular nearby Frida Kahlo Museum at the site of her Coyoacán home, the "Casa Azul." Anahuacalli is seldom described in commercial guidebooks, and few foreign visitors are attracted to the venue. While Rivera's grandiose hopes for the museum never were realized, he nevertheless remains the most celebrated of the great Mexican muralists, an artist deserving of his outstanding reputation.

$\mathcal{E}$

CHAPTER 3

Chilpancingo and Guerrero State: A Gruelling Climb through the Rugged Sierra Madre del Sur Mountain Range

A DIFFICULT JOURNEY UP FROM THE COAST

The three intrepid travellers set off for Mexico City from Acapulco on the morning of 29 March 1803, six days after having touched land in New Spain. Their intermediate destination was the Huacapa River valley and the town of Chilpancingo, "the place of wasps," today the administrative capital of the state of Guerrero. There followed one of the more gruelling trips they were to make, a bold statement given the rough terrain they had already traversed in South America. Their party was large and counted twenty-one mules, thirteen of which carried most of Humboldt's natural history objects gathered in the Andes. Their initial route followed the coastal beach through Coyuca to the north, passing through fields of cotton before turning north-east into the granite hills of the first slopes of the rugged Sierra Madre del Sur. This range covers much of what is now the state of Guerrero and extends south into Oaxaca state. As they began their ascent, they savoured the wonderful aroma of mimosa.

All the way to Mexico City, their journey required them to travel each morning just before sunrise at 5:30 until about 9.30 a.m., when the torrid heat, made worse by hot winds whipping across bare granite rocks, forced a halt each day until 4 p.m. They would then proceed until sunset at 7 p.m. Temperatures in the *tierra caliente*, or torrid lands of the coastal plain, easily surpassed 33°C, but that was to be expected. Soon enough, their tortuous climb took them over the dusty granite rocks of the Sierra Madre del Sur. Although valleys occasionally broke their climb, they too were hot and humid. These difficult conditions did not deter Humboldt and his party from taking their meticulous geological readings and noting the tropical vegetation. They found the region sparsely populated and passed through few settlements until they neared Chilpancingo on 2 April.

The dramatic shift from sweltering humidity to much-appreciated fresh mountain air confirmed one of Humboldt's theories, today so obvious that it is taken for granted. Altitude has as much bearing on flora as does latitude. Not only can there be snow on mountain ranges in the tropics, lines of vegetation can be carefully measured to show these gradients. Using his observations, Humboldt invented maps with isotherms and isobars clearly indicated. A common feature of weather maps today, isotherms are lines connecting points with the same mean temperature. Isobars are lines connecting points with the same barometric pressure for a given time.

This early part of Humboldt's travels in Mexico reflected his lofty scientific goals, as expressed in a letter to his friend David Friedländer just before departing on his American adventure in April 1799: *I will collect flora and fauna; I will investigate the heat, elasticity, and magnetic and electrical charge of the atmosphere, and chemically analyse it; I will determine latitudes and longitudes, and measure mountains. But all this is not the aim of my voyage. My sole true object is to investigate the confluence and interweaving of all physical forces, and the influence of dead nature on the animate animal and plant creation. To this end I have had to instruct myself in every empirical discipline. Thence the complaints of those who have no idea what I am doing, that I'm pursuing too many things at once. We have botanists, we have mineralogists, but no physicists, as B [Bacon] called for.*

To accomplish this Herculean effort to determine the physics of the earth, Humboldt would arm himself with no less than thirty-six of the most modern instruments modern science could provide. To illustrate how specialized some of this equipment was, let us examine some of them. One was the hair hygrometer, which measured humidity according to how much a strand of hair expanded.

Other instruments included four kinds of eudiometers to measure the oxygen content of the atmosphere; a cyanometer to gauge the blueness of the sky; six thermometers; two chronometers; two barometers; a theodolite for measuring angles in the horizontal and vertical planes; sextants of four sizes from four different makers; quadrants; achromatic and reflecting telescopes; a specialized boiler to measure altitude by the boiling point of water; an electrometer to measure the electrical charge of the atmosphere; a Borda repeating circle to make rapid successive measurements of an angle; and an inclinometer to measure the horizontal component of the intensity of the Earth's magnetism.

Like the authorities in the capital, Humboldt was similarly concerned about the perpetual problem of transporting people and goods over the often rugged landscape of New Spain. Within the tablelands, roads were decent, but during the descent from the tablelands to the coastal ports, poor roads made trade more difficult and expensive. (The issue of poor roads in the Veracruz region will be discussed in Chapter 21.) Here in Guerrero, the problems arose in the high plateau at Chilpancingo. Until that point in the journey, the road was *kept in tolerably good order ... but it becomes narrow and extremely bad in advancing toward the capital. The greatest obstacles to communication between the capital and Acapulco arise from the sudden swell of the waters of two rivers, the Papagayo and the Mezcala. Loads are frequently stopped for seven or eight days on the banks of the Papagayo, which the muleteers dare not attempt to ford.*

Humboldt estimated that over 5,000 mules plied the route from Acapulco to Mexico City, completing three return trips annually. The Mezcala River presented similar obstacles, and Humboldt approved of a government plan to build substantial bridges across these two spans. The investment in road improvement, Humboldt argued, would save the colony two or three million piastres on delayed cargo from Manila and Guayaquil to Mexico City.

Humboldt observed what was not evident to others. He noted that while most mountain ranges up and down the Pacific side of North, Central, and South America ran in a north–south line, the Sierra Madres ran sideways from northwest to southeast. For almost 100 kilometres, tropical heat persisted even as the men gained altitude. On 1 April the party at last reached the beginning of the cooler pine forests, but they were never completely free from heat. The ups and downs of valleys and hills meant that later in the day the route would sometimes take them to lower altitudes, such as into the pretty valley of Acaguisotla, where extensive fields of sugar cane grew.

The exhausted travellers finally enjoyed respite when they approached Chilpancingo, on the Huacapa River, where they ate dinner on 2 April. They were now leaving tropical hardwood forest, rich in amate trees, and entering cooler pine and fir forests, adorned with lichens, ferns, and literally dozens of species of orchids found nowhere else in the world. Maize was the main crop cultivated in the pleasant Huacapa valley. Chilpancingo was an attractive town, *surrounded by rich foliage from its abundant willow trees and orchards of lemon trees. The climate is fresh and very pleasant. The Indians decorate the interior of the church with bouquets of flowers ... Near Chilpancingo lies the village of Tixtla, where Indians make crude handkerchiefs.*

After leaving Chilpancingo, the travellers again faced difficult conditions. The road from Acapulco to Chilpancingo had been as decent as those of Europe, even if the terrain and temperatures had made progress difficult. But from Chilpancingo to San Agustín, the road was as bad as the worst Humboldt had seen in South America. From Zumpango and then to the mosquito-ridden village of Zopilote, reached on 3 April, the trail climbing to the Mezcala River was hot and dusty, where the only vegetation to catch Humboldt's eye was immense cacti. Humboldt and his companions found the heat suffocating, as bad as Acapulco, because the rocks held the heat of the day.

AFTER HUMBOLDT:
GUERRERO REMAINS IMPOVERISHED

Chilpancingo and the State of Guerrero were among the most impoverished regions Humboldt visited. The state remains today the least endowed of Mexico's thirty-one federal states, with the exception of Chiapas. Divided into a coastal torrid zone and almost impenetrable mountains in the interior, thinly populated by Indians wracked by disease and abuses of the conquest period, the only portions of Guerrero where Spanish colonial activity was noticeable were in trade, fishing, and pearl gathering along the Acapulco coast and in the silver mining associated with Taxco in the extreme north.

During the early years of the Mexican War of Independence, Guerrero was the scene of important developments. José María Morelos, who had assumed leadership of the struggle for independence after the death of Father Miguel Hidalgo, defeated the royalists at Acapulco but could not hold the town. His insurgents were able to control the centre of the state, where they convened a National Congress (also known as the Congress of Anáhuac) in 1813 at Chilpancingo. Delegates to the congress declared formal independence on 6 November 1813. Morelos was not able to sustain his movement, but the region again became symbolically important in 1821, when the Mexican flag was designed and first sewn in Iguala, Guerrero.

Although Guerrero became a state officially in 1849, it suffered neglect and ruthless exploitation until the Mexican Revolution of 1910 and after. Federal rule benefited only a tiny elite of landholders and mine owners. Public health was non-existent, and education impoverished. Roads were rudimentary, and the first railway linking Acapulco to Mexico City was opened only in the 1890s.

Not surprisingly, Guerrero developed a reputation for dissidence and rebellion. Several unsuccessful revolts sprang up under the dictatorship of Porfirio Díaz between 1877 and 1910 as field labourers rebelled against excessive taxes and usurpation of their lands. Many of the local rebels in Guerrero aligned themselves with the followers of Emiliano Zapata in neighbouring Morelos as the revolution against Díaz erupted in 1910. For a time, the Guerrero rebels fared well, but they had broken with Venustiano Carranza by 1916, and after Zapata's death in 1919, revolt gradually deteriorated into banditry, especially in the 1920s and 1930s. Roads throughout Guerrero became unsafe for travellers, especially after sundown, well into the 1970s.

Rates of illiteracy remain the second worst in Mexico, running over 20 per cent in 2006 and as high as 80 per cent in some rural municipalities. Guerrero's population of 3.2 million is roughly 3 per cent of Mexico's total, but its GDP in 2006 was only 1.6 per cent of the country's total. The United Nations' Human Development Index of 2006 ranked Guerrero only above Chiapas among Mexican states and placed it at a level of *medium human development* comparable to Algeria. Linked to the general lack of education is unemployment in an economy dominated by the tourist industry. For as many as a third of Mexico's population, the solution has been out-migration, mainly to the Chicago area of the United States, where over 300,000 Guer-rerenses live.

While statistics reveal significant rates of poverty and under-development for Guerrero, they do not measure the appalling ne-glect of the Mexican government towards the people of Guerrero. They are the victims of brutality and violence generated by the drug war, where gangsters operate with impunity outside the law. A case in point is the still unsolved massacre in Iguala of forty-three young men, students from Ayotzinapa Rural Teachers' College, in Guerrero in 2014. Though these students had a long history of radical con-frontation with state and federal agents, a thorough 400-page report by the Inter-American Commission on Human Rights exonerates the students and tears to shreds the government's cover-up of the role of the Mexican army and federal police in the murder of the forty-three students and the desecration of their bodies.

Meanwhile, the oppression of young girls by the drug cartels in rural Guerrero continues. Commonly stolen from their homes in remote mountain villages to serve as sex slaves, they are the subject of a critically acclaimed novel by Mexican writer Jennifer Clement. In *Prayers for the Stolen*, first published in English by Hogarth Press in 2014, we learn how women attempt to protect their daughters by naming them males as infants and altering their appearance to make them unattractive and potentially less appealing to marauding kidnappers. While such resistance is usually unsuccessful, Clement masterfully shows how friendship and determination enable her characters to overcome the worst aspects of their abuse.

CHAPTER 4

Humboldt and Colonial Governance
in New Spain

Humboldt's observations on the Spanish colonial regime were deliberately ambiguous. Because he was sponsored by the Bourbon Crown, he seems to have felt obliged to laud his sponsors for creating a prosperous, reform-minded society in New Spain. But a more careful reading reveals a deeper criticism, that centuries of Spanish rule had turned modern descendants of the ancient Aztecs into wretched victims and that the *odious monopoly* of Iberian commercial interests, together with financial mismanagement, had deprived New Spain of its glorious human and commercial potential. Writing in 1808, a time of great political upheaval in Europe in general and in the Iberian world in particular, Humboldt was cautious. His liberal democratic sentiments and his passion for justice for the disinherited classes made him sympathetic to the creole uprisings in Spanish America. But his hope that an enlightened Crown might still achieve some of his vision prevented him from overtly endorsing the rebellions in the colonies. Certainly, no documentation exists in support of the later claim by some that he had supported violent political action. Humboldt had recoiled at the violence generated against members of his own privileged class by the French Revolution's excesses. His first-hand experience of Napoleon did not endear him to military dictatorship, and he was a supporter of the various republican independence movements in Spanish America. He would not, however, have endorsed the mob violence accompanying Father Hidalgo's campaigns in Mexico in 1810. Although naïve

in his speculations about Mexico's future greatness, his idea of a potential transfer of the royal family from Spain to Mexico was not as
far-fetched an idea as it seemed in 1808, since that is exactly what
transpired when the Portuguese royals fled Iberia in favour of Brazil
to avoid capture by Napoleon.

Humboldt's ambiguity enabled him to work for the Spanish Bourbons and, later, for the kings of Prussia while still clinging to his
youthful revolutionary flirtations with republicanism. As the French
historian Charles Minguet argues, Humboldt shared the views of the
Spanish *ilustrados*, progressives who wanted gradual reform under
an enlightened monarchy. After 1815, Humboldt did support revolution in the Americas against reactionary restorations in Europe by
encouraging young radical Spanish-Americans to keep liberalism
alive. Later in his life, in 1848, Humboldt expressed his sadness over
the failures of liberalism in the Americas as well as in Europe.

Two Mexican Creoles whose politics shared much in common
with Humboldt's were Manuel Abad y Queipo and Lucas Alamán.
Abad y Queipo, an enlightened priest whom Humboldt cites frequently in his *Political Essay*, was bishop elect of Michoacán until
he fell from favour with the papacy and the Inquisition in the late
eighteenth century. A student of Adam Smith and Montesquieu,
Abad y Queipo drew on these Enlightenment figures to develop the
first modern analysis of Mexican society. He favoured a reformed
constitutional monarchy, which he believed would address the gross
inequalities of Mexican society, but he stopped well short of opposing Church privilege and property. Brading offers a considered judgment of Abad y Queipo to show the limits of moderate creole
ecclesiastics: "Like many another liberal imperialist, he preferred
good government to self-government, even if its survival depended
on military force."

Born in Guanajuato in 1792 to a prosperous creole family, Lucas
Alamán enjoyed a brilliant career in Mexico as a mining engineer,
capitalist, politician, and historian until his death in 1853. He studied
mining engineering at the School of Mines in Mexico City, which
Humboldt much admired, and was an eye-witness in his native Gua-

najuato to the massacre of creole and Spanish families perpetrated by Father Hidalgo's unruly mob. The experience marked him and reinforced his tepid support for Mexican independence, a position he adopted after 1821. The twenty-seven-year-old Alamán went to Spain in 1819 to serve in the Spanish parliament in Cádiz as a deputy from Mexico, and once in Europe, he actively sought investment and technical assistance for the Mexican mining industry. Back in Mexico in 1822, Alamán co-founded the Conservative Party, and from 1823 to 1825, he occupied the powerful post of minister of interior and external relations in the government of Guadaloupe Victoria. He reoccupied this cabinet position from 1830 to 1832 in the government of Anastasio Bustamante. Troubled by American expansionism, he slowed down US migration to Texas, promoted colonization of the region by Mexicans, and attempted to block a trade treaty with the US. Alamán sponsored ambitious if unrealistic plans for rapid industrialization at a time when depression dominated the Mexican economy. Not all of his initiatives failed. He successfully negotiated national borders in the north with the Americans, and these held right up to the time of the Mexican-American War of 1846. In 1830, he created the first bank in Mexico, the Banco Nacional de Avío. Out of government for the most part after 1832, he served as director for the promotion of industry and devoted himself to research and writing. He created the Natural History Museum in Mexico City and helped found the General National Archive of Mexico. Concerned to put forward a conservative vision of Mexico, he published two monumental histories dealing with independence and the early republic. Finally, consistent with his enduring admiration for the role and memory of Hernán Cortés, whom he considered the founder of the Mexican nation, Alamán administered the estates of the descendants of the Spanish conqueror.

Humboldt followed Alamán's career closely and intersected with him on several occasions. Humboldt shared Alamán's belief that a strong centralized government was needed to industrialize, educate, and modernize Mexican agriculture. He also admired, despite the corruption of the times, how Alamán stood out as a principled and honest citizen. Where Humboldt parted company with Alamán was over the latter's devout Roman Catholic beliefs, which led him to oppose bitterly the secularism of Mexican liberals. Humboldt would have felt more comfortable with the majority of Mexican historians in the 1830s and 1840s, led by Carlos Maria de Bustamante or Lorenzo de Zavala, who viewed independence as the overthrow of three centuries of tyranny.

GOVERNMENT AND POLITICS IN NEW SPAIN

Early in his *Political Essay*, Humboldt offered a mild critique of the administrative division of Mexico into intendancies, a pillar of the Bourbon reforms. Yet, it could be reasonably argued that no political system ever satisfied this sort of rationalist critique: *A country in which the population is dispersed over a vast extent requires that the provincial administration be restricted to smaller portions of ground than those of the Mexican intendancies ... [T]he small intendancy of Guanajuato gives more occupation to an administrator than the provinces of Texas, Coahuila and New Mexico, which are six times more extensive. On the other hand, how is it possible for an intendant of San Luis Potosí ever to know the wants of a province of 28,000 square leagues in extent? How can he, even while he devotes himself with the most patriotic zeal to the duties of his place, superintend the sub-delegates and protect the Indian from the oppressions which are exercised in the villages?*

Towards the end of his *Political Essay*, Humboldt switched his tone to include a series of more substantial criticisms of Spanish colonial government. Discussing revenues, he provided details on the corruption of office holders, as well as on the narrow self-interest of Spanish trading monopolies in Iberia. He was critical of the costs of the frequent petty warfare waged by soldiers stationed on the *presidios* in the north, who separated *warlike and wandering Indians* from settler society, but he found himself unable to judge whether such expenses were justifiable. He showed amazing prescience when he anticipated that Mexico, like other Latin American nations on the Pacific coast, would benefit from Asian immigration as it helped populate the west coast. Overall, he was convinced that a more open society would be much better for Mexico, but he clearly stopped short of declaring his support for the overthrow of the monarchy, even if he was doubtful about whether the reforms he recommended would be implemented: *It might be easy to prove that if Mexico enjoyed a wise administration; if it opened its ports to every friendly nation; if it received Chinese and Malay colonists to people its western coast; if it increased the plantation of cotton, coffee and sugar; and finally if it established a just balance between its agriculture, its mines and its manufacturing industry, it might alone in a very few years afford the crown of Spain a net profit double the amount of what is at present furnished by the whole of Spanish America.*

Humboldt was deeply disappointed by the unfulfilled promises to improve the lot of Indigenous peoples: *We might have hoped that the administration of three enlightened viceroys, animated with the most noble zeal for the public good, the Count of Revillagigedo, Don Teodoro de Croix, and Don Miguel de Azanza, would have produced some happy changes in the political state of the Indians, but these hopes have been frustrated. The power of the viceroys has been singularly diminished of late; they are fettered in all their measures, not only by the junta of finances and by the high court of justice, but also by the government in the mother country which possesses the mania of wishing to govern in the greatest detail provinces at the distance of two thousand leagues, the physical and moral state of which are unknown to them. The philanthropists affirm that it is happy for the Indians that they are neglected in Europe because sad experience has proved that the most part of the measures adopted for their relief have had an opposite effect. The lawyers who detest innovations, and the creole proprietors who frequently find their interest in keeping the cultivator in degradation and misery, maintain that we must not interfere with the natives because on granting them more liberty the whites would have everything to fear from the vindictive spirit and arrogance of the Indian race ... I have heard the same arguments repeated in Mexico, Peru and the kingdom of New*

Granada which in several parts of Germany, Poland, Livonia and Russia are opposed to the abolition of slavery among the peasants.

Humboldt's ambiguity about government and politics in late Bourbon New Spain can be grasped through a sketch of the career of Viceroy José de Iturrigaray, Humboldt's host and sponsor during his visit to New Spain in 1803–04. Iturrigaray gave Humboldt *carte blanche* to travel in Mexico and to access the private government archives in Mexico City, a privilege no foreigner or lay citizen had ever been granted before. The viceroy also invited Humboldt to accompany him on several formal visits through the Valley of Mexico, and he introduced the intrepid explorer to his family and members of the viceregal court.

José de Iturrigaray was born in 1742 to a wealthy Basque merchant family in Cádiz. He became a military officer and participated in the Spanish king Charles III's invasion of Portugal, and in 1793, under Charles IV, he distinguished himself in the war with revolutionary France. He served under Manuel de Godoy as commander in chief of the army in Andalucía in 1801 in the war against Portugal, and Godoy named him viceroy of New Spain, where he served from 4 January 1803 until 16 September 1808. Ambition and venality were two of Iturrigaray's most marked traits. Taking up his appointment, he and his wife, María Inés de Jáuregui y Arístegui, arrived in New Spain at Veracruz with a huge shipment of goods that was duty free because he declared it his personal baggage. When he inspected the mines of La Valenciana and Rayas in 1803, he received a gift of 1,000 ounces of gold because he had offered to request from Spain a sufficient amount of mercury to work the mines more fully.

As viceroy, Iturrigaray carefully cultivated support among Mexican Creoles, making himself a popular contrast to his dour and austere predecessor, Félix Berenguer de Marquina. He received Humboldt graciously and was a progressive supporter of the arts and sciences. On 9 December 1803, Iturrigaray inaugurated Manuel Tolsá's splendid bronze equestrian statue of Charles IV in the *zócalo* of the capital, and in 1804, he allowed one of his sons to be vaccinated against smallpox, though he was disappointedly unenthusiastic about the arrival on 18 March 1804 of Dr Francisco Javier de Balmis with children inoculated with the new smallpox vaccine (see Chapter 22).

Back in Spain in 1808, when Godoy was finally defeated politically and news of the disturbances at Aranjuez reached Mexico, Iturrigaray quickly ingratiated himself with the Creoles to maintain his power. Napoleon had invaded Spain, and the Spanish royal family hurriedly made plans to flee to New Spain, as Humboldt had suggested in the *Political Essay*. The Spanish population took this badly and a riot broke out at Aranjuez on 17 March. The detested Godoy was captured by the crowd and nearly killed; the mob, loyal to Prince Ferdinand, later Ferdinand VII, forced Charles IV to abdicate in favour of his son, who had Godoy arrested. But Charles, Ferdinand, and Godoy were all enticed across the French border, where Napoleon took them prisoner, forced Charles to abdicate in his favour, and then named his brother Joseph king of Spain. On 2 May, the people of Madrid rose up in arms, launching a national revolt against the French. Everywhere provisional juntas were formed, governing in the name of Ferdinand VII. In July, the *cabildo* (municipal government or city hall) in Mexico City declared a provisional, autonomous government for New Spain with Iturrigaray at its head. But the Audiencia, dominated by Spaniards, blocked this attempt and civil war loomed. Iturrigaray had sent 40,000 pesos to the strongly liberal consulate at Veracruz and nominated Creoles to high administrative office. He mobilized the regiment of dragoons from Aguascalientes, stationed in Xalapa and commanded by his close friend Colonel Ignacio Obregón.

The pro-Spanish Audiencia moved more quickly, arrested Iturrigaray and his family, made the populace believe he was being charged with heresy, and confiscated his valuables, stated to be worth over a million pesos and seen to be proof of his venality. Iturrigaray was shipped to Spain on 21 September 1808, but his trial at Cádiz did not end in a conviction, and he was amnestied by the Cortes in 1810. He died in 1815.

Humboldt was silent on Iturrigaray's venality and the dramatic turns of fortune the viceroy experienced as an associate of Godoy's.

To be fair, it would have been inappropriate during the turmoil of Spanish and Mexican politics in the first decade of the nineteenth century for him to have commented. What attracted Humboldt's attention were the politics of slavery, and on this issue he had much to say. Humboldt was impressed that New Spain generally did not rely on African slave labour. He also noted with pleasure that in Mexico City *we meet with a great number of mulatto artisans and free Negroes who by their industry alone procure much more than the necessities of life ... One would say that the mixture of the European and the Negro everywhere produces a race of men more active and more assiduously industrious than the mixture of the whites with the Mexican Indian.*

The kingdom of New Spain is, of all the European colonies under the torrid zone, that in which there are the fewest Negroes. We may almost say that there are no slaves. We may go through the whole city of Mexico without seeing a black countenance. The service of no house is carried on with slaves ... [I]n all New Spain there are not six thousand slaves, of whom the greatest number belong to the ports of Acapulco and Veracruz or the warm regions of the coasts. The slaves are four times more numerous in Caracas which does not contain a sixth of the population of Mexico.

Humboldt noted that enslavement of Indians was forbidden by law in the Spanish colonies, but he deplored the exception among prisoners taken from among the warlike Indians beyond the frontier: *In Mexico the prisoners taken in the petty warfare which is carried out almost without interruption on the frontiers of the* provincias internas *experience an unhappy fate. They are generally of the nation of the Apaches, and they are dragged to Mexico [City] where they languish in the dungeons of a correction house. Their ferocity is increased by solitude and despair. Transported to Vera Cruz and Cuba, they soon perish, like every savage Indian removed from the high table-land into the lower and hotter regions. These prisoners sometimes break from their dungeons and commit the most atrocious cruelties in the surrounding countries. It is high time that the government interested itself in these unfortunate persons whose number is small and their situation so much the easier to be ameliorated.*

In his later years, Humboldt's love affair with the United States became compromised by the US failure to abolish slavery. Humboldt rejected both the rationale for slavery as an economic necessity and the racist notion of inferior peoples. In *Cosmos*, he articulated his position eloquently: *In maintaining the unity of the human race we also reject the disagreeable assumption of superior and inferior peoples. Some peoples are more pliable, more highly educated and ennobled by intellectual culture, but there are no races which are more noble than others. All are equally entitled to freedom: to freedom which in a state of nature belongs to the individual and which in civilization belongs as a right to the entire citizenry through political institutions.*

By mid-century, Humboldt finally had grown weary of holding up the United States as a beacon of liberty and a model for Latin American republics. Speaking to a *New York Times* correspondent shortly before his death in 1859 and just before the outbreak of the American Civil War, the eighty-nine-year-old Humboldt remarked: *I am half American, that is, my aspirations are all with you, but I don't like the present position of your politics. The influence of Slavery is increasing, I fear. So too is the mistaken view of negro inferiority.* According to his protegé Louis Agassiz, Humboldt died sad that the United States had failed to abolish slavery.

Humboldt was among the world's first area specialists, long before such twentieth-century neologisms as "Latin Americanist," "Africanist," or "South Asianist" were coined. What better term than "Latin Americanist" could be used for a man whose range in the social sciences alone included travelogues, literature, anthropology, and art history? The critique so often raised by both critics and admirers that Humboldt's strength did not lie in theory pales before his many profound insights.

ϝ

CHAPTER 5

Taxco: The Baroque Legacy of the First Great Colonial Silver Mine

BORDA, THE SILVER BARON

The first of the mining towns on Humboldt's itinerary was Taxco, where he made a brief overnight stop after his arduous journey through Chilpancingo and the heart of Guerrero. By contrast, he would spend two weeks in Pachuca and an entire month in the richest silver town, Guanajuato.

The Spanish had dug their first mine at Taxco in 1531 searching for tin, but found silver instead, and by the end of the sixteenth century, Taxco was producing more of the precious metal than Bolivia or than anywhere else in the Americas. Bermeja Hill still bears the scars of a cavernous mining tunnel known as the King's Shaft. Cortés and his soldiers also established mining haciendas or refining mills (*haciendas de beneficio*), such as the Hacienda El Chorrillo and the Hacienda San Juan Bautista. Eventually the rich veins petered out and the miners moved on. Taxco fell into decline until 1716, when a Franco-Spanish fortune hunter named Joseph de Laborde, better known as José de la Borda, stumbled upon the great vein of La Cañada. He developed a series of mines, called "Pedregal," "El Coyote," "San Ignacio," and "Cerro Perdido."

Details about Borda's early years are confusing. He was born in 1700 in the Pyrenees, but whether in Spain or across the border in France is unclear. His father was a French army officer at the time of Louis XIV, and his mother was Spanish. His older brother, Francisco, had gone to Taxco to work for two Spanish mine prospectors he had met in Seville. The younger brother, José, came out to New Spain in 1716 to join Francisco in Taxco. In 1720, Borda married Doña Teresa Verdugo Aragonés, his brother's wife's sister. The couple had two children, Manuel, born in 1727, and Ana María, born in 1728. Francisco took his family to Peru in pursuit of mining opportunities, but Borda continued to try his luck in Taxco. Fortune certainly found him there when he discovered the lucrative San Ignacio vein in 1748. Within nine years, it produced 12 million pesos worth of silver, which he used to dedicate the spectacular Santa Prisca Church. But Borda also overspent on houses, schools, and roads, and when the silver began to peter out, he had to reclaim the bejewelled tabernacle of the church to finance his trip north in the hope fortune would shine on him once more.

Now at the advanced age of sixty, Don José de la Borda went off first to Real de Monte and then to Zacatecas, where he hoped to revive the mine called "La Quebradilla," which had been abandoned because of flooding. His debts from lavish building projects, together with failed attempts to drain mines, left him with his last proceeds. Regarded as the most skilled miner of the time, Borda was also a shrewd businessman. In return for tackling the high risk of the deeper mines, he persuaded the reform-minded visitor-general to New Spain, José de Gálvez, and the viceroy, the Marquis of Croix, to grant him full exemption from the silver tithe for the initial years and to provide the state monopoly of mercury at cost price. Borda also reduced the miners' wages. At Zacatecas, he discovered the new Vetagrande lode and opened seven new mines. Now able to afford to invest in superior equipment, he tackled the Quebradilla and enjoyed great success. He revived the wealth of Zacatecas, as well as his own, which now stood at 20 million pesos, but in his seventies and now in failing health, he retired to Cuernavaca, where he died on 30 May 1778. Although his grandchildren eventually lost control of Quebradilla to other entrepreneurs, Borda's success had been due to superior mining techniques. The next generation of Mexican miners

would succeed through heavy capital investment, especially in draining equipment.

Humboldt visited the Taxco silver mines twenty-five years after
Borda's death. He reserved for his *Diario* a rare and candid criticism
of Borda's shabby treatment of his children and of the lavish expen-
ditures made by Borda and other silver barons on a style of architecture Humboldt disdained. Borda, in Humboldt's opinion, *committed
the error of placing his only daughter in a convent. His son was made a
priest, but, in keeping with the custom of the country, this did not prevent him from becoming his father's heir ... Borda built a Church for a
half a million piastres. In the majority of sugar haciendas in Mexico
there are vaulted chapels costing from 20,000 to 40,000 piastres, while
poor, sick slaves are obliged to lie naked on the floor of the infirmary.
The Supreme Being does not require such grandiose masonry in comparison to the tiny surrounding cabins, and it would be more dignified
to imitate the example of His mercy! But the vanity of men makes them
value more visible and durable monuments!*

AFTER HUMBOLDT'S VISIT: HIS MEMORY LINGERS

Humboldt's overnight stay in their town has not prevented Tax-
queños from publicizing, and exaggerating, his visit. They proudly
display the house at 12 Calle Juan Ruiz de Alarcón where Humboldt
and his party lodged for the night. The dwelling at that time offered
the three travellers a fine view of the red-tiled houses and barren hills
as they sat in the evening, enjoying the cool mountain air, the entire
scene illuminated by stars in the night sky. Taxco is well preserved,
and its colourful houses and irregular streets offer visitors sensational
views of the small valleys below the town.

Restored in 1991, the Humboldt House boasts a rich Moorish
façade and a stone-flagged patio leading to a terraced garden decorated with a great variety of flowers. Funded by the state of Guerrero's
Tourism Department, the Viceregal Art Museum of Taxco occupies
most of the Humboldt House. Containing eighteenth-century mem-
orabilia appropriate for Taxco and the Borda family, but very little of

it having to do with Humboldt, the museum's collection has a religious theme, with painted funerary alters, clerical garments embossed with gold or silver thread, and a carved wooden altar. A small room stands apart, displaying a plaque and an attractive bust of the illustrious German visitor. It is accepted lore among locals that Humboldt actually lodged here overnight in 1803, even if there is no evidence that this was the case.

The construction of the Santa Prisca Cathedral was begun in 1751 and completed seven years later. Devoted to Santa Prisca and San Sebastián, this spectacular church boasts paintings by Miguel Cabrera, New Spain's most celebrated artist, and a profusion of gold-leafed saints and cherubs among the twelve highly decorated altars. It is considered one of the finest examples of Mexican churrigueresque baroque architecture extant, a continuation of the exuberant baroque brought to Mexico by the Spanish architect Don José de Churriguera at the beginning of the eighteenth century.

As Humboldt had predicted, Taxco's silver mines did not last forever. Mining in the region in the nineteenth century was not significant, and the town's colonial reputation as a rich silver town declined. Nevertheless, Taxco is today a major tourist destination for the purchase of sophisticated silver products, although silver mining is not responsible for this development. The last mining company operating on the outskirts of town announced in 2007 that it would phase out activities because of depleted reserves. Fortunately, the sale of silver jewellery and silverware continues. It was reinvigorated in Taxco by the arrival in the 1920s of an American, William Spratling, who was impressed with the skills of local silver craftsmen. As discussed in further detail in the next chapter, Spratling developed silver design workshops and began a lucrative export business. A museum named after him near the main plaza contains a significant number of archaeological items from his personal collection.

Tourists can also visit replicas of colonial silver haciendas. The Hacienda El Chorillo is on the north side of town, built beginning in 1534. It offers magnificent views of the valley below and has been exquisitely restored by the state of Guerrero, acting in collaboration with the Universidad Nacional Autónoma de México (UNAM). In 1992,

UNAM converted the site into the Learning Center for Foreigners and made it a campus of the School of Fine Arts. Many of the original structures of the hacienda are still visible, including part of the aqueduct used to provide the large water supply needed to extract silver from ore.

A second hacienda is located in Old Taxco. Hacienda San Juan Bautista, built in the style of a medieval castle in 1543, is now the home of the Regional School of Earth Sciences of the Autonomous University of Guerrero. It houses a small museum containing geological specimens and fossils.

Today's Taxco and environs have other features that Humboldt would have observed. The caves he described are now a part of Grutas de Cacahuampila National Park, one of the largest cave systems in the world. They are located in the extreme northeast of the State of Guerrero, some fifty kilometres from Taxco. Consisting of limestone, as is most of the Sierra Madre del Sur, the caves are called "live" in the sense that groundwater still filters down into them, causing the formations to continue growing. The park receives over 350,000 people a year and is a popular site for spelunking. Rock climbing is also practised nearby. The so-called salons and corridors are enormous, with twenty of the over ninety salons open to the public. They average 130 feet in width and vary in height from 65 to 260 feet. The Acapulco Philharmonic Orchestra occasionally gives concerts in the caves. The caves were used by pre-Hispanic cultures for ceremonial purposes but were kept hidden from colonial rulers until they came to the attention of the Mexican republic in the mid-nineteenth century.

ε

CHAPTER 6

William Spratling and Silver Jewellery Design in Taxco

Despite their many differences, William Spratling, the American-born architect, jewellery designer, and long-time resident of Taxco, shared important characteristics with his German predecessor Alexander von Humboldt. Both men legitimated pre-colonial indigenous culture and shared a love for Mexico. Both enjoyed the company of Mexican intellectuals. And both played important roles as cultural mediators between Mexico and the wider world. In Humboldt's time, this meant western Europe, but for Spratling, it was the United States.

MEXICAN ART AND CULTURE

Spratling's love affair with Mexico began in the summer of 1926 on his first visit, at the age of twenty-six. He soon took up residence in Taxco, and it remained his home until his death in an automobile accident in 1967. He started what is today known as the American School, focusing on silver design. Nicknamed "the Cellini of Taxco," Spratling helped make the remote little town of Taxco famous.

William Spratling grew up in Auburn, Alabama, where he attended high school. Talented in art and drawing, he became an architecture student at the Alabama Polytechnic Institute. After graduating, he worked as an instructor in the Architecture Department of Auburn University. In 1921, the precocious young man became associate professor of architecture at Tulane University in New Orleans, where he lived for most of the 1920s. There, he shared a house with William Faulkner, and they collaborated to produce *Sherwood Anderson and Other Famous Creoles*, a satire of bohemian life in the French Quarter in the 1920s. Spratling also knew John Dos Passos and had many acquaintances in bohemian circles. In addition to his teaching, he published frequently in architecture and travel journals. A restless wanderer, Spratling travelled widely in Italy, Greece, and Egypt from his base in New Orleans, returning each time with a collection of cheap oriental rugs, which he sold at a handsome profit, together with architectural sketches of Venice, Florence, Genoa, and Rome, which he published. Among his other talents was his ability to draw caricatures of famous friends and acquaintances, ranging from Faulkner to Sherwood Anderson. The record reveals a reckless and heavy-drinking party man who enjoyed the bootleg liquor and raucous life of New Orleans, including his discreet but clearly homosexual relationships.

Spratling travelled widely throughout Mexico from 1926 on, a time when it was rare for foreigners to venture much beyond Mexico City and Puebla. On commission from *Architectural Forum* to write articles on Mexican colonial architecture and illustrate them with his own sketches, Spratling went from well-known Puebla and its 365 churches, to Cuernavaca, and then to remote Taxco in the Sierra Madre del Sur, on the northern border of Guerrero. Armed with a letter of introduction to the dynamic, radical muralist Diego Rivera, Spratling began a lifelong friendship with muralist. Through Rivera, he met Miguel Covarrubias, a leading painter, caricaturist, ethnologist, and art historian. Covarrubias was the leading expert on Olmec art in particular, and his knowledge would prove lucrative to both Rivera and Spratling in their activities as dealers in ancient artefacts. In 1928, Spratling introduced American readers to the huge changes rocking the Mexican art world in an article for *Scribner's Magazine* entitled "Figures in a Mexican Renaissance." But his personal discovery of Taxco was to prove life-changing for him and for thousands of others. The mining town had suffered a serious decline typical of many mining centres, and Spratling decided to do something about it.

When Spratling settled in Taxco in 1929, its population – down to only 3,254 – was 25 per cent less than in Borda's heyday. Decay and decline were present everywhere. Windowless small shacks with dirt floors dominated, and overgrown vegetation and collapsing roofs characterized the once-elegant Borda-era houses. Spratling was almost penniless, but he was able to rent accommodation for next to nothing. Through his connection with Diego Rivera and the American ambassador to Mexico, Dwight Morrow, he purchased his own modest place at 23 Calle de las Delicias. The small house, just up from the plaza, was simple, but boasted a large garden bordering on the major ravine or *barranca* in the town.

Diego Rivera was an avid collector of Mexico's ancient art, and he helped Spratling develop a growing appreciation of pre-Columbian art and the collection of artefacts. Gradually, Spratling met others who shared this interest, including Covarrubias. Spratling shifted his interest from colonial architecture to pre-Columbian art and began to frequent remote festivals and gatherings. He undertook a three-day horseback trip to Mexico's second-largest pilgrimage site, at Chalma in the State of Mexico, and met Rivera there the week before Easter. His favourite time of year was March and April, festival time in the states of Morelos and Guerrero.

CULTURAL BROKER BETWEEN MEXICANS
AND AMERICANS

Spratling's friendships with acclaimed muralists Diego Rivera and David Siqueiros were of mutual benefit to all three. With Spratling's support, Rivera garnered the lucrative commission to do the Cuernavaca murals for Dwight Morrow, and Spratling also helped Rivera produce an exhibition of his work at the Metropolitan Museum of Art in New York, funded by the Carnegie Institute. In 1929, Siqueiros was languishing in prison and unable to afford the most basic art materials. He had been jailed for his revolutionary fervour as a senior member of the Mexican Communist Party. Spratling's friendship, encouragement, and financial support enabled the gifted painter to get through the difficult times of the early 1930s. With Spratling's help, Siqueiros persuaded Mexican authorities to release him from prison, on condition that he remain under house arrest in Taxco from 1930 to 1931. Siqueiros was able to resume his art more freely there, and he remained grateful to Spratling for the rest of his life. Also important was Spratling's sponsorship of Siqueiros among American expatriates.

Spratling benefited materially from his role as cultural broker. Diego Rivera tells us in his autobiography that the Morrow commission in 1930 for the Cortés Palace murals was for 30,000 pesos, then US$12,000, with the artist bearing all costs for assistants and materials. "My friend the American architect William Spratling" arranged the commission but would not take an agent's fee. He needed money to live in Mexico, so Rivera used subterfuge, asking Spratling to buy him a house in Taxco, which he then signed over as a gift of 7,000 pesos.

As Spratling helped Taxco revive, its charm and beauty attracted others. Among Mexicans, Moisés Sáenz was entranced and asked Spratling to design a house for him there. Connections between Spratling and the family of US ambassador to Mexico Dwight Whitney Morrow were significant. Morrow's wife, Elizabeth Reeve Cutter, was, like Morrow, a graduate of a distinguished New England college – she was an alumna of Smith and he, of Amherst – and both left endowments and their papers to their alma maters. A close friend of President Calvin Coolidge, Morrow established warm personal relations with Mexican president Plutarco Elías Calles between 1927 and 1930 and helped calm tensions involving the religious rebellion of the Cristeros and Mexican oil policy. The Morrows refurbished an estate in Cuernavaca called "Casa Mañana," now the India Bonita restaurant on a street named after the American ambassador. Morrow was called the "ham and eggs" ambassador because of his private chats with Calles over breakfast. Calles too lived part of the year in Cuernavaca. The Morrows did not look down on Mexicans, and both loved local arts and culture. They were friendly with the bold Rivera, despite his radical Marxism. Their daughter, Anne Morrow Lindbergh, wife of Charles A. Lindbergh, visited Cuernavaca and Taxco frequently, and

Spratling's enthusiasm for flying can be linked to Anne and her famous aviator husband.

Spratling collected pottery, dance masks, and especially pre-Columbian statuary and pottery, and he gave visitors tours of local fiestas. His reputation in the United States as an expatriate who could facilitate interaction with Mexicans grew, and he welcomed a number of celebrated writers to Taxco, among them Hart Crane, Katherine Anne Porter, and John Dos Passos. Many of these luminaries were American women, the most notable of whom was Elizabeth Anderson, just divorced from Sherwood. Spratling built a studio for her in his house, and she remained a permanent resident of Taxco until her death in 1976. Their relationship was very close but platonic. Spratling's lover was an American art student and puppeteer from Minneapolis, Donald Cordry, who arrived in Taxco in 1931. When this romance ended, Spratling took as his lover a Mexican horse trainer who also became his travelling companion and bodyguard.

Spratling's sexuality invites comparisons with Humboldt's. The German traveller too was involved in platonic relationships with a series of attractive women who represented no opportunities for love affairs or marriages. It is guesswork as to whether Humboldt took male lovers. Although some authors, like De Terra and especially Aldrich, are convinced that Humboldt was gay, the discretion of the era led to no convincing evidence of this. For Spratling, on the other hand, one of the great attractions of provincial Mexico in his time was its tolerance for alternative sexual lifestyles.

SILVER ARTISANRY AND BUSINESS, 1932 TO 1944

Spratling developed his artistic skills in silver jewellery design. He began by luring a talented Guerrero silver and goldsmith, Artemio Navarette, from Iguala to Taxco, and providing him with new motifs that went beyond the typical Spanish themes. Soon Spratling and Navarette had established a workshop that attracted young men from the region. By 1932, the Taller de las Delicias was not yet a silver workshop exclusively; its stock also included lamps produced by tinsmiths, simple heavy wood furniture, leather goods, and weavings. Gradually, silver products came to dominate, with Spratling providing designs and the silver acquired from melted silver coins and from artisanal miners selling it door to door. Within two years, there were two teachers, two teaching assistants, and fourteen young apprentices. They liked to work in three dimensions and also mixed silver with ebony, rosewood, and semi-precious stones such as obsidian, malachite, and amethyst quartz. What was emerging was the "Spratling style" of Taxco, an elegantly simple modern style with clean lines and powerful pre-Columbian motifs.

Spratling was also adept at marketing. He stressed the hand-crafted, sometimes erotic nature of the art of silversmithing and kept his prices high, maintaining his Taxco jewellery as a luxury product. By 1938, his workshop was famous as a centre that displayed the creative strength of Mexicans. At its height, the enterprise counted 100 working artisans, 46 of whom were silversmiths.

During the early years of the Second World War, Spratling's enterprise experienced a boom. The importing of silver costume jewellery from Europe to the United States dried up, and imports from Taxco filled the gap. Spratling sold to top-end American stores such as Neiman-Marcus, Bonwit Teller, and Saks Fifth Avenue. Merchants and artisans all benefited, none more so than Spratling, who developed his taste for fast cars and a lavish lifestyle, which included owning a yacht and a beach house in Acapulco. To raise more capital to meet increased production, Spratling took on twelve Mexican and two American partners, selling them 75 per cent of his stock and changing the name of the company from Taller de las Delicias to Spratling y Artesanos. The new ventures included a wholesale line of silver for the less upscale Montgomery Ward catalogue and the manufacture of heavy silver ID bracelets for the US military. Space was lacking for the growing number of employees, so he expanded to an abandoned hacienda at La Florida, near the northern entrance to Taxco.

Figure 6.1
The Spratling logo. (Author's photo)

COMMERCIAL SETBACKS, 1943–1950

Spratling's business decisions were not always sound, and he risked losing control of his company should the boom slow down, as it was bound to do. He hoped his partners would put up more money, but they insisted he use his own cash from the proceeds of his sale of the company's stock. Productivity increased but quality declined with a growing reliance on the shoddy machine-made production of silver beads and trinkets. By 1943, the town of Taxco had a total of 1,200 silver-smiths, four times the pre-war number, and Spratling y Artesanos accounted for over 300. But disputes over the company's direction led his partners to remove him from control. In March 1944, he was forced to accept a contract as managing director, a euphemism for a salaried employee. In July 1945, Spratling left the company, which soon went bankrupt thanks to the short-sighted greed of its bosses.

Broke but still keeping up appearances, Spratling moved to a six-acre chicken farm in Taxco El Viejo that he had bought a few years before. He became something of a recluse, travelling up to the town rarely and usually at night. He accepted a one-year project with the US government's Department of the Interior to teach silver making to seven indigenous students in Alaska, using the proceeds to purchase a plane, which he flew solo to Alaska and back in 1948.

The Alaska project failed, though Spratling developed hundreds of brilliant designs, with some Alaskan motifs entering into his work. Influenced also by George Jensen, the brilliant Scandinavian designer, Spratling evolved a new style with a new hallmark, the ws intertwined in script, and opened a small workshop at his ranch with a new company that he called "William Spratling S.A." Production was limited and sold in Acapulco and Mexico City. Most visitors to Taxco bought from merchants there, and Spratling was unable to lure more than a handful down the ten kilometres to Taxco El Viejo. Money continued to be a problem, and Spratling sold his yacht, though he kept his plane.

OTHER SILVER MASTERS AND WORKSHOPS IN TAXCO

In *Silver Masters of Mexico*, a brilliantly illustrated book that has become essential for collectors of Mexican and especially Taxco silver, American art historian Penny Morrill has provided an invaluable portrait of the many silver artists whom Spratling inspired. Spratling created an industry based on good design and fine craftsmanship. He was generous with his advice and instruction and did not resent it when some of his talented artists chose to leave Las Delicias in order to set up their own workshops. By the time of the Second World War, silver production was widespread throughout Taxco. Perhaps the most prominent of his disciples was Héctor Aguilar, who, with his American wife Lois Cartwright, opened an atelier of their own in Taxco in 1939 after working with Spratling at Las Delicias. They renovated the historic Casa Borda on the *zócalo* of Taxco and made it into a workshop and store with the name "Taller Borda." Aguilar was the principal designer, but others included the painter Valentín Vidaurreta and several *maestros* and apprentices who had formerly worked for Spratling. This community of silversmiths, carpenters, designers, leatherworkers, and coppersmiths remained together for twenty-four years. When the Taller disbanded, many continued working in small workshops in their homes. Those still active today, according to Morrill, look back fondly "with [the] satisfaction that comes from a life devoted to the pursuit of beauty."

Héctor Aguilar was born near Puebla in 1905 to a prominent Mexican family and educated in Mexico City. He worked as a photographer, tour guide, and adventurer as a young man. Versed in art and archaeology, Aguilar met Spratling when he brought one of his tour groups to Taxco, and after marrying the widowed Lois Cartwright in 1937, he went to work for Spratling for two years as manager of the Las Delicias workshop. In 1939, the couple went into business on their own but with the financial support of friends, opening the Taller Borda workshop and store, with Lois serving as business manager. The workshop store and living quarters were at the Casa Borda, which had fallen into a ruinous condition since its heyday as the private residence of the flamboyant silver entrepreneur José de la Borda. Aguilar began using his hallmark H R to produce wonderful silver jewellery – necklaces, brooches, bracelets, earrings, and ensembles. His work remained popular for many years. It included such technical innovations as concealed swivel hinges for his bracelets, much copied by other silversmiths. Aguilar was a brilliant designer, and his work featured not only pre-Columbian motifs typical of Spratling's work, but also modern abstractions. He also worked in copper and encouraged carpentry ironworks and copper workshops at the Taller Borda. During the Second World War, his workshop adopted machine production, producing military insignia and silver costume jewellery on a large scale. The popularity of Taller Borda products soared in the 1940s and 1950s. Two important customers were Rosa Covarrubias, wife of the painter and art historian Miguel Covarrubias, and her friend the accomplished American artist Georgia O'Keeffe, who was a lover of Taxco silver and leatherware.

Aguilar's behaviour in Taxco touched on *noblesse oblige*. He was active in Mexico as one of founders of the Union of Silver Industrialists, bringing order and standards to the exportation process by regulating wholesalers and guaranteeing purity of silver content. On the other hand, he was a strongly paternalist employer. In the late 1950s, the Taxco silver business began to suffer from an inevitable decline. First, the opening of the new Mexico City–Acapulco highway in 1954 bypassed Taxco, reducing tourist traffic somewhat. More importantly, in 1958, the Federal Department of Social Security built a hospital in Taxco, and the government required Taller owners to pay social security on behalf of their employees monthly. Bankruptcy was the response of many workshops, while others cut their workforce by as much as a half. Workers formed a union and called a strike that lasted four months. On 24 December 1962, the Aguilars locked out their workers and declared bankruptcy. Forty-odd workers formed a union, hired lawyers, and secured the support of Guerrero's Department of Labour in the form of compensation. In April 1963, the workers tried to reopen the Taller Borda, but the request was turned down by the Aguilars' lawyers. The Aguilars finally reached a settlement by selling off assets. They sold their store in 1966 and moved to Zihuatanejo. Lois passed away in 1978, and Héctor in 1986.

In addition to the Taller Borda, two other workshops grew out of Spratling's initiative at Las Delicias. Los Castillo, founded by Antonio Castillo and his three brothers, was Taxco's largest workshop. At its height in the 1940s, it comprised 350 artisans and designers, who produced roughly 200 kilograms of silver jewellery and decorative objects every week. Antonio, his three brothers, and a cousin had begun with Spratling, and in 1939, they moved out to form their own workshop. Their work was highly innovative and experimental, at its best when marrying different metals to produce trays and pitchers with very little soldering.

The third workshop linked to Spratling was a much smaller operation. It owed its existence and name to Reveriano Castillo, a silvermaster with ties to both Spratling and Aguilar. In 1934, at age ten, Castillo began as a helper for Las Delicias and Spratling. In 1939, he was one of ten young men who left with Aguilar to join the Taller Borda. Later, Castillo formed his own workshop with fifteen to twenty workers, called "Reveri," in a store located across the street from the Taller Borda. Reveriano Castillo possessed his own hallmark, and his designs were whimsical, inspired by Aztec art and highlighted, for example, by wonderful caterpillar and starfish pins. His work is well represented in private collections.

Three important silver artists who did not create their own workshops were Valentín Vidaurreta, Rafael Ruiz Saucedo, and Enrique Ledesma. Vidaurreta was a well-known Mexican Cubist painter, friendly with Spratling, Covarrubias, and the wealthy art collector Dolores Olmedo Patiño. By the early 1930s, he had become interested in silver design and had begun working for Spratling at Las Delicias. Like Aguilar but unlike Spratling, Vidaurreta found inspiration in the baroque era of Taxco. He also took commissions for architectural renovation in Taxco and Cuernavaca, including the old colonial hacienda San Juan Bautista on the edge of Taxco, which he purchased in 1935. After the Aguilars went into business for themselves, Vidaurreta worked as a designer at the Taller Borda. He died suddenly of a heart attack in 1959.

Rafael Ruiz Saucedo was a master silversmith and *jefe*, or administrator, of the Los Castillo workshop. Originally from Michoacán, he moved with his brother to Mexico City and then to Taxco in 1938. They joined Las Delicias, worked for Aguilar briefly in the 1950s, and then joined Los Castillo. Rafael Saucedo was lured away by Spratling in 1963 to work at the ranch, which he did until Spratling's death in 1967. Rafael lived in semi-retirement until his death in 1990.

Enrique Ledesma was a painter, silversmith, and lapidary who began his training in Mexico City at the prestigious San Carlos Academy. He then apprenticed at his father's silver workshop and at a large workshop while in art school. Sometime in the 1930s, he joined Spratling at Las Delicias. After 1945, Ledesma moved to the

Taller Borda, where he did lapidary work. In 1949, Spratling asked him to help train Alaskans, and in 1950, when that experiment had clearly failed, he put together his own workshop. Ledesma's designs are modern and elegant, mixing silver with obsidian and other media. One of his remarkable creations is a beautiful silver and tortoise-shell ensemble.

SPRATLING'S LATER YEARS, 1950–1967

By 1950, Spratling had become a collector and dealer in antiquities rather than a full-time jeweller. Covarrubias was the acknowledged expert on Olmec antiquities. In 1944, Covarrubias labelled art from the middle Rio Balsas area – where many of the artefacts were found – as "Mezcala." Rivera and Spratling concentrated on these western Mexican pieces, building up large personal collections as well as selling off pieces to well-heeled collectors. The buying and selling of Mexican antiquities was not illegal until 1973, but it was frowned upon, especially on a large scale or when the pieces were known to be fakes cleverly reproduced by special shops in Taxco. Rivera was untroubled by the practice, declaring, "Same clay, same Indians" when asked about it.

Spratling was an exporter on a large scale and found himself in trouble with Mexican authorities on several occasions. In his autobiography, he justified his activities by arguing that exceptional pieces would have ended up in museums in any case, thus convincing himself he was preventing plundering and abuses. But his sometimes shady practices strained his friendship with the artist Rufino Tamayo, for example, who bought a piece from Spratling that proved to be fake. The sums involved could be large. Nelson Rockefeller was an enthusiastic customer and purchased pieces that ran to $10,000 or more. One gold piece, which sold for $25,000, later proved to be fake, and Spratling was obliged to return the money. Spratling's reputation in Taxco was affected, and some local broadsides denounced him as a thief. On the other hand, he remained a celebrated figure among

Americans. He enjoyed meeting with Hollywood celebrities like John Huston and Marilyn Monroe, who visited his ranch six months before her death. Other visitors included Richard and Pat Nixon.

His last years at Taxco El Viejo were absorbed in an extravagant routine. He entertained with good food, indulged his taste for alcohol, and drove weekly to Mexico City to sell and barter antiquities. At his ranch, he showed customers his special rooms for gold, silver, and regular objects. With an eye on the customer's purse, Spratling directed them to the appropriate room. He served wealthy visitors champagne in the gold room and tequila in the silver room, while others made do with soft drinks in a third room. Taxi drivers and others were given commissions on sales for bringing in people. He bred Great Dane dogs and had up to twenty-three at his ranch at times. A year before his death, he underwent a prostate operation and survived a plane crash while flying solo to Mexico City, yet his death in 1967 was the result of a car accident. Although he and his chauffeur survived the crash, Spratling died of a heart attack before he could be treated in hospital.

Spratling's funeral in Taxco recalled the larger-than-life days of José de la Borda. Over 20,000 people attended, filling Santa Prisca and beyond. Speakers at the funeral recognized how Spratling had turned Taxco around as a town, and the town he had barely visited in the last decade of his life now honoured him as one of its famous sons.

After Spratling's death, his friend Alberto Ulrich purchased the ranch at Taxco El Viejo, the hallmark, and all the designs through his new company, Sucesores de William Spratling. The company remains in the Ulrich family. Two sisters, Violante and Consuelo Ulrich, live in Mexico City and visit the ranch occasionally, hoping to find more jewellery available for customers; they have made Mexican cooking lessons available and offer to rent the facility to groups.

The Ulrichs continue to keep Spratling's legacy alive. In January 2013, they loaned hundreds of Spratling pieces to the Franz Mayer Museum in Mexico City for an excellent exhibit of Spratling's work entitled *William Spratling, Designer: Legacy in Silver.* While his silver designs

are clearly outstanding, the beauty of his furniture shows his importance in the Art Nouveau movement and the influence of another architect and designer, the Glaswegian Charles Rennie Macintosh.

What little silver production there is today at Taxco El Viejo fails
to measure up to the standards of Spratling in his prime. Though
now run down, the ranch remains a beautiful site, with a mountain
rising right behind the hacienda. Rushing water in the stream irri-
gates the luxuriant foliage Spratling originally planted. In their cages,
macaws, parrots, and even an alligator enliven the ranch, but the
Great Danes are long gone.

CHAPTER 7

Cuernavaca: A Brief Stay in the Valley of Eternal Spring

After leaving Taxco, Humboldt and his companions spent a short time in the fertile Cuernavaca valley on 9 and 10 April, which they entered through Puente de Ixtla. They would have observed sugar plantations until they were just north of the town, where limestone mountains, called the "Sierra de Chichinautzín," separated the Cuernavaca valley from that of Mexico City itself, only a day's ride away. Humboldt was eager to climb to the height of the *sierra* at 13,000 feet and at last glimpse the "City of Palaces," which Cortés had observed almost 300 years earlier from this very spot. Humboldt lingered only a few hours in the town of Cuernavaca, barely long enough to give it the label "City of Eternal Spring," by which it is still known.

The travellers spent an uncomfortable first night in the Cuernavaca valley, having become accustomed to temperatures of around 34°C; yet the thermometer dipped at night to 10°C or below. Moving through large pine forests, Humboldt and his companions were once more struck by the natural beauty they observed: *The sunset is glorious. We glide over the great plains of San Gabriel, Ixtla and Cuernavaca, framed all along the eastern horizon by the two snow-capped mountains of Puebla and a few grotesque basalt hills with large and attractive columns. The bottom of the plain is very green, rich with abundant crops of sugar, maize, and wheat, and adorned by a multitude of small villages, each with pretty white stone churches. Many of these date back to the time of Hernán Cortés, who erected walls of immense thickness, similar to those of the temples of Mexico City, to serve as defensive barriers in case of attack.*

XOCHICALCO AND THE CUERNAVACA VALLEY FROM MESOAMERICAN TIMES TO HUMBOLDT'S VISIT

In his *Vues des Cordillères*, Humboldt described the archaeological site of Xochicalco, a pre-Hispanic ceremonial centre one day's journey south of Cuernavaca and just off the road leading from Puente de Ixtla to Cuernavaca. In a hurry to reach Mexico City, the travellers elected not to visit the ruins, but Humboldt offered this description: *From the heights of Cuernavaca we can see the ruins of the great pyramid of Xochicalco. Within this pyramid are found pelts which men prepared for sacrifices, and horns of impressive size. The only similar find exists in the archives of the viceroy of México. The horns are over seven feet long and weigh from thirteen to fifteen pounds. They are said to be the antlers of a stag but what great size! They have seven points and cannot be those of an elk or moose. Rather, they are likely the antlers of an antediluvian ancestor of a stag. The inside of the horn resembles ivory.*

Humboldt could well have consulted a landmark publication on Xochicalco, the first illustrated study in Mexico in what would be the emerging field of archaeology. The essay appeared in the Mexican *Gaceta de literatura* in 1791 and was written by the cleric José Antonio de Alzate y Ramírez, who had independently visited the recently discovered site of Xochicalco in 1777.

Xochicalco is one of the finest restored archaeological sites in Central Mexico, only thirty-eight kilometres southwest of Cuernavaca and an easy day trip from Mexico City. The name is Nahuatl for "house of flowers," and it emerged as a late classical ceremonial centre after the fall of Teotihuacán in around 300 CE. It is likely to have been founded by Olmec priests fleeing the invasion of the Valley of Mexico by Toltec desert nomads. At its height 300 years later, Xochicalco's inhabitants may have numbered 20,000 and nearly all the standing architecture was built by that time.

The architectural style shows the strong influence of Teotihuacán. The site contains one of the largest ball courts in Mesoamerica, and a vivid representation of Quetzalcóatl sits along the sides of the main pyramid, known as the Temple of the Feathered Serpent. Also adding drama to this large ruin are two smaller ball courts, sweat-baths, a row of circular altars, some free-standing sculptured stelae, and especially a cave with steps carved into it. The cave was decorated in several colours, with a hexagonal chimney at the top. The chimney's slight slope allowed the sun's rays to be projected on the floor of the cave during the 105 days running from 30 April to 15 August, when the sun moves on towards the Tropic of Cancer. On 15 May and 29 July, the beam of light from the sun falls directly through the chimney, projecting the image of the sun on the floor of the cave. As if this were not spectacular enough, Xochicalco's main pyramid marks the sunrise azimuth at summer solstice, when the sun passes directly above the summit of Popocatépetl, and another pyramid aligns with the sunrise azimuth of the winter solstice.

Chosen for its defensive attributes as well as for its remarkable astronomical features, the site commands the old Mesoamerican trade roads to and from modern-day Taxco, Cuernavaca, and Puebla. Archaeological evidence shows that Xochicalco was burned and destroyed around 900 CE and quickly abandoned. A remnant population lived on the lower slopes, and by 1200, a smaller, more rustic town had emerged. A steady stream of mainly Mexican archaeologists have worked at Xochicalco since the late nineteenth century, and many superb artefacts have been unearthed. Supervision, preservation, and display of the site and its treasures are the responsibility of the INAH, the National Institute of Anthropology and History, a public institution of which Humboldt would have been proud. As it does in many other locales, the INAH maintains a highly attractive museum close to the site and organizes spectacular summer viewings of celestial events. Xochicalco, perhaps more than any other single ceremonial centre, deserves to be visited when the heavens reveal their secrets, as they have been doing for Mesoamericans for millennia.

Long after Xochicalco's glory years had passed, other new arrivals in the valleys of Mexico and Cuernavaca discovered the attractions of this pleasant region. After first conquering the Cuernavaca valley in the thirteenth century, Aztec emperors established a winter residence in Cuauhnáhuac ("surrounded by trees," as they called it in Nahuatl) to escape from the colder winter nights of Tenochtitlán (Mexico City). The Spanish name "Cuernavaca" is a mispronunciation of the Nahuatl; the town has nothing to do with "the horns of a cow," but the name has stuck.

Two centuries later, the Spanish conquerors found Cuernavaca just as attractive as the defeated Aztecs had, and for the same reasons. The warm and densely populated city, with its large farms and plentiful labour in the surrounding valleys, prompted Hernán Cortés to make the city his favourite residence after 1523. Cortés and his heirs engaged in numerous projects. They used Indian forced labour liberally for construction and agriculture, introducing Caribbean-style sugar cane cultivation, even introducing African slaves as labourers to supplement production. The family's first sugar hacienda was located in Atlacomulco, now a suburb of Cuernavaca, and is used as an attractive hotel and concert site. The conqueror's wife, Juana de Zúñiga, lived in the magnificent Palacio de Cortés, which her husband began constructing in 1526 and finished nine years later. It is one of the most impressive buildings of the conquest era, built in the Renaissance style, with a series of arches on the central terrace and thick-walled battlements. Cortés and his descendants would inhabit the building for several centuries. Later, it served as a warehouse, a jail, a military barracks, and the state of Morelos's government building until 1969. During the War of Independence, José María Morelos spent some days imprisoned there until his execution in 1815.

Cortés also started construction of the Cathedral of Cuernavaca as the church within the monastery of the Franciscan Order in 1529. The cathedral, like other churches in Morelos, was to double as a fortress and had cannons mounted above the buttresses. The main sanctuary is stark, as are frescoes dating from the sixteenth century depicting the persecution and martyrdom of San Felipe de Jesús and his companions in Japan.

The Taxco silver baron José de la Borda also contributed to Cuernavaca's lustre. He bought a house in the city that his son, Manuel de Borda y Verdugo, transformed into a beautiful property, filled with flowers and fruit trees, fountains and artificial lakes. Don Manuel's portrait is in the kitchen of the residence. The house is still known as the Borda Garden and is open to the public.

All in all, late colonial Cuernavaca's architecture, climate, and natural beauty combined to make it a very attractive place. One creole natural scientist who had spent time in Spain, Lieutenant Antonio Pineda y Ramírez, had training as a botanist and visited Central Mexico on special assignment to the Royal Museum of Natural Science in 1791. He found Cuernavaca and its valley abundant in water, and its graceful tree-lined avenues and cultivated fruit trees reminded him of the beauty of Granada.

CUERNAVACA AFTER HUMBOLDT'S BRIEF VISIT

Beginning at least with Humboldt if not well before, officials in Cuernavaca have not been averse to embellishing the city's association with famous figures. There is a Humboldt Street in town, as well as a Privada Humboldt, or Humboldt Lane, south of the city centre. A house in this lane has a plaque in one of its bedrooms announcing in German that the famous naturalist slept there. If the implication is that Humboldt spent the night, it is incorrect, but of course he could easily have taken his daily *siesta* here before resuming the trek to Mexico City. Right around the corner, off Rufino Tamayo Street, lies another lane, Privada Rufino Tamayo, proudly indicating that the great Mexican painter made his home here in his later years. Just down the road leading to one of the city's major ravines is yet another modern shrine, this one claiming to be the former residence of Diego Rivera when he visited the valley.

Cuernavaca deserves its reputation for having a benign climate. It enjoys mild year-round temperatures that only exceed 28 degrees in April and May, just before the rains arrive. The rains last until September, but they fall in the late afternoon or evening so that residents have the whole day to enjoy the flowers and abundant greenery that thrive in the spring-like temperatures. Altitude makes a huge difference, and the northern part of the city, at 6,000 feet, is considerably cooler than the southern end at 4,500 feet, as the entire city is sloped northeast to southwest and is divided by several sharp ravines and marked by numerous microclimates. On a clear day and from certain vantage points, two of Mexico's spectacular active volcanoes, Ixtaccíhuatl (Sleeping Woman) and Popocatépetl (Smoking Mountain) may be visible. Hence the title of Malcolm Lowry's novel *Under the Volcano*, set in Cuernavaca in the 1930s. Living here in 1939, Lowry counted no less than eighteen churches and found "the streets and lanes tortuous and broken, the roads winding." During the rainy season, water flooded the lower roads near the series of ravines, or *barrancas*, which were ubiquitous in the town. In Humboldt's day, the town and valley counted about 40,000 people, but greater Cuernavaca today numbers well over a million, though as to how many are permanent residents, how many are daily commuters to the Federal District, and how many are weekenders from Mexico City, no one is certain.

During his brief time as emperor of Mexico, the Austrian Archduke Maximilian converted the Borda Garden into a summer residence for himself and his wife, Carlota Amalia. In 1865, he bought land in nearby Acapantzingo on which to construct a chalet for his mistress, "La India Bonita." Today, the property has become an excellent botanical garden, run by the INAH. It contains a fine collection of Mexican orchids, many of which Humboldt first identified 200 years ago.

Labour coercion continued to be a feature of life in the Cuernavaca valley, at least until the Mexican Revolution of 1910. Under the dictatorship of Porfirio Díaz, powerful landowners living in Mexico City steadily dispossessed small peasant landowners and imposed a virtual serfdom on them. The great champion of agrarian reform, Emiliano Zapata, who was born in a small village near Cuautla in the heart of the state of Morelos, rose up in defence of the dispossessed with his cry of *"Tierra y libertad!"* (land and liberty) and developed a powerful base in the state until he was assassinated in 1919. A large equestrian statue of Zapata dominates the northern entrance to the city.

People seeking to escape the cold winter temperatures and polluted air of Mexico City have continued to seek shelter in Cuernavaca in contemporary times. The list includes the Mexican actor Mario Moreno, better known as Cantinflas, and several Americans, such as artist and collector Robert Brady, us ambassador to Mexico Dwight Morrow, who was posted to the republic from 1927 to 1930, and Barbara Hutton, the Woolworth heiress. Cantinflas resided near the centre of Cuernavaca and engaged his friend Diego Rivera to decorate his swimming pool with a design of a pre-Hispanic goddess, done in Venetian-style mosaic.

Diego Rivera, too, appreciated Cuernavaca's warm weather, and his hand can be seen throughout the city. In addition to the Cantinflas swimming pool, his most spectacular contribution is his stunning mural in the Palacio de Cortés. Its largest images are full-length portraits of José María Morelos and Emiliano Zapata. As in other instances, Rivera's communist ideology did not cause him to reject commissions from wealthy capitalists, so long as he could express his beliefs freely. Morrow paid Rivera $12,000 in 1930 to do the Cuernavaca mural, which the ambassador then turned over to the state as a gift.

Robert Brady transformed his home and private artworks and collectibles into a museum celebrating Mexico's rich tradition of popular arts and crafts. On his death in 1986, his estate bequeathed the home and collection to the city. Its eclectic holdings include oil paintings by Frida Kahlo and Rufino Tamayo, Mexican colonial and popular art, and handicrafts from Africa and India.

Last but by no means least, in 1959, Barbara Hutton built a lavish estate named "Sumiya" eleven kilometres south of Cuernavaca with materials, craftsmen, and an architect brought in from Japan. The main house, a series of large connected rooms and decks, overlooks thirty acres of grounds that contain Japanese as well as native Mexican plants and trees. The property even boasts a kabuki-style theatre and a gorgeous Zen meditation garden. Its details satisfy Japanese tourists as well as experts on Japan, who often express their astonishment at the accuracy of the construction. Sometime after Hutton's death, the Camino Real Hotel chain took over the property and turned Sumiya into a luxurious hotel and convention centre.

CHAPTER 8

Ecological and Economic History in the Mexican Tableland Valleys of Anáhuac (Toluca, Mexico, and Puebla)

An ever-present danger in writing biography lies in losing sight of the subject's shortcomings. Despite his awareness of Mexico's history of water management and of potential fuel shortages from deforestation, Humboldt did not fully appreciate the dramatic transformation of Mexico's ecology. Perhaps, as a member of the gentry, however liberal he was, he could also be a romantic idealist, unable to see Mexico's flaws. Instead, he documented a prosperous Mexico, a country where the land was fertile, the air pure, the people and culture admirable.

Drawing especially on the work of John Richards and of Arij Ouweneel, we can see what Humboldt could not, even as we recognize that both researchers, writing 200 years later, had the benefit of new understandings of ecological change. Richards notes that Mexico and Central America experienced a dry period from the early sixteenth to the early nineteenth century, marked by growing drought and famine. Increasing scarcities of food, fuel, water, and fertile land pointed to a serious ecological crises. Extreme droughts after 1785–86 took place in four-year sequences, such that crop failures brought famine conditions at the onset of the Mexican Revolution in 1811. Late spring droughts in 1791, 1793, and 1797 caused harvest failures and increased mortality. Humboldt, travelling in between these years of hardship, missed these trends.

After the Spanish conquest of Mexico, land became less rather than more intensively used as a result of a dispersed and dwindling

Indian population. Migrants from Europe and Africa were insufficient to replace three centuries of die-off before the Indigenous population began slowly to recover. In addition, silver profits and their lure drove frontier expansion in colonial New Spain well beyond settled frontiers. Settlements then caught up to the mining regions, bringing new roads and transport. Mines produced their own peculiar form of pollution, and the commercial ranching of sheep and cattle wrought huge ecological change as well. In sum, agriculture in New Spain could never be described as intense. Humboldt did mention that drought and famine had struck before his visit in 1803–04, but he did not see a larger trend and tended to support the notion – indeed, to be one of the sources – for those historians who argued that the Spanish Bourbon reforms had led to an economic boom in the last quarter of the eighteenth century.

Ouweneel offers his own highly original environmental analysis through his examination of the role of landscape and precipitation, combined with the composition and development of the population. He begins with a criticism of the new ecological history, many of whose proponents were once Marxists, "reds becoming greens" in his colourful phrasing. These writers focus on the history of environmental degradation resulting from the forces of political economy. It is assumed that wealthy Spanish colonists imposed a heavy ecological burden on the environment, especially under colonialism. Poor people, on the other hand, generated local indigenous movements of resistance against extractive economies. Ouweneel, however, suggests that ecological history should not be deterministic and that a mature ecosystem might be one in which the nutrient supply is in equilibrium – that is, with little loss.

Ouweneel takes as his study the Mexican tablelands, called "Anáhuac," consisting of three large valleys: Toluca in the west, Mexico in the centre, and Puebla in the east, all enclosed by rugged and impenetrable mountains. Each area had a high population density; the two large cities of Mexico City and Puebla also benefited from a strong central government and a well-integrated market in the late eighteenth century. Nevertheless, three "shadows" fell over the three valleys of Anáhuac between 1780 and 1810: a demographic one, based on relative overpopulation in the peasant communities; a climatological one, manifested by a series of late spring droughts; and a political one, the result of Bourbon reforms and changes in landholding to the detriment of the Indian communities.

Ouweneel borrows a metaphor from historians to characterize the period as one of contrast and contradiction between the very rich and the very poor, comparing the lavish churrigueresque style exemplified by the churches of Santa Prisca, Tepotzlán, and La Valenciana with the beggars in the streets. True, New Spain did undergo economic growth and increasing territorial integration, but it also experienced impoverishment because its prosperity was not generalized.

Ouweneel's three valleys stand at altitudes ranging from 7,000 to 8,500 feet and are distinguished from other regions of New Spain such as Michoacán, Guadalajara, and Oaxaca, which are lower. The three valleys are surrounded by the neo-volcanic axis, which cuts Mexico in two along an east–west axis. These ridges deflect rain clouds from the plains so that precipitation falls directly in this mountain area but less frequently in the larger highland plateaus. Second, the flat plateaus from which four enormous volcanoes rise are generally fertile in the valleys between the mountain ridges and the highland volcanoes. This prevents an expansion of agricultural territory to deal with expanding population. Third, natural irrigation channels fed by streams running off the great volcanoes are dry for much of the year.

Access to the valleys from the coast was always difficult. The ascent from Veracruz to the Puebla valley was the most severe. A climb of 6,500 feet was necessary over only 100 kilometres, the last part of which lay in thick mist because of perpetual low-hanging clouds. The main obstacle was called "Soldier's Mountain" near Xalapa. The mountain track was so narrow and slippery that every caravan lost a few mules, which went crashing down the slopes. Ropes and pulleys were required at this spot to haul both mules and loads up the slope.

Ouweneel offers this sketch of the three valleys in the Central Mexican Plateau. Toluca is the most inclement, since its average height is 8,500 feet, 650 feet higher than Mexico City and 1,300 feet

TABLE 8.1
Rainfall in seven cities of Anáhuac, 1976

Cities	Altitude (metres)	Rainfall (millimetres)	Average Annual Temperature (Celsius)
Toluca	2,675	800.2	12.7
Tlaxcala	2,552	802.3	16.2
México	2,240	720.8	15.1
Puebla	2,209	822.9	17.1
Pachuca	2,435	386.8	14.2
Cuernavaca	1,529	1,061.0*	20.7
Xalapa	1,487	1,514.8**	17.9

Source: *Nuevo atlas porrua de la República Mexicana* (Mexico City: 1980), adapted from Table 3, in Ouweneel, *Shadows over Anáhuac*, 78.
*Note that Arij Ouweneel considers the southern edge of Cuernavaca subtropical.
**Xalapa is very humid on its northeastern flanks because of clouds gathering there.

above Puebla. It has twice as many nights of frost as Puebla. Its narrow strip of agricultural land is only sixty kilometres wide, much of it unusable because of marshes, which were more numerous 200 years ago. Poor drainage sends lots of water into the more central lower parts of the valley in the rainy season. A marshy lake is the source of the Lerma River. The valley had a population estimated at forty persons per square kilometre in 1800. The volcano in the Toluca valley is called the "Nevado de Toluca" and its summit sits at 15,000 feet.

The Valley of Mexico also has poor drainage, but its strip of farming land is larger than Toluca's, running 60 kilometres wide and 100 kilometres long. In colonial times, there were large lakes – Chalco, Texcoco, Xaltocan, and Zumpango. Mexico City was plagued by muddy streets and inundations well into the eighteenth century because the colonial regime filled in most of the canals. A specialist was called in but did not finish his improvements until the end of the eighteenth century. In the meantime, embankments were used to keep the lakes contained. Evaporation made the banks brackish. The villages of Xochimilco and Ixtapalapa laid out fields and vegetable gardens (*chinampas*) on the shores. The many ducks and water birds provided food. Population density was lower than for Toluca and ran at thirty-six persons per square kilometre in 1800.

The Puebla valley was the lowest, the largest, and the best drained of the three. The valley sat at just below 6,500 feet, was drained by the Atoyac River, and ran 150 kilometres long and 100 kilometres wide. Its estimated density of sixteen people per square kilometre made it the least crowded of the three valleys. Since the city of Puebla was situated among the five major volcanoes of highland Mexico, people living there could view all of these beautiful mountains on a clear day. Moreover, because the Puebla volcanoes are close to one another, they draw more rainfall for this valley than the other two.

ECONOMY OF NEW SPAIN

While modern geographers and ecologists have offered useful analyses of late colonial Mexico's economy, it is important to contextualize Humboldt's understanding of the relationship of agriculture to mining and to Bourbon policy in New Spain. Humboldt was well versed in the new economic philosophies of the eighteenth century, especially those in France and Scotland. His thoughts on agriculture owed most to the French physiocrats. Leading French physiocrats such as François Quesnay, Jacques Turgot, and Pierre Samuel du Pont de Nemour, whose school flourished in the 1750s but was in decline by 1768, stressed productive work as the source of national wealth. They challenged mercantilism, which focused on the ruler's wealth, the accumulation of gold, or the balance of trade. The flaw in this analysis was that they considered only agriculture and its labour as valuable, as opposed to other productive activities that also added to the national income. They advocated labour and commerce freed from all government restraint and deplored the mercantilist idea of increasing state wealth and power through rules, coin, and bullion manipulation. Humboldt was attracted to their application of scientific method to economics, and while he valued agriculture above mining, he was far less doctrinaire than the physiocrats about non-agricultural production.

The views of Scottish Enlightenment leaders, the philosopher David Hume and especially the political economist Adam Smith, were deeply embedded in Humboldt's thinking as filtered through German Romanticism. Hume strove to create a "science of man" that examined the psychological basis of human nature, in stark opposition to the rationalists who preceded him, especially Descartes. Passion, not reason, accounted for human behaviour in Hume's view. It followed that ethics were based on feelings rather than on abstract moral principles.

Primary among Adam Smith's many contributions to economic theory are his notions of the free market, the division of labour, and the "invisible hand." In his monumental work, *The Wealth of Nations*, published in 1776, he argued that "human nature," which, like Hume and others, he took as universal and unchanging, made self-preservation and self-interest paramount. But what resulted in actions for the common good flowed from "an invisible hand" that directed men to "advance the interests of society." The three classes in society – labourers, landlords, and manufacturers – divided up profits from the annual production of goods and services, the true wealth of nations. Competition was the mechanism through which the passionate pursuit of bettering one's own condition was turned into a socially beneficial agency. This competition drove prices down to a natural level. Workers received wages, landlords rents, and manufacturers profits.

HUMBOLDT'S *POLITICAL ESSAY*

Humboldt mentioned Adam Smith twice in his *Political Essay*, though not by name. Referring to *The Wealth of Nations*, Humboldt acknowledged that he had borrowed from Smith the technique of calculating territorial land production from the land tax and tithes paid to the clergy. Influenced both by Smith and the physiocrats, Humboldt believed that silver mining in Mexico, while essential to the country, nevertheless did not represent the true wealth of the country, which was agriculture. He also noted that many had acquired their wealth through land, not mining. Clearly an independent thinker, Humboldt sometimes found himself in disagreement with Smith, *a justly celebrated author who had the soundest ideas relative to the exchange of metals, [but] who defended the duties of seigniorage.* Humboldt was implying correctly that this state duty was the kind of mercantilist tax that Smith normally opposed.

Humboldt had absolutely no doubt as to *the true national wealth of Mexico because the produce of the earth is in fact the sole basis of permanent opulence. It is consolatory to see that the labor of man for half a century has been more directed to this fertile and inexhaustible source than towards the working of mines, of which wealth has not so direct an influence on the public prosperity, and merely changes the nominal value of the annual produce of the earth.*

Humboldt also made it clear that many individuals had grown rich as landlords rather than from mining: *The mines have undoubtedly been the principal sources of the great fortunes of Mexico. Many miners have laid out their wealth in purchasing land and have addicted themselves with great zeal to agriculture. But there is also a considerable number of very powerful families who have never had the working of any lucrative mines. Such are the rich descendants of Cortés. The Duke of Monteleone, a Neapolitan lord who is now the head of the house of Cortés, possesses superb estates in the province of Oaxaca, near Toluca, and at Cuernavaca. The net produce of his rents is actually no more than 23,000 pounds, the king having deprived the duke of the collection of the alcabala and the duties on tobacco. However, several governors of the marquesado have become singularly wealthy.*

While not without risk, of course, agriculture in the Mexican tableland was highly successful: *On the ridge and declivity of the Cordilleras the temperature of each table-land varies as it is more or less elevated; whole provinces spontaneously produce alpine plants; and the cultivator inhabiting the torrid zone frequently loses the hopes of his harvest from the effects of frost or the abundance of snow. From this*

order of things we may conceive that the variety of indigenous produc-
tion must be immense, and that there hardly exists a plant in the rest of
the globe which cannot be cultivated in some part of New Spain.

Not all agriculture, Humboldt argued, was worthy of support, because it was sometimes associated with servile labour, as was the case
with plantation labour carried out by slaves in the Caribbean. There,
[r]ural life loses its charm when it is inseparable from the sufferings of
our species. But in the interior of Mexico the word agriculture suggests
ideas of a less afflicting nature. The Indian cultivator is poor, but he is
free. His state is even greatly preferable to that of the peasantry in a great
part of the north of Europe. There are neither corvées nor villeinage in
New Spain, and the number of slaves is next to nothing. Sugar is chiefly
the product of free hands. There the principal objects of agriculture are
not the productions to which European luxury has assigned a variable
and arbitrary value, but cereals, nutritive roots and agave, the vine of
the Indians. The appearance of the country proclaims to the traveler
that the soil nourishes him who cultivates it, and that the true prosper-
ity of the Mexican people neither depends on the accidents of foreign
commerce nor on the unruly politics of Europe.

Those who only know the interior of the Spanish colonies from the
vague and uncertain notions hitherto published will have some diffi-
culty in believing that the principal sources of the Mexican riches are
by no means the mines, but an agriculture which has been gradually
ameliorating since the end of the last century. Without reflecting on the
immense extent of the country, and especially on the great number of
provinces which appear totally destitute of precious metals, we gener-
ally imagine that all the activity of the Mexican population is directed
to the working of mines. Because agriculture has made very considerable
progress wherever the mountains are accounted poor in mineral pro-
ductions, it has been inferred that it is to the working of the mines that
we are to attribute the small care bestowed on the cultivation of the soil
in other parts of the Spanish colonies. But in Mexico the best cultivated
fields surround the richest mines in the known world. Wherever metal-
lic seams have been discovered in the most uncultivated parts of the
Cordilleras, on the insulated and desert table-lands, the working of

mines, far from impeding the cultivation of the soil, has been singularly favorable to it. Farms are established in the neighborhood of the mine. The high price of provision, from the competition of the purchasers, indemnifies the cultivator for the privations to which he is exposed from the hard life of the mountains. Thus from the hope of gain alone, and the motives of mutual interest which are the most powerful bonds of society without any interference on the part of the government, a mine which first appeared insulated in the midst of the wild and desert mountains becomes in a short time connected with lands under cultivation.

Advancing toward the central tableland are fields of maize all the way from the coast to the valley of Toluca, which is more than 2,800 metres above the level of the ocean. The year in which the maize harvest fails is a year of famine and misery for the inhabitants of Mexico. Maize suffers from the cold whenever the mean temperature does not reach 7 or 8 degrees of the centigrade thermometer. We therefore see rye and especially barley vegetate vigorously on the ridge of the Cordilleras at heights where the cultivation of maize would be attended by no success. But, on the other hand, the latter descends to the warmest regions of the torrid zone, even to the plains where wheat, barley and rye cannot develop. Hence on the scale of different kinds of cultivation, maize at present occupies a much greater extent in the equinoctial part of America than the cereals of the old continent.

The fecundity of the tlaolli, or Mexican maize, is beyond anything that can be imagined in Europe. The plant, favored by strong heats and much humidity, acquires a height of from two to three metres. In the beautiful plains which extend from San Juan del Río to Querétaro, one fanega [1.6 bushels] of maize produces sometimes eight hundred. Fertile lands yield from three to four hundred. In the environs of Valladolid a harvest is reckoned bad which yields the seed of only 130 or 150 fold. Where the soil is most sterile it still returns from sixty to eighty grains for one. It is believed that we may estimate the produce of maize in general at a hundred and fifty to one.

Although a great quantity of other grain is cultivated in Mexico, maize must be considered the principal food of the people and of most of the domestic animals. The price of this commodity modifies that of all *the others. When the harvest is poor, either from the want of rain or from premature frost, the famine is general and produces the most fatal consequences. Fowl, turkeys, and even the larger cattle, equally suffer from it. The dearth of provisions is especially felt close to the Mexican mines; in those of Guanajuato, for example, where fourteen thousand mules annually consume an enormous quantity of maize.*

In warm and very humid regions maize will yield from two to three harvests annually, but generally only one is taken ... The actual produce of maize in all New Spain amounts to more than 17 millions of fanegas or more than 800 millions of kilograms of weight. This grain will keep for more than three years in Mexico in the temperate climes; for five or six years where the mean temperature is below 14 degrees centigrade, especially if the dry stalk is not cut before the ripe grain has been somewhat struck with the frost. In good years the kingdom of New Spain produces much more maize than it can consume.

The harvests of wheat are rich in proportion to the water taken from the rivers by means of irrigation canals. This system is particularly common in the fine plains which border the Santiago River, and in those between Salamanca, Irapuato, and the villa de Léon. Canals of irrigation, reservoirs of water, and the hydraulical machines called norias *are objects of the greatest importance for Mexican agriculture.*

Humboldt was critical of Mexican society for spending excessively on comfort and luxury rather than on *constructing machines, dikes, and* canals to address irrigation needs of agriculture. He praised the example of the well-watered wheat fields he observed near Celaya, and maintained that when the new road from the tableland of Perote to Veracruz was completed, Mexican flour could be exported to Bordeaux, Hamburg, and Bremen: *The Mexicans will then possess a double advantage over the inhabitants of the United States, that of greater fertility of territory and that of a lower price of labor. Mexican wheat is of the very best quality; it is very large, very white and very nutritive, especially from farms where watering is employed.*

Finally, Humboldt praised the clergy for having spread the cultivation of fruits and vegetable gardens from their convents and monasteries to the Indian villages. Clearly, though, the variety and yield on church property was important. In the Valley of Mexico, he noted particularly the gardens of San Agustín de las Cuevas, the garden of the Convent of Carmen en San Angel, and those of the bishop of Tacubaya, where olive trees yielded 2,300 kilograms of excellent oil yearly.

The central table-land produces cherries, prunes, peaches, apricots, figs, grapes, oranges, melons, apples and pears in great abundance … The traveler is astonished to see in Mexico, Peru, and New Granada the tables of the wealthy inhabitants loaded with at once the fruits of temperate Europe and the production of the torrid zone.

Humboldt devoted less space in his writing to crafts and manufacturing, but he did report on what he saw, especially the working conditions. In his several visits to factories and workshops, Humboldt found that working conditions were often poor. In Querétaro, for example, he inspected a cigar factory with 3,000 workers, of whom 1,900 were women. *The halls are very neat but badly aired, very small and consequently excessively warm.* He also observed wool workshops in the same city but was outraged, *not only with the great imperfection of the technical process in the preparation of dyeing, but in a particular manner also with the unhealthiness of the situation, and the bad treatment to which the workers are exposed. Free men, Indians, and people of color are confounded with the criminals distributed by the courts among the factories, in order to be compelled to work. All appear half naked, covered with rags, meager, and deformed. Every workshop resembles a dark prison. The doors, which are double, remain constantly shut, and the workmen are not permitted to quit the house. Those who are married are only allowed to see their families on Sunday. All are unmercifully flogged, if they commit the smallest trespass on the order established in the factory.* To recruit Indians, employers advance a small sum of money. Should the unfortunate man consume all the money in drink over a few days, he then is shut up in workshop on pretence of repaying his debt. The use of cloth and brandy as a means of keeping workers in perpetual debt was a serious abuse that needed redress.

Puebla had long been a major centre of manufacturing, even if production declined in the late eighteenth century as cheaper foreign imports challenged local products. The Puebla region's cloth work-shops were extensive, with many looms to be found in Puebla, Cholula, Huexocingo, and Tlaxcala, which boasted the oldest cloth factory. Long a centre of glass and porcelain manufacture and of Delftware and hats, Puebla was badly hit by colonial policy between 1793 and 1802. The colonial government imposed mercantilist legislation restricting the colonial manufacture of fine textiles and generally encouraged the mining sector, so manufacturers were poorly served.

Humboldt praised some of the reforms of the late Bourbons, who hoped to reverse this trend: *Virtuous men have from time to time raised their voices to enlighten the government as to its true interest; and they have endeavored to impress the mother country with the idea that it would be more useful to encourage the manufacturing industry of the colonies than to allow the treasures of Peru and Mexico to be spent on the purchase of foreign commodities.* But the powerful lobby of a few maritime towns in Spain (he gave no names, but Seville and Cádiz were obvious candidates), favoured by great wealth, kept up their intrigue at court. Still, progress was being made. Manufacturing in New Spain was worth 7 or 8 million piastres (1.5 million pounds sterling) annually.

Humboldt also provided an account of the royal monopoly at the mint in Mexico City. *The mint of Mexico, which is the largest and rich-est in the world, is a building of very simple architecture belonging to the palace of the viceroys.* It employed up to 400, and it was a great advantage for a country to control this production. After offering a very long technical account of the chemistry of production, Hum-boldt deplored the fact that no pupils of the School of Mines were employed either at the mint or in the processing of ore.

The manufacture of luxury items also caught his eye. He admired handsome carriages, musical instruments ranging from strings to harpsichords and piano-fortes, and lovely furniture *remarkable for their form and color and polish of the wood, which is procured from the equinoctial region adjoining the coast.* Such products were built not only in Mexico City, but in the internal provinces as well. In general, however, Humboldt commented little or not at all on crafts and pro-duction of which he did not approve. For example, religious art and elaborate pieces associated with the Mexican baroque he regarded as excessive displays. The one concession he did make was to applaud locally crafted chandeliers in gilt bronze produced for the new cathedral in Puebla. Humboldt was happier with more prosaic items, such as small toys crafted in bone, wood, and wax by patient Indian artisans. One day, Humboldt predicted, these items would become popular exports.

ƒ

CHAPTER 9

Mexico City: Humboldt's Stay in the City of Palaces

Humboldt enjoyed his stay in the ancient Mexican capital enormously, feeling at home in its beautiful urban space. As he states in his *Diario*, this *city of palaces* took his breath away. *There is no city in all of Europe which in general appears more beautiful than Mexico. It has the elegance, regularity, and uniformity of structures of Turin and Milan, and the attractive neighbourhoods of Paris and Berlin. All the streets are very wide and straight, running east to west or north to south.* He credits these achievements to the Count of Revillagigedo, who replaced the *chaos and confusion in and around the great central plaza from the time of Cortés.* Humboldt approved of the earlier decisions to pave over the canals, which were reportedly very dirty and forced streets to remain narrower than they are now. *The streets are cleaner than the majority of the cities of Europe thanks to the ordinances of the Count of Revillagigedo. Security is good and the cleanliness contributes significantly to the beauty of the city. What a difference compared to Lima and Santa Fé [de Bogotá], where dead dogs remain in the streets. At night, illumination is attractive. The lamps are of Argand, but are not placed in the middle of the streets.*

Humboldt loved the beautiful and decorous appearance of the city, admiring the colour to be seen in the market: *Indian merchants are seen sitting in a wall of greenery. A hedge three feet high and made of fresh grasses ... surrounds like a semi-circular wall the fruit being sold to the public; the back, of a uniform green, is divided by flower garlands arranged so as to be parallel to one another; small bouquets, placed sym-*

metrically between the festoons, give this wall the look of a carpet scattered with flowers … [and] the fruit are arranged with great care and elegance in small boxes made of very light wood. Like Cortés three centuries before him and Diego Rivera over a century after him, Humboldt greatly admired the Indians' love of flowers and decoration.

The city's urban layout and architecture impressed Humboldt as it did other visitors to the capital of New Spain. The Spanish had established their great central square, the *zócalo*, where the Aztec ceremonial centre had once been located. The baroque cathedral stood on the northern side, on top of a rack where thousands of sacrificial skulls had been displayed, while on the west side stood the viceroy's palace, where Moctezuma's residence had been. Mexico City counted hundreds of religious buildings ranging from churches to monasteries, to convents, to hospitals and shelters for the poor, but Humboldt much preferred to discuss the impressive secular buildings he found. These included a university, a public library, a botanical garden, an academy of fine arts, the royal mint, and a spanking-new school of mines.

What a number of beautiful edifices are to be seen at Mexico! Nay, even in provincial towns like Guanajuato and Querétaro! These monuments, which frequently cost a million or a million and a half francs, would appear to advantage in the finest streets of Paris, Berlin and Petersburg. M. Tolsá, professor of sculpture at Mexico, was even able to cast an equestrian statue of King Charles IV; a work which with the exception of the Marcus Aurelius at Rome, surpasses in beauty and purity of style everything which remains in this way in Europe.

Sightseeing was a pleasant diversion for Humboldt and his companions. The highest point of land in Mexico City is Chapultepec Hill. Humboldt climbed up several times to glimpse the snow-capped volcanoes surrounding the city. On one occasion, he wrote: *The morning of our visit to Chapultepec with the Viceroy's sons was one of the most gorgeous we ever had. The songs of the birds, the quantity of turtle doves, and of rabbits … everything was in a state of splendid animation. The view from the castle over the city of Mexico highlighted the two fresh water aqueducts leading to Lake Texcoco, and the convent of Nuestra Señora de Guadalupe, framed by jasper mountains, the volcanoes covered by permanent snow caps and the groves of fruit trees of San Agustín de las Cuevas, of San Ángel and of Tacubaya, the imposing number of houses and churches dispersed among well worked fields, large and beautiful avenues which from all directions end up at city gates, all of this forms a portrait as varied as it is interesting ... There are few palaces in the world with a more beautiful vista. The exterior is imposing enough, but the interior design is above any criticism. Today the government is thinking of selling the castle, but in the meantime, they are selling the windows at a time when crystal glass is very expensive. What vandalism! It seems to me imprudent not to conserve this site, the only fortress in the entire valley and where records and money, as well as the viceroys and their families themselves can be sheltered in the unfortunate case of a revolutionary crisis.*

Ironically, given how polluted the air of Mexico City would later become, Humboldt waxed poetic about conditions he found there: *The vista of these volcanoes is what makes the Mexican scene so majestic and unique. This great capital possesses a more impressive window than any other in America or Europe ... Above all, in the months from November to January for fifteen or sixteen consecutive days we did not see a single cloud and the sky was of a transparency inconceivable in Europe because of the thin air here. November is when the volcanoes can be seen in all their majesty.*

Against a stream of compliments, Humboldt's *Diario* also offered one less than flattering comparison of Mexico City with European urban locales, especially among the poor: *There is no city in Europe where so much misery can be observed in the streets. From 30,000 to 40,000 men (Indians) completely naked save for a woolen blanket or rags. An aspect as sad as it is repulsive. An abundance of lice! An extreme inequality of wealth. Why such poverty? I think it has pre-Hispanic origins. The governance of Mexico was despotic. In the time of Montezuma there were a large number of poor without property. This class has been unable to acquire any since then.*

Finally, Humboldt left his readers with an intriguing suggestion. Given its beauty, sophistication, and centrality, Mexico City could, in an emergency such as Napoleon's invasion of Spain, double as a new capital for the Empire. The idea was not far-fetched, for the

Portuguese Crown would exercise a similar option when it abandoned the Iberian Peninsula for the safer shores of Brazil: *The physical situation of the city of Mexico possesses inestimable advantages, if we consider it in relation to its communications with the rest of the civilized world. Placed on an isthmus, washed by the South Sea and the Atlantic Ocean, Mexico appears destined to possess a powerful influence over the political events which agitate the two continents. A king of Spain resident in the capital of Mexico might transmit his orders to the Peninsula in Europe, and in six weeks to the Philippine Islands in Asia. The vast kingdom of New Spain, under a careful cultivation, would alone produce all the commercial collects together from the rest of the globe, sugar, cochineal, cocoa, cotton, coffee, wheat, hemp, flax, silk, oil and wine. It would furnish every metal without even the exception of mercury.*

MODERN MEXICO CITY

In the two centuries since Humboldt's visit, Mexico City has changed beyond recognition, although then as now it was one of the largest urban concentrations in the world. In 1803, with a population of roughly 250,000, Mexico City was arguably second only to greater London with its 1.1 million people. Its population in 2010 of 20.5 million people placed it only behind Tokyo at 32.5 million and Seoul at 20.6 million (London, at 12.9 million, now ranks eighteenth according to worldatlas.com). Dense traffic and the internal combustion engine have given rise to haze and pollution, such that the transparent skies Humboldt observed are non-existent and only rarely can the snow-capped volcanoes be viewed. In 1980, as the population topped 14 million and the fleet of cars, trucks, and buses reached 2 million, pollution levels reached crisis levels.

Because Mexico City is situated at a high altitude, its oxygen is less plentiful and vehicles run less efficiently than at sea level, generating more ozone and carbon monoxide. The abundance of sunshine produces smog, which, when added to the air inversions that occur frequently between November and May, has made a bad situation worse. As well, Mexico City accounted for 30 per cent of the entire national industry by 1980. Pollution was so bad that the World Health Organization (WHO) sounded an alert and newspapers began publishing daily pollution levels and WHO-sanctioned guidelines. The government, too, took steps, including limiting the days per week that cars were allowed to circulate. By 1990, improvements were noticeable. Sulfur dioxide, carbon monoxide, and lead concentrations were no longer above guidelines. It should also be recalled that in London in 1952, when the population was over 8 million, the "Great Smog" struck, playing a role in the death of over 4,000 people. Today, strict environmental controls and the move away from dirty coal have made London's air and atmosphere comfortable.

Despite the profound impact of modernity, Mexico City's core still resonates with the beauty of sites dating back to Humboldt's visit. Consider the legacy of Manuel Tolsá. He designed the School of Mines (now the Palacio de Minería) at 5 Tacuba Street. This gorgeous building with three arches is now part of the UNAM's Faculty of Engineering. It had special appeal for Humboldt because his friend and classmate from his Freiberg days, Andrés del Río, was the school's director. Close to the school stands a plaza now named after Tolsá, and nearby is his marvelous statue of Charles IV, *El Caballito*, originally cast in 1803, facing the National Museum of Art on Tacuba Street where it meets Bellas Artes.

Born in Enguera, Valencia, Spain, in 1757, Manuel Tolsá was a prolific neoclassical sculptor and architect who doubled as a hydraulics engineer and a master craftsman of furniture, coaches, church altars, and urban design. He studied art and sculpture at the royal academies in Valencia and Madrid. After succeeding as a sculptor at the royal court in Madrid, in 1790 he was named director of sculpture at the recently created Academy of San Carlos in Mexico City. On the king's instructions, he sailed from Cádiz in February 1791 with books, instruments, and plaster copies of classic sculptures from the Vatican Museum. In Mexico he would donate a collection of moulds and figures and 300 medals and coins to the Academy of San Carlos. His outstanding works include the completion of the Cathedral of Mexico City, including statuary (cupola and façade) in 1813; the Palacio de

Figure 9.1
Central square and Tolsá's *El Caballito* statue, cast in 1803. (Author's photo)

Minería, from 1797 to 1813; and the main altar of the Church of San Felipe Neri, known as "La Profesa" (English, "the professed house").

La Profesa, a parish church, was established in the late sixteenth century by the Jesuits. It exhibits an important transitional style, from a more sober baroque to the extreme decoration of eighteenth-century Mexican baroque. Located at the corner of Madero and Isabel la Católica Streets in the Historic Center (Centro Histórico), the church has had a colourful history. A flood in 1629 almost completely destroyed the original building, but it was rebuilt in 1720. When the Jesuits were expelled in 1767, all Jesuit property was turned over to the colonial government, which in turn granted the church to the Congregation of the Oratory of Saint Philip Neri. Manuel Tolsá redecorated the interior of the church, finishing work on his wonderful neoclassical altar in 1802.

During the War of Independence, the "Profesa Conspiracy" unfolded at the church. This was a conservative movement that favoured the Spanish Crown over republican government, was opposed to the Spanish Constitution of 1812, and helped anoint Agustín de Itúrbide as emperor of Mexico in 1821. The church has an important colonial art collection and is favoured by wealthy Mexicans as a site for marriages. It was here that deliberations began over the beatification of the Mexican Indigenous saint Juan Diego.

Chapultepec Castle, whose view Humboldt so admired, sits atop the highest point in Mexico City at 7,600 feet. Meaning "grasshoppers' hill" in Nahuatl, it was a sacred locale for the Aztecs and has served variously in Mexican history as a military academy, an imperial residence, a presidential palace, an observatory, and, currently, the National Museum of History.

In 1725, Viceroy Bernardo de Gálvez ordered a country house built for him on this highest point. A castle-like fortress evolved, but the project was delayed and remained unfinished when Humboldt visited the castle in 1803. Abandoned during the War of Independence, Chapultepec Castle became a military academy in 1833 and acquired fame in Mexico as a result of the American invasion of 1847. The cadets there became immortalized as "Niños Héroes" when some were martyred defending the site against an attack by American marines. The castle also became part of American lore as the "Halls of Montezuma" in the "Marines' Hymn."

Emperor Maximilian chose the castle as his regal home in 1864 and modelled an elaborate boulevard after the Vienna Ringstrasse and the Champs-Elysées, naming it after his wife, the Empress Carlotta, as the Paseo de la Emperatriz. After Maximilian's defeat and execution, President Juárez renamed the grand avenue Paseo de la Reforma. Under President Porfirio Díaz, in 1882, Chapultepec Castle

Figure 9.2
Humboldt's house, 3 Calle de San Agustín, today,
80 Calle de Uruguay. (Author's photo)

underwent several structural changes as it became his residence. Subsequent presidents continued to reside there until, in 1939, President Lázaro Cárdenas established it as the National Museum of History, which opened in 1944. Cárdenas never lived in the castle and instead moved into Los Pinos, the new presidential residence nearby.

Mexico City's core is replete with traces of Alexander von Humboldt's long visit in 1803–04. During this time, he posed for an oil portrait by Rafael Ximeno y Planes, a Spanish painter living in Mexico. The painting is part of the national patrimony and hangs in the small collection of the Palacio de Minería on Tacuba Street. On 80 Uruguay Street stands the house where Humboldt lodged, a short walk from the National Archives, the public library, and other centrally located sites. Somewhat dilapidated now, the lower floor of the house is occupied by a fast-food café featuring "shwarma" and other

Figure 9.3
Statue of Humboldt, donated by Emperor Wilhelm II and erected in 1910
on the grounds of the Convent of San Agustín, corner of Uruguay
and Isabella la Católica Streets, Mexico City. (Author's photo)

Lebanese dishes. Two statues of Humboldt have also been erected. The first, inaugurated in 1910 with funding from the German Empire to mark Mexico's centenary, can be found at the site of the old public library on the grounds of the Convent of San Agustín, on the corner of Uruguay and Isabel la Católica Streets, only half a block from the house where Humboldt had resided. The statue is large and ponderous, quite unflattering to Humboldt, who was a small and lithe man. A newer and more attractive representation of Humboldt was sculpted by Antonio Castellanos Basich in 1999. It is located in the western corner of Alameda Park, set off by itself and with no attractive greenery around it.

The Museum of Anthropology in Chapultepec Park houses the so-called Aztec Calendar, more properly called "Stone of the Sun." Excavated back in December 1790 in the Plaza Mayor, the circular disc includes names of the days and cosmogonic suns but was in fact an unfinished *temalacatl*, or large gladiatorial sacrificial altar. The stone dominates the Mexica (Aztec) Room at the back of the museum and is replicated for tourist consumption on key chains, postcards, T-shirts, even a mouse pad!

CHAPTER 10

Culture and Higher Learning
in Humboldt's Mexico

Humboldt championed the study of the humanities in Mexico and was as proud of the achievements of the classical cultures of pre-Hispanic Mexico as he was of those developed by contemporaries in the late colonial period. He demonstrated a sustained research interest in the subject, seeing his role as the godfather of this dazzling but little-known or -appreciated cultural tradition in the wider European world. He basked in the architectural pleasures of Mexico City and delighted in its importance as a centre of education and learning.

ARTS

Humboldt's artistic flair was pronounced. He excelled at drawing, and his sketches, maps, illustrations, and engravings were often spectacular, especially in those non-specialized publications devoted to what he described as "views" of natural phenomena and archaeology. As previously noted, his innovative isoline cartography offered a new way of observing nature. Humboldt sketched some of the excavated sculptures he examined in the colonial archives. He later reproduced them in his *Vues des Cordillères et monuments des peuples indigènes de l'Amérique*, first published in 1810 and marking in many ways Europeans' introduction to the fascinating cultures of pre-Hispanic Americans.

Figure 10.1 *Top*
Humboldt's sketch of volcanoes of Puebla. (In ATG)

Figure 10.2 *Bottom*
Humboldt's sketch of the peak of Orizaba. (In ATG)

Figure 10.3
Velatri codex hieroglyphs in Borgia Museum, Velatri. (In HCU)

His powers of careful observation helped him grasp the significance of the Mexican archaeological record. He visited the immense ruins at Teotihuacán, some forty-eight kilometres north of the city centre, and correctly concluded that this "Place of the Gods" was much older than the Toltec culture, predecessor of the Aztecs, which dominated the Valley of Mexico from about 900 CE. Later archaeology would confirm that Teotihuacán did indeed flourish from roughly 300 CE, when it was the largest city in the New World, dominating an empire that reached from North-Central Mexico to Guatemala. Although he did not spend more than a day at the Cholula site near Puebla, he did describe it, along with Mitla and Xochicalco, in his *Vues des Cordillères*.

Humboldt, who was openly subjective about aesthetics, considered classical Greece as the gold standard. His critics have dwelt at length on his preference for Western norms of beauty and his frugal, Protestant-inspired distaste for what he considered baroque embellishment. Mesoamerican architecture and religion, he wrote, needed to overcome the ugly oppressiveness of Aztec theocracy: *American architecture, we cannot too often repeat, can cause no astonishment, either by the magnitude of its works, or the elegance of its form, but it is highly interesting, as it throws light on the history of the primitive civilization of the inhabitants of the mountains of the new continent. [While in Greece], religions became the chief support of the fine arts, among the Aztecs, the primitive cult of death results in monuments whose only goal is to produce terror and dismay.*

A product of the Western Enlightenment, Humboldt inherited this era's cultural aesthetic, but he was deeply admiring of pre-Columbian achievements and did more than any other person of his time to validate this world. He thought deeply about how this world's records could be rediscovered and preserved. After colonial labourers dug up the so-called Aztec Calendar in 1790, he predicted that Aztec achievements *will become particularly interesting if a government, anxious to throw light on the remote civilization of the Americans, should make researches by digging round the cathedral in the chief square of the ancient*

Tenochtitlan. Sure enough, 150 years later, in the 1970s, a team of electrical workers came across the Great Temple of the Aztecs very close to the place where Humboldt had suggested a major find was possible.

Humboldt was never a cultural relativist, or worse, an apologist for barbarism. He did not disguise his horror over the brutal human sacrifices perpetrated on a scale of mass murder by the Toltecs and especially by the Aztecs well after the "golden age" of Mesoamerican civilization had been reached in the sixth century CE. Impressed as he was by the priestly "scientists" who accomplished so much in calendrics and mathematics, Humboldt deplored how militarists replaced this earlier elite at the top of the social hierarchy.

Eloise Quiñones Keber, a well-respected expert on Aztec art, exempts Humboldt from the post-modern criticism imposed by a European-based value system by recognizing Humboldt's "prodigious contribution to the nascent field of pre-Columbian, and especially, Aztec art. Informed by his scientific training, Humboldt's methodology combined intense, firsthand observation, profound knowledge of documentary sources, wide-ranging comparative studies, and broad theoretical frameworks, interpretive strategies that would be utilized by later generations of art historians, anthropologists, and others studying ancient Mexican monuments. If his scientific or philosophical interests and incessant cross-cultural comparisons sometimes overburden his discussions of Aztec art, we must recall that Humboldt was a scientist, not an art historian." Especiallyin *Vues des Cordillères*, Humboldt helped promote a growing interest in pre-Columbian artworks and their creators by enthusiastically acknowledging the contributions of pioneering specialists and his discussions with them, by drawing attention to the public and private objects he viewed, and by tenaciously searching for sources in European archives.

Humboldt's various publications reveal his deep fascination and strongly asserted claims for American antiquity. In *Personal Narrative*, he offered for the first time a serious comparative analysis of Aztec culture, art, and architecture as subjects worthy of investigation and on a level of accomplishment equal to other global wonders. He claimed that the sense of history possessed by ancient Mexicans was

Figure 10.4
Sun Stone, popularly called the "Calendar Stone," unearthed in 1790. (In HCU)

Figure 10.5
Coatlicue (Serpent Skirt). (In HCU)

as sharp as that of ancient Israel. His examination of Mexican codices
and drawings convinced him that not only were these rich in history,
but they also continued right up to the period of the Spanish conquest, where the brutality of the military clashes become obvious
from the illustrations. He compared the Mexican belief in four re-
generations of the world to the four ages of Hesiod, and the New
World pyramids to those of ancient Egypt. Not content to investigate

what could be found in Mexico, Humboldt continued his research quest upon his return to Europe. He read the letters of Cortés and Clavigero's *Historia Antigua de México.* As he tells us in his *Vues des Cordillières*, in his indefatigable quest for Aztec codices and other records, he searched the archives of Rome, Veletri, Vienna, and Dresden. He was truly a tenacious scholar.

Not everybody was happy with his claims and comparisons. An unfriendly British reviewer in the British journal *Quarterly Review* in 1816 could not contain his hostility: the Mexican codices were "unintelligible daubings," even if they were "of first rate importance [to] M. de Humboldt ... We do not mean to deny that the first attempts, however rude, of an unenlightened people to register events, communicate ideas and render visible the operations of the mind, are void of interest ... but we wish to discountenance the perverse ingenuity which would mould and twist them to its own purposes and give them a meaning which they never intended to bear; the Mexicans may have advanced but, we believe, not a great way beyond the village children, the landladies and the bushmen."

Humboldt was the first non-state official to be granted access to the colonial archives, and he made the most of this privilege. In addition to his research on culture, he pored over raw economic and geographic information, which he would publish in his later writings. Among the unpublished documents were those pertaining to the far north of America, from California to Nootka. These included documents relating to the voyages of Malaspina and of Bodega y Quadra, as well as their maps and diaries. He described beautiful colonial paintings that would fetch a fortune on the London market and a treasure trove of Indian paintings done at the time of Cortés on subjects ranging from genealogical trees to important battles. He was, however, disappointed by the lack of documents on Cortés's administration and on the sixteenth century in general.

Among his predecessors in art, sites, and monuments were the Jesuit Francisco Clavigero and his student the cleric José Antonio de Alzate y Ramírez, who pioneered in the emerging study of archaeology by writing in 1791 about the recently discovered site of Xochicalco. In exile after the expulsion of the Jesuits, Clavigero wrote a four-volume *Historia Antigua de México*, first published in Italian in 1780–81 and quickly translated into English in 1787 and German in 1789. Also useful to Humboldt was Scottish historian William P. Robertson's more general and critical history, *The History of America*, published in two volumes in London in 1777. While they often disagreed, both Robertson and Clavigero discussed ancient Mexican sculpture and manuscripts.

Humboldt admired recently discovered Aztec sculptures that a Mexican savant, Antonio de León y Gama, had written about. He had observed a great sculptural figure, that of Motecuhzoma Xocoyotzin the Younger, carved in the rocky cliffs of Chapultepec in pre-Hispanic times. León y Gama also wrote at length of two artefacts unearthed accidentally in 1790 in the Plaza Mayor in Mexico City. The first of these was the now famous Sun Stone, known more popularly as the Calendar Stone; the second was a gigantic statue of the fearsome earth goddess Coatlicue, or Serpent Skirt. León y Gama discussed these figures in his *Descripción histórica y cronológica de las dos piedras*, published in 1792 and again posthumously in 1832.

Humboldt was invariably generous to others with historical and archaeological interests, and he never failed to cite the work of those who had come before him, no matter their obscurity in the rest of Europe. One such individual was Father José Antonio Pichardo, affiliated with the Church of San Felipe Neri. Father Pichardo had copied out *El Libro del Cabildo*, begun 8 March 1524 and finished in 1529, one of the oldest codices to have survived the burnings and destruction of the early conquest period. It tells the sad story of how none of the Indians' property was respected when Cortés laid out the city of Mexico. Humboldt describes Father Pichardo as *very erudite in Greek, and the most knowledgeable, distinguished and communicative person on the subject of Mexican antiquities which still existed.* Pichardo had also sent texts to Rome for safekeeping, but he had invested a small fortune in building his own collection of Aztec codices as well, and he allowed Humboldt access to it.

Probably the most renowned of all Aztec sculptures, the Sun Stone first described by León y Gama was an enormous basalt disk with a schematic solar depiction and other calendric symbols carved in high

Figure 9.2
Humboldt's house, 3 Calle de San Agustín, today, 80 Calle de Uruguay.
(Author's photo)

Figure 2.2
Diego Rivera, *Nude with Calla Lilies*, 1944, in AKR. (Photo courtesy of Rafael Doniz)

Figure 16.1
Gerardo Murillo (Dr Atl), *Popocatépetl*, 1908. (In ADM)

Figure 10.2 *Right*
Humboldt's sketch of the peak of Orizaba. (In ATG)

Figure 16.2 *Below*
Luis Nishizawa, *El Regresso*. (In ADM)

Pic d'Orizaba,

vu depuis la Forêt de Xalapa.

Figure 2.1
Diego Rivera, *The Creation*, 1922–23, in the Museum of San Ildefonso, Mexico City.
(Photo courtesy of Rafael Doniz)

Figure 9.3
Statue of Humboldt, donated by Emperor Wilhelm II and erected in 1910 on the grounds of the Convent of San Agustín, corner of Uruguay and Isabella la Católica Streets, Mexico City. (Author's photo)

relief on its surface. After it was unearthed in 1790, the enlightened viceroy, the Count of Revillagigedo, ordered that it be displayed publicly against the bell tower of the cathedral. Although some later critics have found Humboldt's lengthy discussion of the stone naïve at best and highly prejudiced at worst, Quiñones Keber argues instead that Humboldt's research and writings on the stone represent his genuine efforts to understand the complexity of this sculpture in light of contemporary near ignorance, and that Humboldt helped publicize León y Gama's pioneering scholarship for a much wider audience of antequarians and travellers. Humboldt considered the Sun Stone a fine example of the *universal ingenuity of mankind*. The Sun Stone now forms the centrepiece of the Aztec or Mixteca gallery in the National Museum of Anthropology in Chapultepec Park. In a nearby site, a second stone was discovered much more recently. Late twentieth-century reconstruction in the Centro Histórico has enabled visitors to inspect the site and admire the outstanding museum, which now houses this stone together with a host of more recently excavated treasures.

Humboldt described the eighteen months and twenty days of an Aztec year as far different from any European or African calendar, but closer to an Asian model in its division of time, zodiac signs, and epochs of nature. He described as ingenious the Mexican cycles of fifty-two years, divided into four periods of thirteen years, as was the definition of days and months, not with numbers but with astrological signs.

Not the least of Humboldt's contributions to Mexican arts and culture were his activities as cultural patron in Paris. In 1826, he wrote Latour-Allard to congratulate him on the opening of his collection of American antiquities at the Louvre, the first time such an exhibition had been mounted. Eventually, the collection made its way to the Trocadero Museum. In later years, his correspondence shows how he continued to express his delight in the growth in European appreciation of American cultural traditions.

HIGHER LEARNING IN MEXICO

Humboldt was greatly impressed with the quality of higher education and training in Mexico City. His account of the state of arts and science and of the men who taught these subjects is brimming with superlatives: *No city of the new continent, without even excepting those of the United States, can display such great and solid scientific establishments as the capital of Mexico. I shall content myself here with naming the School of Mines, to which we shall return ... the Botanic Garden and the Academy of Painting and Sculpture. This academy owes its existence to the patriotism of several Mexicans and to the protection of the minister José de Gálvez, Marqués de la Sonora. The government assigned it a spacious building in which there is a much finer and more complete collection of casts than is to be found in any part of Germany. We are astonished on seeing that [casts of] the Appollo of the Belvedere, the Lacocoon, and still more colossal statues, have been conveyed through narrow mountainous roads, and we are surprised at finding these masterpieces of antiquity collected together under the torrid zone in a table land higher than the convent of the great St. Bernard.*

Instruction is communicated gratis *at the Academy of Fine Arts. It is not confined alone to the drawing of landscapes and figures; they have had the good sense to employ other means for exciting the national industry. The academy labors successfully to introduce among the artisans a taste for elegance and beautiful forms. Large rooms, well lighted by Argand lamps, contain every evening some hundreds of young people, of whom some draw from rilievo or living models, while others copy drawings of furniture, chandeliers or other ornaments in bronze. In this assemblage (and this is very remarkable in the midst of a country where the prejudices of the nobility against the castes are so inveterate) rank, color and race is confounded. We see the Indian and the mestizo sitting beside the white, and the son of a poor artisan in emulation with the children of the great lords of the country. It is a consolation to observe that under every zone the cultivation of science and art establishes a certain equality among men and obliterates, for a time at least, all those petty passions of which the effects are so prejudicial to social happiness.*

*Since the close of the reign of Charles III, and under that of Charles
IV, the study of the physical sciences has made great progress, not only
in Mexico but in general in all the Spanish colonies. No European government has sacrificed greater sums to advance the knowledge of the
vegetable kingdom than the Spanish government. Three botanical expeditions, in Peru, New Grenada and New Spain, have cost the state
nearly eighty-five thousand pounds sterling. All these researches, conducted during twenty years in the most fertile regions of the new continent, have not only enriched science with more than four thousand new
species of plants, but have also contributed much to diffuse a taste for
natural history among the inhabitants of the country. The city of Mexico exhibits a very interesting botanical garden within the very precincts
of the viceroy's palace. Professor Cervantes gives annual courses there
which are very well attended.*

*This savant possesses, besides his herbs, a rich collection of Mexican
minerals.*

*The principles of the new chemistry, which is known in the Spanish
colonies by the equivocal appellation of new philosophy, are more dif-
fused in Mexico than in many parts of the peninsula. A European traveler cannot but be surprised to meet in the interior of the country on the
very borders of California with young Mexicans who reason on the de-
composition of water in the process of amalgamation with free air. The
School of Mines possesses a chemical laboratory; a geological collection
arranged according to the system of Werner; a physical cabinet, in which
we not only find the valuable instruments of Ramsden, Adams, Le Noir,
and Louis Berthoud, but also models executed in the capital with the
greatest precision and from the finest wood in the country. The best min-
eralogical work in the Spanish language was printed at Mexico. I mean
the* Manual of Oryctognosy, *composed by Don Andrés Mariano del Río
according to the principles of the school of Freiberg in which the author
was formed. I cite these isolated facts because they give us the measure
of the ardour with which the exact sciences are begun to be studied in the
capital of New Spain. This ardour is much greater than that with which
they addict themselves to the study of languages and ancient literature.*

*Instruction in mathematics is less carefully attended to in the
university of Mexico than in the School of Mines. The pupils of this last*

establishment go farther into analysis; they are instructed in integral and differential calculi. On the return of peace and full intercourse with Europe, when astronomical instruments shall become more common, young men will be found in the most remote parts of the kingdom capable of making observations and calculating them after the most recent methods. The taste for astronomy is very old in Mexico. Three distinguished men, Velásquez, Gama and Alzate, did honour to their country towards the end of the last century. All three made a great number of astronomical observations, especially of eclipses of the satellites of Jupiter. José Antonio Alzate, the worst informed of them, was the correspondent of the Academy of Sciences at Paris. Inaccurate as an observer and frequently impetuous, he gave himself up to too many objects at a time. He is entitled to the real merit, however, of having excited his countrymen to the study of the physical sciences. The Gazetta de Litteratura, *which he published for a long time in Mexico City, contributed singularly to give encouragement and impulsion to the Mexican youth.*

The most remarkable geometrician produced in New Spain since the time of Siguenza was Don Joaquín Luciano Velásquez de Léon. All the astronomical and geodesical labors of this indefatigable savant bear the stamp of the greatest precision. He was born on 21 July 1732, in the interior of the country. An uncle, parish priest of Xaltocan, took care of his education. Placed in Mexico in the Tridentine college, he found neither professor nor books nor instruments. With the small assistance which he could obtain, he fortified himself in the study of mathematics and the ancient languages. A lucky accident threw into his hands the works of Newton and Bacon. He drew from one a taste for astronomy and from the other an acquaintance with the true methods of philosophizing. While poor and unable to find any instrument even in Mexico, he set himself with his friend M. Guadalajara (now professor of mathematics in the Academy of Painting) to construct telescopes and quadrants. He followed at the same time the profession of law, an occupation which in Mexico as well as elsewhere is much more lucrative than that of looking at the stars. What he gained by his professional labors was disbursed in purchasing instruments in England. After being named professor in the university, he accompanied the visitador *Don José de Gálvez in his journey to Sonoro[a]. Sent on a commission to California, he profited by the*

serenity of the sky in that peninsula to make a great number of astronomical observations. He first observed there that in all the maps for
centuries, through an enormous error of longitude, this part of the new
continent had always been marked several degrees farther west than it
really was. The most essential service which this indefatigable man rendered to his country was the establishment of the Tribunal de Minería
and the School of Mines, the plans for which he presented to the court.
He finished his laborious career on 6 March 1786, while first director-
general of the Tribunal.

   After mentioning the labors of Alzate and Velásquez, it would be un-
just to pass over the name of Gama, the friend and fellow laborer of the
latter. Without fortune and compelled to support a numerous family by
a troublesome and almost mechanical labor, unknown and neglected
during his life by his fellow citizens who loaded him with eulogies after
his death, Gama became by his own unassisted efforts an able and well-
informed astronomer. He published several memoirs on eclipses of the
moon, on the satellites of Jupiter, on the almanac and chronology of the
ancient Mexicans, and on the climate of New Spain; all of which demonstrate a great precision of ideas and accuracy of observation. If I have allowed myself to enter into these details on the merit of three Mexican
savants, it is merely for the sake of proving from their example that the
ignorance which European pride has thought proper to attach to the
Creoles is neither the effect of the climate nor a want of moral energy;
but that this ignorance, where it is still observable, is solely the effect of
the insulation and the defects in the social institutions of the colonies.

PART TWO

Visits to the Mexican Heartland,
14 May to 10 October 1803:
Silver Mines and Active Volcanoes

CHAPTER II

Pachuca, Land of Mines, and Mining Haciendas

Pachuca was the second silver-mining region visited by Humboldt in 1803. It owed its prominence to the discoveries of Pedro Romero de Terreros, a Spaniard who was another of the larger than life personalities in the history of colonial Mexican mining. After the usual pattern of decline had taken place, significant increases in silver production occurred in the early eighteenth century. A mercantile company owned the Pachuca mines, and by 1760, Romero had emerged as the sole owner at Real del Monte.

Romero was born to a prominent family on 10 July 1710 in Cartagena, Spain. He studied at the University of Salamanca and in 1730 went to Mexico to resolve the estate of a deceased brother. He settled in Querétaro, where his uncle, who was ill, lived, and he took over the successful business of transporting goods from Veracruz throughout Mexico. For a time, he was mayor of Querétaro, but when a Real del Monte miner named José Alejandro Bustamante needed more capital to extend his mine, Romero joined him in the venture.

The mines in Pachuca formed part of the Veta Vezcaína. Three times, owners had abandoned these mines because of flooding. It was a risky investment, and some miners had even purchased English machinery costing 100,000 pesos in an unsuccessful effort to return the mines to profitability. Romero's efforts became the very model of successful renovation of an older mine. When Bustamante died, Romero inherited his debts and assets in Pachuca. He built a huge tunnel, an expensive undertaking lasting thirteen years, as well as a vast refining mill costing nearly 500,000 pesos. It had two covered patios, water wheels, and furnaces. He recruited voluntary workers, but also drafted Indian labour from villages within a fifty-kilometre radius of Real del Monte. Romero was opposed by Indian *alcaldes*, Spanish and creole landowners, and parish priests of the area who insisted Indian labour was best suited to agriculture. Drafted Indian labour had declined to negligible proportions during the course of the eighteenth century.

In 1776, when Romero attempted to cut wages, a major strike closed down the mines and workers murdered the local magistrate who tried to arbitrate. Nine years later, Romero was obliged to back down. His difficulties with labour notwithstanding, Romero was a highly successful entrepreneur. His success demonstrated that mining once again attracted investors. Romero invested only in Real del Monte and in the purchase of local haciendas, unlike other mining barons who invested in other silver mines. Among his properties in Real del Monte were the Hacienda San Miguel Regla, the Santa María Regla, and the San Antonio. He also bought confiscated Jesuit estates in Tepotzotlán and Mexico City from the Crown to give to his sons, turning a tidy profit in this way.

Romero bought a title for himself and became the Count of Regla in 1769. He purchased two others for his sons, who became the marquises of San Cristóbal and San Francisco. The Count of Regla died at the age of seventy-two on 27 November 1781 at San Miguel Regla and was buried in El Baño de Condesa, part of the beautiful park on the hacienda. Under his son the second Count of Regla, silver production fell off because of water problems and the high cost of annual drainage. Nevertheless, the second Count of Regla revived the mines between 1794 and 1801, and they were again profitable. But Real del Monte required twenty-eight hoists to keep the water controlled, and they now cost 250,000 pesos a year. When the British blockade interrupted mercury delivery, he could not meet huge overheads and he closed the mine. His son the third Count of Regla tried to start it up again, but his efforts were cut short by the 1810 uprising.

When Humboldt passed through Real del Monte and Pachuca in

1803, he elaborated on the technical problems but spoke of the mine's great potential. His enthusiasm made it easy to raise money in Europe in 1824 for new investment and a new start-up. (Details of how an English company from Cornwall took the initiative form the subject of Chapter 12.) Humboldt's description of his visit to the Pachuca region is one of the most vivid he has left. For twelve days in May of 1803, he and his companions travelled north to the edge of the valley and into the mountains of Pachuca and Real del Monte, ostensibly to inspect the mines and refining mills of the second Count of Regla. In his *Diario*, where Humboldt devotes considerable space to this trip, he is enthralled by the varied and colourful countryside to be found less than 100 kilometres from the colonial metropolis. He confides that his plans to climb the two snow-capped volcanoes of Popocatépetl and Iztaccíhuatl on the return portion of the excursion would have to be postponed because of the onset of the rainy season.

On his way north, Humboldt was struck by the great density of the population and speculated that his party was travelling through one of the most populated belts on the planet. Arriving in the town of Pachuca on 15 May, he was impressed with its cleanliness and declared it a healthier city than the crowded colonial capital. Its views were splendid, but the town – the location of the oldest mine in New Spain – was now very quiet. Most of the mines had been abandoned because of a shortage of mercury, and the miners had dispersed. Mining activity, he found, was hampered by flooding and the lack of new investment in machinery to address these issues. Proceeding the short distance from the silver mines down to the refining mills or haciendas belonging to the Count of Regla on 20 May, Humboldt and his companions entered into one of the most spectacular small valleys in the entire highlands, blessed with aromatic pine forests, unique natural basalt formations, and waterfalls. He found traces of obsidian in the region and commented that this product had been mined in prehistoric times to craft arrow tips. The region also yielded significant water, while firewood could be had for very low prices. He was as unimpressed with the refining mills here as he had been with those in Taxco a month earlier.

Figure 11.1
San Miguel Regla Hacienda. (Public domain)

The changing weather marked by the approaching rainy season elicited comments. One day, the party climbed to the summit of El Cerro de Zumate where they had hoped for views of Mexico City, but a *tropical deluge … soaked them to the bones.* When it was time to return to Mexico City, Humboldt and his party chose a circular route, heading northwest to Atotonilco and Actopan before turning back south. They were amazed at how quickly the landscape could change. At first, the country on the route to Atotonilco was *very gentle, attractive and densely farmed.* Conditions soon deteriorated as they entered a more desolate and arid region. On 22 May, they slept in Baños de Atotonilco after travelling on *horrible roads* near Puente de la Madre de Dios. Humboldt declared he had not seen such terrible paths since he had taken poor Andean roads near Cajamarca in Peru. In a rare moment, he complained about his accommodation and his treatment by local Indian *alcaldes: What a terrible night we spent in the village of Magdalena! Hardly any Indian could speak Spanish. We lacked beds or a meal. We had decided to rendez-vous at a hut on the road but we missed noticing it entirely. The village was deserted as in the majority of cases, with people off working in their fields, leaving only dogs and small children, who stood watching us from their huts. When night fell it was totally dark. We were searching for our mule train over bare rocks and horrible precipices. We marched two leagues on foot without finding the mules. The porters, it turned out, had decided to continue on their own to Actopan and wait for our arrival there the next day. Exhausted, we retraced our steps, dying of thirst and hunger. We took shelter in a small chapel, resting our heads on our saddles. What an interminable night! Over 24 hours we had only drunk some very bad water, and eaten a little corn flour. That evening, the Indian* alcaldes, *drunk as usual, but very surprised at our appearance in the chapel, then bothered us over our passports, which were with our baggage heading for Actopan.*

Fortunately, the next day, 23 May, brought them relief. Descending on empty stomachs into the attractive Actopan valley, they not only met with their mule train, but enjoyed the hospitality of the curate Manuel Lino Guerra, former secretary to Archbishop Haro. Humboldt found him amiable, learned, and friendly to foreigners. His home was a former convent, and his library well stocked with *classical authors. The property was embellished with attractive doors, and marble. It contained gardens of olives, and a large reservoir of water, which the curate had ordered built for the benefit of the people.*

Resuscitated from their ordeal, the travellers resumed their return trip to Mexico City on 24 May. They inspected the Actopan region, and Humboldt gave geological descriptions of the striking, dark Mexican quartz called *pórfido* and an iron oxide volcanic rock of reddish hue called *tezoncle*. Next, their route took them to Carpio, and on the morning of 26 May, they entered Mexico City.

MODERN PACHUCA

Today's Pachuca, with a population of 300,000, is called "La Bella Airosa," "the windy beauty," after the strong winds that whip into the valley through canyons north of the city. The city, standing at 7,900 feet, is perched on rugged terrain that forms part of the Trans-

Mexican Volcanic Belt. The hills surrounding the city are honey-combed with tunnels and slag pits from centuries of mining, but no mines are active today.

Pachuca was once one of the centres of production of a traditional Mexican beverage called *pulque*. This milk-coloured, somewhat viscous alcoholic drink derives from maguey or agave, a plant that grows best in the cold, dry climate of the rocky central highlands of the states of Hidalgo and Tlaxcala. *Pulque* has its origins in the early Mesoamerican period and remained popular through the colonial period and after. Its consumption reached its peak early in the twentieth century. Although it remains popular, consumption has declined as tastes have migrated to beer.

In 1866, the first railway between Veracruz and Mexico City began operations, crossing through Hidalgo. Known as the "*pulque* train," since it brought in fresh supplies of the drink daily, this means of rapid transport made the region rich and gave rise to a "*pulque* aristocracy" of as many as 300 *pulque* hacienda owners. Once fashionable among all classes, the drink gradually became associated with lower-class consumers, with excessive drunkenness, and with lack of sanitation in its production in comparison to beer, which European immigrant beer brewers marketed as rigorously hygienic and modern. Moreover, in the 1930s, the government of Lázaro Cárdenas campaigned against *pulque* in an effort to reduce alcohol consumption in general. In Mexico City at the beginning of the twentieth century, there were over 1,000 bars or *pulquerías*, some of them places of elegance. Today, they have dwindled, and the few still operating are small and shabby establishments. A similar pattern exists in the rest of the country, although a high proportion of *pulquerías* can still be found in the poor rural districts of Hidalgo and Tlaxcala. Maguey fields are being replaced by barley.

One of *pulque*'s limitations had been that it could not be stored for long periods or shipped abroad. Recently, *pulque* makers have found a way to preserve the beverage in cans, and they have started touting its value as a healthy product. Modern analysis of the liquid has revealed it to be rich in vitamins C, B-complex, D, and E, amino acids, and minerals such as iron and phosphorus. Athletes and body builders have endorsed the product, and it is becoming popular in the US among Mexican-American men under the brand name "Nectar del Razo."

For all of its efforts to revive *pulque* production and develop barley to replace maguey, the state of Hidalgo suffered a disastrous economic slump in the 1960s and 1970s, resulting in a significant out-migration among the local inhabitants. Today, Pachuca is a quiet provincial city only an hour and a half by bus from Mexico City but inhabiting another world. The town is modern and well maintained, and people are proud that it is the home of the Santa Clara Dairy, a food chain that originated in Pachuca in 1924 and is found throughout Mexico.

Its red-roofed houses, or *casas coloradas*, erected in the late eighteenth century by the silver baron, the Count of Regla, are a striking feature of the town. A former school in this style now houses government offices. A second building constructed by the Count of Regla in the same period is today the location the Museum of Mining. Behind its austere red façade lies an elegant building where visitors can see documents and machinery illustrating the mining history of the area, as well as personal effects of the miners.

The Royal Vaults, or *Cajas Reales*, were still another testimonial to Pachuca silver in the colonial era. They were built in the mid-seventeenth century to safeguard the "royal fifth," the 20 per cent of silver belonging to the Crown. This vault also stored and sold the state monopoly, mercury, in the refining process. It has two storeys and a central patio. The façade contains two towers that flank the main entrance and the north side to serve as guard stations. The building has housed the offices of the Real del Monte y Pachuca Company since 1850.

Some of the most spectacular sites in all of Mexico await the visitor to the Pachuca/Real del Monte region, just as they attracted Humboldt two centuries ago. In the Huasca River valley, about thirty kilometres beyond and below Real del Monte, lie the town of San Miguel Regla and its satellite village, Huasca de Ocampo. This area was chosen by the first Count of Regla for his refining mills or haciendas. Here was more open terrain, abundant water from the river,

Figure 11.2
Basalt formations and falls. (Public domain)

and an ample supply of wood. Elaborate canals, aqueducts, and other hydraulic installations still stand. Churches in the haciendas of San Miguel Regla and Santa María are still being used locally. San Miguel occupied some fifteen acres and included workshops, housing for workers, and food production. The count and his family clearly lived well, enjoying a private theatre and banquet halls. Today, the Hacienda of San Miguel Regla is a handsome hotel with swimming pools and other modern attractions, while preserving wherever possible the architecture and atmosphere of a working refining mill and an elegant residence. The next chapter examines the considerable impact that English, and specifically Cornish, immigrants to Pachuca have had in the region.

f

CHAPTER 12

Cornishmen and Women Settle in the Pachuca Region

ARRIVAL OF THE ENGLISH IN THE 1820S

Despite Humboldt's optimism about silver mining in the Pachuca region, Mexico's silver production plummeted during the War of Independence. Both sides in the conflict targeted mines for sabotage, and these actions led to further flooding and disrepair. Nevertheless, Mexican mining entrepreneurs were certainly interested in resuming production and thus directed their efforts towards attracting foreign capital to joint ventures. A leader in these initiatives was Humboldt's admirer Lucas Alamán, the young Guanajuato mining engineer and conservative creole politician. His involvement in mining ventures with English investors in the early 1820s is discussed in Chapter 14.

Other joint Mexican and English initiatives soon followed Alamán's. In 1824, the third Count of Regla allied with English mining interests to repair and modernize the mines in the Pachuca region. What emerged eventually was the Real del Monte Company, when the colourfully named "Adventurers in the Mines of Real del Monte," directed by an established English mining engineer John Taylor, joined forces with Mexican investors. By 1826, Mexico counted no less than ten foreign mining companies, seven British, two American, and one German. In addition to Pachuca, the British were also active in Jalisco, Michoacán, Guanajuato, San Luis Potosí, and Zacatecas.

So much money poured into mining ventures that the sector became a bubble resembling the earlier tulipomania in Holland. By 1830, a single share of Real del Monte reached the astronomical price of 1,500 pounds before collapsing. Anticipating this result much earlier, reputable miners like John Taylor defended their own undertakings. In 1825, Taylor published his "Statements respecting the profits of mining in Mexico." In a letter to Sir Thomas Fowell Buxton, principal shareholder in the Real del Monte Company, Taylor warned that "prudent enterprise" was required to bring "the number both of able managers and experienced workmen" to a level necessary for success. Taylor did succeed in Pachuca in the 1820s, and Real del Monte did reward its long-term investors. His company imported some 1,500 tons of mining equipment from England and sponsored the immigration of Cornish miners in particular to transform production.

The contribution to mining by settlers from villages in the Cornwall region of England is an integral part of the history of silver mining in post-independence Pachuca. Cornish expertise extended well beyond Pachuca. In the 1820s, the Cornish engineer Richard Trevithick designed the famous pumping engines driven by high-pressure steam, which transformed many of the water-logged mines into lucrative silver producers once more. In fact, Cornish mining technology, which addressed the previously costly and often insurmountable problem of flooding in the mine shafts, was also exported to Australia, South Africa, and South America throughout the nineteenth century. The miners came predominantly from the Cornish mining villages of Camborne, Redruth, and Gwennap, and sailed from the port of Falmouth.

The struggles of these early Cornish miners to revive the Real del Monte mines have been preserved in Cornish historical records on the website "Poldark Mine, the Cornish miner in Mexico." The harrowing adventures of John Buchan, one of the members of the first transport party, were recorded in a diary he kept of the journey, which lasted from 28 May 1825 to 1 May 1826. The company's task was to survey the mines and introduce new machinery for draining, to negotiate for mules and labour, and to build roads where there were only mule tracks. The company bought 150 heavy-duty military wagons from the British government as surplus from the Peninsular War against Napoleon. All the gear was loaded on four ships, but since the Spanish still held the castle of San Juan de Ulúa at Veracruz, the English were obliged to land their gear on the open beach and surf of Mocambo. The equipment included two powerful steam engines for pumping water and columns of iron pipes to enable them to reach the bottom of the mines.

Buchan describes the hardships of dealing with terrible roads and, especially, the onset of the yellow fever season: "We had the very difficult task of landing our machinery on the open beach and then transporting it through the jungles to our first depot at Santa Fe ... Whilst doing this the sickly season commenced and the yellow fever made sad ravages amongst both English and Mexicans. We fought hard against these difficulties and by the end of August all our machinery was landed and the greater part moved to Santa Fe ... Everything was now abandoned and we retreated to the higher and more healthy position of Xalapa ... This fearful campaign had cost us the lives of one third of our officers, one half of our English workmen, and of those who escaped nearly all had been at death's door. The number of Mexicans who perished we had no means of judging, but I should estimate them at no less than two hundred ... On the 13th February (1825) ... we took the road on our second transport campaign (to) our second depot, the Hacienda of Encero, situated at the foot of the great ascent to Xalapa, but being some 4,491 feet above sea ... and therefore considered to be quite out of the region of the yellow fever. We immediately commenced with 50 wagons, 550 mules and 120 men, to remove all our heavy machinery (some 350 tons) from our old station at Santa Fe. This required four journeys with our whole force over very bad roads, but by the end of March, to our great joy, this heavy task was successfully completed."

The convoy's third and final depot was the Hacienda of Guatemape, near the town of Perote, 7,400 feet above sea level, which they reached on 8 April. They hoped to reach the silver mines at Real del Monte at 9,000 feet quickly, but the rains began early that year and "the plains became vast lakes where our heavy wagons sank to their very axles." At last, on the first of May 1825, the convoy made their "grand entry into Real del Monte ... It was a lovely day and crowds of Mexicans from near and far assembled to welcome the first entry of a steam engine into any of the mining districts of Mexico. Bells were ringing, bands playing and everyone in holiday attire. Truly it was a day of rejoicing and triumph."

The new arrivals from Cornwall would leave a strong imprint on the region. As the Cornish immigrants married into Mexican families, their descendants often preserved the Cornish patronymics but lost their English mother tongue. The Cornish-Mexican Cultural Society has sought to maintain this unique history and to cement ties by publicizing Pachuca as "Mexico's Little Cornwall." The society runs a website featuring the history of Cornish involvement in Pachuca/Real del Monte.

"PEOPLE WITH FAIR HAIR AND BLUE EYES": FANNY CALDERÓN DE LA BARCA VISITS PACHUCA

Yet another rich source for the growing Cornish influence in the Pachuca region comes from the remarkable pen of the Scottish-born wife of the Spanish ambassador to Mexico, Fanny Calderón de la Barca. She accompanied her husband, Angel, on his diplomatic mission from 1839 to 1842, travelling widely with him. In her excellent memoir entitled *Life in Mexico*, she provides a colourful story of her encounters with carrot-topped, blue-eyed Mexicans as she met with the English wives of the mine managers on the former refining mills and haciendas of the Count of Regla for English breakfast and tea. Like Humboldt four decades earlier, Mrs Calderón de la Barca was dazzled by the beauty of the area and the comforts of hacienda guests. She was also able to visit the outstanding basalt prisms of Huasca de Ocampo, which had so bewitched Humboldt in 1803 and are now considered one of the "thirteen wonders of Mexico," attracting large numbers of visitors on weekends and holidays.

Here is her dramatic account: "The scenery was magnificent. On one side mountains covered with oak and pine, and carpeted by the brightest-coloured flowers; goats climbing up the perpendicular rocks, and looking down upon us from their vantage-ground; fresh clear rivulets, flinging themselves from rock to rock, and here and there little Indian huts perched among the cliffs; on the other, the deep valley with its bending forests and gushing river; while far above, we caught a glimpse of Real itself, with its sloping roofs and large church, standing in the very midst of forests and mountains. We began to see people with fair hair and blue eyes, and one individual with a shock of fiery red hair and an undeniable Scotch twang I felt the greatest inclination to claim as a countryman. The Indians here looked cleaner than those in or near Mexico, and were not more than half naked. The whole country here, as well as the mines, formerly belonged to the Count de Regla ...

"We arrived at Real del Monte about nine o'clock, and drove to the director's house, which is extremely pretty, commanding a most beautiful and extensive view, and where we found a large fire burning in the grate – very agreeable, as the morning was still somewhat chill, and which had a look of home and comfort that made it still more acceptable. We were received with the greatest cordiality by the director, Mr. Rule, and his lady, and invited to partake of the most delicious breakfast that I have seen for a long while, a happy *mélange* of English and Mexican. The snow-white table-cloth, smoking tea-urn, hot rolls, fresh eggs, coffee, tea, and toast looked very much *à l'Anglaise*, while there were numbers of substantial dishes *à l'Espagnole*, and delicious fresh cream-cheeses, to all of which our party did ample justice.

"After breakfast, we went out to visit the mines, and it was curious to see English children, clean and pretty, with their white hair and rosy cheeks, and neat straw bonnets, mingled with the little copper-coloured Indians."

Mrs Calderón de la Barca goes on to tell of how Lucas Alamán went to England and successfully raised capital that set off a speculative boom, and refers her readers "to Humboldt and Ward" for the scientific treatment of technical mining issues. She ends her account of this day with a colourful description of the stunning basalt formations and the refining haciendas: "Down in a steep barranca, encircled by basalt cliffs, it lies, a mighty pile of building, which seems as if it might have been constructed by some philosophical giant or necromancer; – so that one is not prepared to find there an English director and his wife, and the unpoetic comforts of roast mutton and potatoes!

"All is on a gigantic scale: the immense vaulted store-houses for the silver ore; the great smelting-furnaces and covered buildings where we saw the process of amalgamation going on; the water-wheels; in short all the necessary machinery for the smelting and amalgamation of metal. We walked to see the great cascade, with its row of basaltic columns, and found a seat on a piece of broken pillar beside the rushing river, where we had a fine view of the lofty cliffs, covered with the wildest and most luxuriant vegetation."

FOOTBALL AND PUB FOOD

The man mentioned as manager of Real del Monte was Francis Rule. A native of Camborne, Cornwall, Rule became a multi-millionaire with numerous interests in the mines of the area. As powerful as he was, Rule could not prevent the Real del Monte Company from changing hands, though he remained a partner. In 1848, the Mexican-American War obliged his company to sell its interests to a joint Mexican and American mining conglomerate called "Mackintosh, Escondón, Beistegui and John Rule." Political events once more led to changed ownership in the Real del Monte/Pachuca region during the Mexican Revolution of 1910. Various factions in the fighting hoped to gain control, but American mining interests ultimately prevailed. In the period from the revolution until 1947, the United States Smelting, Refining and Mining Company became the primary producer, with output reaching a peak in the 1930s. The cost of production after the Second World War rose as labour demands and the falling world price of silver saw the Americans leave the scene, selling their interest to the Mexican government in 1965.

Today, Real de Monte is virtually a suburb of Pachuca. It has narrow, steep cobblestone streets and buildings reminiscent of a Cornish village. Designated a *pueblo mágico* by the Mexican government,

Real del Monte boasts of houses adorned with colourful fresh paint and of Mexican tourists arriving in large numbers on weekends to eat *pastes* at one of the countless tiny establishments that vie for this trade. The antiseptic, fairy-tale atmosphere belies the town's history as a hardscrabble mining locale. The same idealized gloss permeates tours and museums dedicated to the history of mining in both Real del Monte and Pachuca.

The English (and specifically Cornish) heritage is close to the surface. A tranquil English Methodist cemetery occupies a summit just to the east of Real del Monte, where family names such as Bell, Rule, and Buchan dominate. Myth has it that all graves face east towards Cornwall, but a visit to the site is enough to debunk this story.

The larger centre of Pachuca also has an English heritage, even if the language has long since disappeared from usage. One of its landmarks dates from a hundred years after independence. The clock in the central square, built to commemorate Mexico's centenary in 1910, was a gift of the English mining magnate John Rule, who made his fortune in Pachuca, and was modelled after London's Big Ben. Dining in Pachuca reflects the regional culture of Hidalgo and the later English presence. A comfortable hotel on the *zócalo* is the Hotel Emily. Its restaurant has the unpromising name of "Chip's," but in fact it serves tasty Hidalgo dishes, many of them called *mineros,* as in *caldo minero,* or *enchiladas mineras.* Close by is La Blanca Restaurant, named after a local mine and opened almost sixty years ago. So common are the Cornish-style meat pies or "pasties" (*pastes* in Spanish) that they are automatically served to patrons as they are in many English pubs. Each pasty consumed bears a modest charge of ten pesos, again much like the English custom, though its fillings are much more Mexican, and spicy, than the traditional English palate would have preferred.

Football as well as pub food comes to mind when many Mexicans think of Pachuca. It is home to the Pachuca Athletic Club, Mexico's oldest professional soccer team. Established in 1900, when many of its players would have been descendants of Cornish miners, the team has won many Mexican championships and proudly proclaims itself the "cradle" of Mexican soccer.

CHAPTER 13

Guanajuato: An Exhausting Month at New Spain's Richest Silver Mine

Of all the mining regions of New Spain, none surpassed Guanajuato. It is no wonder that Humboldt would spend an entire month here, literally exhausting himself as he descended shafts and climbed summits. All the mines here, including the Valenciana, were part of a central lode, the Veta Madre, running in a straight line southeast to northwest of the town. The Valenciana mine was the richest of them all, a virtual underground city of many work tunnels at all depths and directions. At its peak, it employed over 3,000 workers. Uniquely among mining centres, Guanajuato's mine proprietors were fiscally autonomous, relying on local sources of credit and investment. Records for Guanajuato were destroyed during the upheavals of the early independence years after 1810, so Humboldt's description of 1803 is especially valuable: *In the centre of the intendancy of Guanajuato on a ridge of the Cordillera of Anáhuac, rises a group of summits known by the name of the Sierra de Santa Rosa. This group of mountains, partly arid and partly covered with strawberry plants and evergreen oaks, is surrounded by fertile and well cultivated fields. To the north of the Sierra the plains of San Felipe extend as far as the eye can see, and to the south the plains of Irapuato and Salamanca exhibit the delightful spectacle of a rich and populous country. The famous vein of Guanajuato, which has alone produced a mass of silver equal to over fifty-seven million pounds sterling since the end of the sixteenth century, crosses the southern slope of the Sierra de Santa Rosa. At the foot of the Sierra we discover a nar-*

row ravine, dangerous to pass at the period of the great swells, which leads to the town of Guanajuato. The population of that town is more than 70,000 souls. One is astonished to see in this wild spot large and beautiful edifices in the midst of miserable Indian huts. The house of Colonel Don Diego Rul, who is one of the proprietors of the mine of Valenciana, would be an ornament to the finest streets of Paris and Naples. It is fronted with ionic columns, and the architecture is simple and remarkable for its great purity of style. The erection of this edifice, which is almost uninhabited, cost more than 33,000 pounds, a considerable sum in a country where the price of labor and materials is very moderate ... The production of the Guanajuato vein is almost double that of Potosí. Valenciana, in the Guanajuato district, is almost the sole example of a mine which for forty years has never yielded less to its proprietors than 80,000 to 125,000 pounds of annual profit. The year 1803 promised great advantages to the proprietors, and they reckoned on a net profit of more than 109,000 pounds. The profit distributed annually among the shareholders of the district of Freiberg only amounts to 10,417 pounds.

Humboldt had little time to enjoy Guanajuato's diversions. Though he left extensive technical accounts of mining there, only in his *Diario* are we afforded a candid admission from such an indefatigable traveller that his visit was one of the most exhausting in his life. He chose to resume his usual reticence about his efforts to recover from an injury he sustained during his inspections: *I climbed all mountains using my barometer ... In Valenciana I descended three times to the bottom of the mine, twice in Rayas, in Mellado, in Fraustros, in Animas, and in San Bruno. I visited the mine of Villalpando, spent two days in Santa Rosa and in Los Alamos ... I had a dangerous fall on my back at Fraustros, and experienced extreme pain for fourteen days due to a strain at the base of my spine!*

The driving force behind Guanajuato mining was not a Spaniard, but a third-generation Creole named Antonio de Obregón y Alcocer, Count of Valenciana, a title he purchased in 1780. His early partner was a modest Guanajuato trader named Pedro Luciano de Otero. Both Obregón and Otero were grandsons of men from the mountains of Santander who had emigrated from Spain in the 1680s. Obregón was not an ignorant dilettante as he is sometimes depicted. He was the only son of his father's first marriage, received his baccalaureate in 1742, and applied to enter lesser clerical orders at Valladolid. He had a change of heart and, instead, married and set out with his wife to seek his fortune in the silver mines of Guanajuato.

In 1760, Obregón opened the Valenciana mine on a section of the lode previously thought to be only of base metal. The popular assumption was correct, but only to a depth of 180 feet. It took him eight years to cut a shaft to the rich middle region of the lode. He and Otero had a bonanza on their hands, but they needed capital for shafts, whims, and refining mills. They cut labour costs and sold their own ore to independent refiners. Obregón was very generous to his workers, his kinsmen, and the Spanish Crown. The two partners kept twenty-two of the twenty-eight shareholders in their families, all of them staunch members of the Guanajuato creole elite. Obregón himself became a municipal magistrate and then mayor of Guanajuato. His two daughters were courted by men from Santander who dominated Guanajuato's immigrant and mercantile community by the late eighteenth century. One was Antonio Pérez Gálvez and the other Diego Rul. Obregón's son, the second Count of Valenciana, was a spendthrift and did little to distinguish himself. At his death in 1786, Obregón left an estate of over 1.5 million pesos, which would increase to over 4 million pesos by 1791, the year of its division among his heirs. Otero's inheritance was not so well managed, but when Humboldt met the two younger sons of Otero at Guanajuato in 1803, they were still very rich men.

The trajectory of Colonel Diego Rul, first Count of Casa Rul and Obregón's preferred son-in-law, illustrates how family background and an advantageous marriage could favour fortunes. A well-educated man from Málaga, Rul amassed a fortune in mining, and as a landowner, he purchased the title of Count of Casa Rul in 1804. He paid for the privilege of taking the title of "colonel" by financing one of the newly levied militia regiments of Guanajuato. Rul bought three great haciendas, San Jacinto de Ciénega Grande, Cieneguilla, and Santa Rita de Tetillas, all within the Zacatecas intendancy. At one time Jesuit property, these lands had been purchased by the Count of

Regla, whose son sold them to Rul. As Humboldt noted, Rul also built a fine house in Guanajuato. Rul was wise to invest most of his capital in land, since the silver mines would soon decline. His descendants did not have much success in mining ventures. Rul was one of a small group of enlightened Spaniards, and he befriended a few young men who ran into difficulties with the Spanish Inquisition, as he also did, though the charges against him were dropped.

AFTER HUMBOLDT: MODERN GUANAJUATO

Traces of Humboldt's visit to Guanajuato can easily be found today. There is a small museum at the entrance to the San Ramón mine shaft that contains texts of Humboldt pertinent to mining in the region. It must be said that the museum's focus is on mining materials from the years after Mexican independence was achieved, in 1821. A guide there, Daniel Rivera Granados, states that few know about Humboldt or are interested in his role in the history of mining in Guanajuato. Similarly, in the heart of Guanajuato, close to the university, there stands an obscure alley named the "Humboldt Passage." It contains a small plaque indicating his visit in 1803. The University of Guanajuato has made an effort to commemorate Humboldt as well. In 2003, it celebrated the bicentenary of his visit by sponsoring an academic conference and offering a handsome publication entitled *Bicentenario de Humboldt en Guanajuato (1803–2003)*, edited by José Luis Lara Valdés, a historian at the university.

Unlike his practice elsewhere, Humboldt did not comment on the haciendas and estates of Guanajuato. One magnificent property still stands to the south, below the old centre of Guanajuato. The Hacienda San Gabriel de Barrera was built during the heyday of colonial Guanajuato in the second half of the eighteenth century by the Barrera family, relations of Doña Guadalupe Barrera y Torrescano, the wife of Antonio Obregón y Alcocer, the first Count of Valenciana. Now a museum open to the public, this ex-hacienda offers fine displays of the outdoor gardens on its grounds and a lovely view of the town of Guanajuato and its hills above.

Guanajuato is a charming cultural centre, surrounded by green hills, quiet parks and plazas, ornate colonial buildings, colonial mansions, and a flourishing artistic tradition, home to many Mexican and international university students. By Mexican standards, the town is small, roughly the same size it was when Humboldt visited, with a population of only 80,000. Sitting at 6,500 feet and located 370 kilometres from Mexico City, it has become one of the country's leading tourist attractions in the Mexican high plateau. UNESCO (United Nations Organization for Education, Science and Culture) declared it a World Heritage Site in 1988. The University of Guanajuato received its charter in 1945, but Guanajuato's reputation as an important centre of learning is much older, dating back to the establishment of a Jesuit seminary in 1732. Humboldt was impressed with the quality of scientists and teachers in Guanajuato and thought that, given its proximity to rich silver mines, the city would have made a better locale for the nation's School of Mines than Mexico City.

Guanajuato's name derives from Quanaxhuato, meaning "hill of frogs," and owes its foundation to mining discoveries in 1548. Silver made the town one of the most prosperous in New Spain, a fact reflected in its residents' bourgeois lifestyle bolstered by great mansions and churches erected with silver profits. As the state capital, Guanajuato played an important role in the early days of the struggle for independence. Shortly before noon on 28 September 1810, Father Miguel Hidalgo y Costilla ordered his army, now a mob joined by hundreds of workers from the surrounding silver mines, to advance on the massive town granary, called the "Alhóndiga de Granaditas," where greatly outnumbered Spanish royalists, mining barons, and members of the landowning elite had taken refuge. The defenders fired and killed hundreds in the first assault. The attackers used ignited soft-pine torches on the wooden gate and charged through, and within an hour, most of the elite, Spaniards and Creoles alike, were dead. Their bodies were dragged through the streets and buried in a makeshift cemetery. Looting, disorder, and drunkenness followed for a day and a half. Over 500 Spaniards and 2,000 Indians were killed. Although the revolutionaries had won their first victory, their bloody triumph was short-lived. The royalist revenge was swift and decisive.

Within a year, Hidalgo and three other revolutionary leaders were executed, decapitated, and their heads publicly displayed in Guanajuato until independence was achieved in 1821.

The event certainly traumatized eighteen-year-old Lucas Alamán, who gave this account three decades later in his *Historia*: "This pillage was more merciless than would have been expected of a foreign army. The miserable scene of that sad night was lighted by torches. All that could be heard was the pounding by which doors were opened and the ferocious howls of the rabble when the doors gave way. They dashed in triumph to rob commercial products, furniture, everyday clothing, and all manner of things. The women fled terrorized to the houses of neighbors, climbing along the roof tops without yet knowing if that afternoon they had lost a father or husband at the granary … The plaza and the streets were littered with broken pieces of furniture and other things robbed from the stores, of liquor spilled after the masses had drunk themselves into a stupor."

The layout of Guanajuato differs from that of any other Mexican town. Other locales have narrow and twisting streets, of course, but nowhere else was an underground system built to deal with serious periodic flooding. The old riverbed became a road that winds into the old downtown, with cantilevered houses jutting out high above the automobiles that now use these routes.

The area around the Valenciana mine in the northern part of the city offers several tourist attractions. Not least is another Mexican baroque specimen, the Church of El Cayetano, built in the late colonial period, with an opulent interior replete with dazzling gilded carvings that are illuminated by the mid-afternoon sun. Further west is the old house of the Count of La Valenciana and the principal opening to this spectacular mine, which has only recently ceased operations. Visitors will find an eight-sided vertical shaft 1,650 feet deep, surrounded by a tall stone wall in the shape of a crown, with large wooden doors and a miners' chapel at the entrance.

The Valenciana mine ceased to be profitable towards the end of the twentieth century. With the rise in the price of silver, Valenciana was purchased by Endeavour, a Canadian mining company, in 2005, and it has been closed to the public. Tours of a shaft of the vast mine are still available at Bocamina San Ramón in the same northern suburb of Guanajuato.

The Church of El Cayetano is an extreme example of Mexican baroque, and it is no surprise that Humboldt chose not to comment at all on the building, even if he did express elsewhere in his writings his dislike for what he considered the extravagance of the baroque. Taste is subjective, but it cannot be denied that religious symbols like El Cayetano, though they may not have guaranteed their donor a place in heaven, did provide remunerative work for talented artists and craftsmen. Besides, it can be argued, the money would otherwise have been swallowed up by the Crown for military adventures and not used to benefit the deserving poor. A second symbol of the baroque is the Church of San Diego, built under the direction of Franciscan missionaries in 1633 but almost destroyed by a major flood in 1760. Reconstruction, largely paid for by the Count of La Valenciana, turned the more austere original into a flamboyant example of Mexican baroque, especially its pink cantera stone façade.

Guanajuato's importance as a cultural centre has grown since Humboldt's day. Near the university stands the attractive Teatro Juárez, built in the late nineteenth century to emphasize the wealth of the city. Its ornate exterior façade displays Doric columns and large statues of the nine muses. Inside, the theatre's walls are hung with red and gold velvet panels featuring French and Italian operatic themes. The layout of the seats resembles famous European models, especially La Scala in Milan. The Teatro Juárez now serves as the main venue of the annual Cervantes Festival, held in mid-October. Running for three weeks, this international festival of the arts, named after the immortal Spanish writer Miguel de Cervantes, attracts students from across Central Mexico as well as international participants and spectators.

Yet another reason for Guanajuato's prestige as a cultural centre is its link to Diego Rivera, arguably Mexico's greatest muralist. He was born here on 8 December 1886 in a house that has become a museum named after him. Here, many of his early works and representations of his famous murals can be viewed.

CHAPTER 14

Humboldt the Mining Inspector and Mexican Silver Mining

Well before Humboldt began his American voyages, he had demonstrated both his scientific and his humanitarian skills in the applied field of mining and metallurgy. The Prussian administration had hired him as chief mining officer of the newly annexed principality of Ansbach-Bayreuth in 1792, when he was only twenty-three, and his mine inspections in this backward northeastern region of Germany were concerned not only to increase production, but also to improve the lives of the miners. He invented safety devices for miners, established a pension fund for them, and provided some applied education. Moreover, in 1794, on his own penny, he opened the Free Royal Mining School at Steben. Though limited in the classes it offered, the school preceded by some years the free schools of Pestalozzi in Switzerland and of Robert Owen in Britain.

Mining was clearly one of Humboldt's principal areas of expertise and a significant reason for the Spanish Crown's decision to give him a free hand in visiting Mexico. The subject of Mexican silver mining, its technical aspects, its labour and sanitary conditions, its economic importance to New Spain, and its future prospects occupy a considerable portion of the *Political Essay*. The attention it gives mining helps explain the popularity of the book when it first appeared – especially among potential English investors – and its enduring value some 200 years later.

Humboldt was proud of his mining expertise, and his self-confidence shone through in his writing. He made it a point to visit three of the four leading mining centres of New Spain, missing only Zacatecas, the most northerly of the great silver mines: *Having been engaged from my earliest youth in the study of mining, and having myself for several years directed subterranean operations in a part of Germany which contains a great variety of minerals, I was doubly interested in examining with care the state of the mines and their management in New Spain. I had occasion to visit the celebrated mines of Taxco, Pachuca and Guanajuato. I resided for more than a month in Guanajuato, where the veins exceed in richness all that has hitherto been discovered in other parts of the world, and I had it in my power to compare the different methods of mining practiced in Mexico with those I had observed in Peru ... The vein of Guanajuato alone yields more than a fourth of the silver of Mexico and a sixth of the produce of all America.*

HUMBOLDT'S TECHNICAL ASSESSMENT
OF MEXICAN SILVER MINING

The Mexican mines had a long history of exploitation. Pre-Hispanic cultures extracted precious and semi-precious stones for ritual and decorative purposes. Mining at the four major silver mines, concentrated within the central high plateau of Mexico, was intensified by Cortés and his fellow Spaniards around the middle of the sixteenth century, Taxco in 1531, Zacatecas in 1546, Guanajuato in 1550, and Real del Monte and Pachuca in 1552. Humboldt saw an advantage to this geographical concentration.

Mexican silver mining consisted of three phases: extraction, refining, and conversion into silver coinage. Early colonial operations were technically unsophisticated and came to trail behind evolving European methods. By the mid-eighteenth century, however, mainly through the adoption of blasting cartridges using gunpowder to engineer deep and wide shafts, Mexican engineers were able to develop mines surpassing those of Europe in depth and magnitude. The major technological innovation was the use of whims, windlass hoists drawn by teams of four or more horses and mules, to haul ore up the shaft or to assist drainage by hauling up buckets of water. The scale of such changes could be great. The great Quebradilla mine in Zacatecas required 800 horses to operate fourteen to sixteen whims.

Humboldt did not lack opinions on various technical aspects of mining operations, always keeping an eye on costs and profits. He was impressed with the engineering of tunnels and shafts, but not with the way gunpowder was used in blasting: *I could not praise the method of blowing with powder. The holes for the reception of the cartridges are generally too deep, and the miners are not sufficiently careful in stripping the part of the rock intended to yield to the explosion. A great waste of powder results ... Lining with wood is very carelessly performed, though it ought to engage the consideration of the proprietors as wood is becoming year after year more scarce on the table-land of Mexico. The masonry employed in the pits and galleries, and especially the walling with lime, deserves a great deal of praise. The arches are formed with great care, and in this respect the mines of Guanajuato compare favorably with the best methods at Freiberg ... The greatest fault observable in the mines of New Spain, and which renders the working of them extremely expensive, is the want of communication between different works. They resemble ill-constructed buildings, in which we must go round the whole house to pass from one adjoining room to another. They are true sacks, with only one opening at the top and without any lateral communication.*

Nor did Humboldt approve of drainage techniques: *We have already spoken of the truly barbarous custom of drawing off water from the deepest mines by means of bags attached to ropes which are drawn by winches using horses. The same bags are sometimes used in drawing up the water, and sometimes the mineral; they rub against the walls of the pit and it is very expensive to uphold them. At the Real del Monte for example, one of these bags only lasts seven or eight days, and it commonly costs from one and a half to two pounds. As wood is very scarce on the ridge of the Cordilleras, and coal has been discovered only in New Mexico, they are unfortunately precluded from employing the steam engine, the use of which would be of such service in the inundated mines.*

It is in the drawing off the water that we particularly feel the indispensable necessity of having plans drawn up by subterraneous surveyors ... Moreover, in the district of Guanajuato nearly two hundred and fifty workmen perished in the space of a few minutes on June 14, 1780, because, not having measured the distance between the works of San Ramón and the old works of Santo Cristo de Burgos, they had imprudently approached this last mine while carrying on a gallery of investigation in that direction. The water with which the works of Santo Cristo were full, flowed without impediment through this new gallery of San Ramón into the mine of Valenciana. Many of the workmen perished by the effect of the sudden compression of the air, which in taking a vent threw (to immense distances) beams and large pieces of rock. This accident would not have happened if in regulating the operations they could have consulted a plan of the mines.

Refining was the second step in silver mining. It consisted of amalgamating the mercury in silver by means of the patio process. This was by far the most efficient method to recover silver from relatively low-grade ores until it was replaced in the twentieth century by the new process using *cianuro* (cyanide). The German mining expert Friedrich Sonneschmidt, sent out in the late eighteenth century by Bourbon reformers to improve colonial mining technology, declared the system excellent and well suited to New Spain's conditions.

When particles of silver came into contact with mercury, they dissolved in the mercury and formed an alloy called "amalgam." Each Mexican mine required a refining mill, or *hacienda de beneficio*, with stamping mills driven by water or animal power to crush the concentrate to the consistency of sand. Workers heaped the milled ore in piles of up to two metric tons on a patio, a stone-paved flat surface; next, they added water to produce a thick slime; then they added three reagents, salt, iron pyrites, and mercury; and lastly, they spread the mix out in a thin layer over the stones. For a period from six weeks to three months, workers or sometimes mules periodically walked barefoot over the muddy mix to agitate it. Eventually, the heavy amalgam settled and the lighter waste floated away. Then the workers heated the amalgam, allowing the mercury to vaporize, leaving pure silver behind. The residual silver was then poured into bars or ingots.

Humboldt's concerns about Mexican refining haciendas were related to the cost of raw materials. While the salt and pyrites were easily found on the Central Mexican Plateau, mercury was another matter. It was imported from Spain until 1572, when a major discovery at the Huancavalica mine in Peru came into play. Nevertheless, the trip was long and the supply could be disrupted, as was the case during the War of Independence shortly after Humboldt's departure. Then, silver production ceased, either because of the unavailability of mercury or through sabotage of the mining operations. The colonial mills were major industrial enterprises, requiring a gallery to house the stamp mills, a large patio, furnaces, washing sheds, storage rooms for mercury and the other reagents, and stables for the mules. Humboldt found that the Mexican processing method, while having the advantage of simplicity, nevertheless would benefit from adopting better European practices. The local practice caused *an enormous waste of mercury. In the method of amalgamation followed in Europe, the silver is extracted in the space of 24 hours, and eight times less mercury is consumed.*

Humboldt concluded that young Mexican engineers at the School of Mines in Mexico City were pioneers of applied knowledge. Their innovations, he argued, would lead to improved health for workers: *The art of mining is daily improving and the pupils of the school of mines at Mexico gradually diffuse correct notions respecting the circulation of air in pits and galleries. Machines are beginning to be introduced in place of the old method of carrying minerals and water on men's backs up rapidly ascending stairs. As the mines of New Spain come to resemble more and more those of Freiberg, the miner's health will be less affected.*

CONDITIONS IN THE MINES

The issues of labour conditions, health, and wages in the mines were closely linked to technology. Humboldt contextualized labour conditions in New Spain by comparing the early years after conquest with what he knew of the mines of northern Europe. For the time, he wrote knowledgably about wages and conditions of workers, but on the subject of their health, he shared medical assumptions of the turn of the nineteenth century that did not take account of the impact of adverse environmental factors. Pollution caused by mercury and other toxic agents was a subject neither Humboldt nor others addressed. Further, however admiring and sympathetic he was towards workers, Humboldt was a mining engineer who saw things from a capitalist's perspective: *The working of the mines has long been regarded as one of the principal causes of the depopulation of America. It will be difficult to call into question that at the first epoch of the conquest, and even in the seventeenth century, many Indians perished from the excessive labour to which they were compelled in the mines. They perished without posterity, as thousands of African slaves annually perish in the West Indian plantations, from fatigue, defective nourishment, and want of sleep. In Peru, at least in the most southern part, the country is depopulated by the mines because the barbarous law of the* mita *is still in existence which compels the Indians to leave their homes for distant provinces where hands are wanted for extracting the subterranean wealth. But it is not so much the labor as the sudden change of climate which renders the* mita *so pernicious to the health of the Indians. The health of copper-colored man suffers infinitely when he is transported from a warm to a cold climate, particularly when he is forced to descend from the elevation of the Cordillera into those narrow and humid valleys where all the miasmatic air of the neighboring regions appear to be deposited.*

The mortality among the miners of Mexico is not much greater than what is observed among the other classes. We may be easily convinced of this by examining the bills of mortality in the different parishes of Guanajuato and Zacatecas. This is remarkable, as the miner in several of these mines is exposed to a temperature 6 degrees above the mean temperature of Jamaica. I found the centigrade thermometer reading 34 degrees at the bottom of the mine of Valenciana, while at the mouth of the pit in the open air the same thermometer sinks in winter to 4 or 5 degrees above zero. The Mexican miner is consequently exposed to a change in temperature of more than 30 degrees.

Indian porters [tenateros], *the beasts of burden in the mines of Mexico, remain loaded with a weight of from 225 to 350 pounds for a space of six hours. In the galleries of Valenciana they are exposed to a temperature of from 22 to 25 degrees, and during this time they ascend and descend several thousands of steps in pits of an inclination of 45 degrees ... To protect their shoulders (for the miners are generally naked to the waist) they place a woolen covering under this bag. We meet in the mines with files of fifty or sixty of these porters, among whom are men above sixty and boys of ten or twelve years of age. In ascending the stairs they throw the body forwards, and rest on a staff which is generally not more than a foot in length. They walk in a zigzag direction, because they have found from long experience (as they affirm) that their respiration is less impeded when they traverse obliquely the current of air which enters the pits from without.*

The appearance of these robust and laborious men would have brought about a change in the opinion of a number of authors, however estimable in other respects, who have been pleased to declaim against the degeneracy of our species in the torrid zone. This occupation [carrying] is accounted unhealthy if they enter the mines more than three times a week. But the labor which most rapidly ruins the most robust constitutions is that of the barrenadores *who blow up the rock with powder. These men rarely pass the age of 35 if from a thirst of gain they continue their severe labor for the whole week. They generally pass no more than five or six years at this occupation and then move to other employment less injurious to health.*

We cannot sufficiently admire the muscular strength of the Indian and mestizo tenateros of Guanajuato, especially when we feel ourselves oppressed with fatigue in ascending from the bottom of the mine of Valenciana without carrying the smallest weight ... These enormous expenses of transportation would be perhaps diminished more than two-thirds if the works communicated with one another by interior pits or by galleries adapted for conveyance by wheel barrows and dogs.

Humboldt's naïveté about the health of miners is apparent in the following remarks: *From five to six thousand persons are employed in the amalgamation of the minerals or the preparatory labor. A great number of these individuals pass their lives in walking barefooted over heaps of brayed metal, moistened and mixed with muriate of soda, sulphate of iron and oxide of mercury. It is a remarkable phenomenon to see these men enjoy the most perfect health. The physicians who practise in places where there are mines unanimously assert that the nervous affections which might be attributed to the effect of an absorption of oxide of mercury very rarely occur.*

Opinions today about the history of health in the mining sector are far less benign. Environmental historians like John Richards have very recently turned their attention to environmental degradation in the early modern world. Richards states: "Over three centuries of uninterrupted colonial Spanish operation, silver mining altered soil, water, plants, and birds. The human population of the mining centers found their lives shaped by the resources demanded by the mines and by rampant industrial pollution, primarily from mercury wastes … It is likely that mercury pollution from the mines of Mexico and Peru constituted the single largest source of industrial pollution in the early modern world." Much of the mercury used dissipated into the air, but the patio process required workers to touch the product and they absorbed mercury through their skin, especially into cuts and lesions. Acute mercury poisoning causes lung damage, heightened blood pressure, and even death from respiratory failure. While mercury poisoning was the most obvious risk, mining was never a risk-free enterprise anywhere in the world. Underground accidents, the buildup of noxious gases, and the persistent dust generated caused long-term silicosis everywhere. While there are no studies to confirm rates, the amalgamation process of refining silver generated large quantities of dust that damaged the lungs of thousands.

Turning to the legal status and wages of the miner, Humboldt noted that Indian mine labour in Mexico was not compulsory: *The labor of a miner is entirely free throughout the whole kingdom of New Spain, and no Indian or mestizo can be forced to dedicate himself to the working of the mines. It is absolutely false, though the assertion has been repeated in works of the greatest estimation, that the court of Madrid sends out galley slaves to America to work in the gold and silver mines.*

The miner was well paid and free to choose his employer, but Humboldt deplored the tendency towards larceny: *The Mexican*

miner is the best paid of all miners, [but] honesty is by no means so com-
mon among the Mexican as among the German or Swedish miners, and
they make use of a thousand tricks to steal very rich minerals. As they are
almost naked, and are searched on leaving the mine in the most inde-
cent manner, they conceal small morsels of silver in their hair, under
their arm pits, and in their mouths, and they even lodge in their anus
cylinders of clay which contain the metal. These cylinders are sometimes
five inches long. It is a most shocking spectacle to see hundreds of work-
men, among whom there are a great number of very respectable men,
searched on leaving the pit or gallery. A register is kept of the minerals
found in the hair, in the mouth, or other parts of the miners' bodies. In
the mine of Valenciana between 1774 and 1787 the value of these stolen
minerals amounted to 37,000 pounds sterling.

THE VALUE OF THE MEXICAN MINES

Mexican silver was truly a bonanza for the Spanish Crown, and it became the engine of the economy of New Spain, as Humboldt made
very clear in his *Political Essay*. The need to furnish the mines with
human and animal labour, raw materials, and food to sustain these
efforts stimulated the growth of colonial agriculture and pastoral-
ism. The need to transport resources from distant regions to the mining centres led to the growth of a substantial transport industry. New
Spain produced on average about two million pounds of silver annually, ten times the volume produced by all of Europe combined.
Production did fall off by the end of the seventeenth century, only to
be revived, and dramatically expanded, in the eighteenth century for
a combination of reasons. Reforms of the Spanish Bourbons under
Charles III and Charles IV offered incentives to entrepreneurs and
measures to overcome technological backwardness in the mining industry. The drop in the price of the state monopoly of mercury along
with tax incentives to revive old mines or open new ones encouraged
Mexican capitalists to put their profits back into mining. A reduc-
tion in the cost of labour was also a factor.

Humboldt naturally recognized mining's importance, but he was also concerned that it occupied too large a place in the economy of New Spain. Mining bred a conservatism among capitalists that needed to be addressed so that his favourite sector of the economy – agriculture – could advance: *It is not then, as has too long been believed, from the intrinsic wealth of the minerals but rather from the great abundance in which they are to be found in the bowels of the earth and the facility with which they can be obtained that the mines of America are to be distinguished from those of Europe.*

If we consider the people of New Spain and their commercial connections with Europe, it cannot be denied that in the present state of things the abundance of the precious metals has a powerful influence on the national prosperity. It is from this abundance that America is enabled to pay in specie for the produce of foreign industry, and to share in the enjoyments of the most civilized nations of the old continent. Notwithstanding this real advantage, it is to be sincerely wished that the Mexicans, enlightened as to their true interest, may recollect that the only capital of which value increases with time consists in the produce of agriculture, and that nominal wealth becomes illusory whenever a nation does not possess those raw materials which serve for the subsistence of man or as employment for his industry.

In taking a general view of the mineral wealth of New Spain, far from being struck with the value of the actual produce, we are astonished that it is not much more considerable. But we must repeat here that changes can only take place very slowly among a people who are not fond of innovations, and a country where the government possesses so little influence on the works which are generally the property of individuals, and not of shareholders. It is a prejudice to imagine that on account of their wealth the mines of New Spain do not require the same intelligence and economy which are necessary to the preservation of the mines of Saxony.

A major consequence of Humboldt's *Political Essay* on New Spain was the attention it drew in northern Europe to the immense mineral resources of Mexico. Humboldt spoke so glowingly of silver-mining production and how it could be expanded to yield even greater profits if properly exploited that the result almost inevitably was a frenzy of investing in Paris and especially in London. His book was immediately translated from the original French to English in 1811, and its publication led directly to uncontrolled speculative investment once Mexico became independent in 1821. At that time, Humboldt was approached by French financiers to act as a consultant for a large mining operation in Mexico, but nothing came of it. In a letter to his brother Wilhelm in 1824, he expressed bitterness at having been excluded from financial rewards: *Without my work it would have been impossible for English financiers to put up three million pounds sterling for investments in Mexico. It is grotesque that one should be unable to profit from fame. Virtue is of little use in life.*

Although some of these mining ventures were successful, speculation and unscrupulous operators created a bubble that burst in 1830, ruined many, and brought undeserved discredit to Humboldt's reputation. Having acted in good faith, Humboldt deeply resented the charge in the English press that "the ingenious Humboldt" had led on investors with his "exaggerated view" of Mexico's mining potential. He defended himself by insisting that he had never offered investment advice or sought to profit from his knowledge. Nevertheless, excerpts from his glowing descriptions of Mexican mines were used in investment prospectuses. What Humboldt and potential investors had not anticipated was that many mines became flooded or were otherwise rendered inoperable during the War of Independence and that a large capital investment was required to restore production.

Mexican mining entrepreneurs were certainly interested in attracting foreign capital to exploit the silver mines. The first enterprise to start up in 1822 in Paris was the initiative of Lucas Alamán. His expertise as a graduate of the School of Mines and his presence in Europe as a delegate to the Cádiz parliament lent him credibility, and he was able to raise 160,000 pounds sterling for his venture, the Franco-Mexican Association. The company offered Humboldt the position of chairman of the board of directors and European consultant in exchange for a gift of shares worth 20,000 pounds sterling. Humboldt refused the offer and Alamán became director of the Franco-Mexican Association, capitalized at 240,000 pounds sterling held in 600 shares. Unable to attract enough interest in Paris, Alamán turned to London and formed a new company, the United Mexican Association. It purchased ore and dealt with smelting and silver refining.

$\mathcal{E}$

CHAPTER 15

Morelia (Colonial Valladolid): Colonial Crafts and the Ascent of a Live Volcano

Humboldt enjoyed his visit to Michoacán and to the still smouldering volcano fields known as El Jorullo. He especially admired the skilled work of Tarascan master craftspeople and spoke highly of the work he saw in and around Lake Pátzcuaro, close to the site of the ancient Tarascan capital. Sitting at over 7,000 feet, it is one of the highest lakes in Mexico. The site is beautiful, with fir trees visible in the distance and the shore dotted with many tiny Tarascan villages, accessible only by boat. Humboldt regarded the Tarascans as one of the most gifted peoples in the Americas, industrious, clever with their hands, and producers of great carvings, musical instruments, and colourful textiles.

Humboldt's recognition of the uniqueness of the Tarascans, or "Purépecha" as they called themselves, was consistent with later constructs of their Mesoamerican past. In about the ninth century BCE, their ancestors arrived by sea on the coast of Michoacán with a knowledge of metallurgy. Finding the Pacific lowlands here hot and dry, they moved inland and up into the volcanic highlands. The land boasted plentiful fish and birds, productive soils, and pine-clad mountains, so they established themselves in highland Michoacán's more hospitable environment. The language of the newcomers, their dress, and their adornment were totally different from those of the local Toltec or Mixtec populations they encountered. Nor did they have a calendric tradition, mathematics, or astronomical curiosity. What they did display were superior skills as metallurgists and weapon makers, enabling them to fend off several Aztec attempts to conquer Michoacán.

What Humboldt praised as Tarascan industriousness was also, in part, a legacy of the far-sighted Spanish bishop Vasco de Quiroga. He encouraged each village to expand upon or develop a craft specialty, and to this day, the crafts of Michoacán are among the strongest in Mexico. Quiroga's rival, the Spanish viceroy Antonio de Mendoza, wanted a politically based settlement that favoured the Spanish settlers over the ecclesiastics, and in 1541, he authorized the founding of Valladolid, renamed "Morelia" after independence. It won out in its rivalry with Pátzcuaro in 1580 when it became the capital of the province. At independence, Morelia was a city of 20,000, with a major cathedral and aqueduct.

Humboldt's detailed account of the ascent of El Jorullo on 19 September 1803 provides rich documentation of the region and its peoples, as well as a short account of the eruption on 29 September 1759 that created this new volcano. After a series of earth tremors and subterranean explosions, El Jorullo rose from its surrounding fields, spewing hot ash and lava, triggering mudslides, and reaching over 800 feet after six weeks. When it finished erupting fifteen years later, in 1774, it stood an amazing 4,400 feet above the surrounding plain, its crater measuring over a mile in diameter. When Humboldt and his companions arrived in September 1803, the volcano was still sputtering, and cones all around it emitted a dense vapour, making the air unbearably hot. Humboldt was delighted at the opportunity to measure the temperature of the volcanic gases. He also interrogated locals and concluded, erroneously as it happened, that El Jorullo's eruption supported the idea then held by volcanologists that volcanoes were created by the upwelling of subterranean gases.

Humboldt described a local notion with religious connotations for which he, as a man of the Enlightenment, had contempt. A group of Capuchin missionaries had been poorly received in the region: *In [the Indians'] opinion, the volcanic eruption was the work of monks, the greatest, no doubt, which they have ever produced in this hemisphere! The monks prophesied that the farm would be consumed by fire, and that soon afterward the air would cool off so that all the mountains would be covered with snow and ice. The first of these maledictions having come true, the Indians regard the gradual cooling of the volcano as a sinister foreboding of perpetual winter. It is in this manner that the Church preys on the credulity of the natives so as to render their ignorant minds the more submissive.*

Humboldt was struck by the great variety of physical phenomena he observed in his climb of El Jorullo. He found the bright-green growth of vegetation in these mountains and plains magnificent, and he especially admired the world of salvia plants and begonias. In the fertile volcanic deposits found in the plains surrounding El Jorullo, local farmers grew indigo, a labour-intensive but very profitable product. Humboldt noted the *hornos*, small oven-like breaks in the soil found all over and erroneously also called "craters." Some were small, no more than three or four feet, while a few were giants of 2,000 feet.

On the other hand, while a few Spaniards benefited from the richness of the volcanic landscape, Humboldt observed wretched conditions among local Indians in the hot and humid valley: *In the small Indian cabin which we observed in the Jorullo plain, we encountered an old man and three small children sick with fever. Completely nude and partially covered with an animal hide, without any medicine even though lime juice is very common here.*

Humboldt was careful to acknowledge the assistance of local residents. He cited the 1782 publication *Rusticatio Mexicana* by a Guatemalan Jesuit, Raphael Landívar, who gave a flowery account of the fertility of El Jorullo in the wake of its eruption. Typically, however, Humboldt could not resist correcting the priest's calculations of the height of the volcano and of the temperature of the thermal waters left behind. In their ascent of El Jorullo via the northeast route, Humboldt's party consisted of himself, Bonpland, a Basque settler named Ramón Epelde, and two Indian servants. The intrepid Epelde owned a small indigo plantation in the area and had been the first to reach the summit around 1780 when others had failed, having been gripped by panic, terror, and superstition. At that time, the heat and gases were true deterrents, but over the ensuing fifteen years, the heat and vapours were significantly diminished.

Figure 15.1
Humboldt and his companions near El Jorullo volcano, after a sketch
by Alexander von Humboldt. (In LUW)

That is not to say the ascent was easy. Heat and the steepness of
the path made for difficult climbing: *The route is not recommended
for those with vertigo. Several parts are dangerous and require leaps of
over a foot to avoid holes filled with sulphur. The entire volcano is an
enormous repository of sulphur. There is not an ounce of pyrites. Our
faces were completely burned. I had a cough and horrible rheumatism
brought on by the cold of Guanajuato; I thought myself cured by this
steam bath. But it seems the sulphur increased the irritation. I was much
worse the following evening.*

On the return trip to Mexico City soon after the ascent of El
Jorullo, Humboldt and his companions set their sights on the Nevado
de Toluca. They followed a route back to Valladolid, and then, via
Zinapécuaro, Ucareo, Acámbaro, Maravatío, and Ixtlahuaca, they
arrived at the city of Toluca on 28 September. In passing, Humboldt
remarked that Zinapécuaro was a very industrious wool-producing

town situated at the foot of the Ucareo mountains. The Toluca valley was one of prettiest and most fertile in the highlands, in spite of its cold. It was a significant maize producer and of great interest botanically, as it was the site of one of the only Devil's hand trees (*árbol de las manitas* in Spanish and *Chiranthodendron pentadactylon* in Latin) in all of New Spain. (The tree is native to Guatemala and Southern Mexico and is now cultivated in gardens around the world.) Toluca was full of plantations of maguey, yielding an abundance of pulque, which was drunk primarily in Mexico City.

The travelling party then spent the next day, 29 September 1803, from 4 a.m. to 8 p.m., on the slopes of the Nevado de Toluca, becoming the first Europeans on record to scale the extinct snow-capped volcano. The early morning was a cold four degrees as they left Toluca on horseback. After two hours, they reached the end of the valley and entered the forest where, in winter, mountain snow crept right to the forest edge. Next, they entered an immense valley called "la puerta del volcán." There, a river flowed with clean and delicious water. Pine trees still flourished, but some had become dwarfed and distorted higher up, badly treated by the wind and eternal snow. By now, having dismounted, they followed a fine track through the valley for two more hours, making excellent progress. Near the summit, however, they met with strong winds, cloud, and fog. Here, as well, they found caves and signs of how Indians harvested ice, which they sold in the lowlands.

MODERN MORELIA

Colonial Valladolid changed its name to Morelia in 1828 to honour its most famous son, José María Morelos y Pavón. He was born in Valladolid in 1765 to humble mestizo labourers and rose to become a martyred hero in the War of Independence. His birthday on 30 September is celebrated with parades and fireworks. Today, Morelia is a prosperous city of roughly 700,000, located at 6,200 feet, whose well-preserved colonial architecture helped it gain recognition by UNESCO in 1991 as a World Heritage Site. Its strong Spanish flavour has earned it the label "Aristocrat of Colonial Cities." Strict building ordinances require all new construction to conform to an architectural plan that honours the city's richly decorated seventeenth- and eighteenth-century buildings. Early urban planners laid out wide and straight boulevards that can still handle today's vehicle traffic. A twin in some ways of colonial gems like Guanajuato and Querétaro, Morelia also used an elaborate aqueduct to supply itself with water. Built in 1789, extending almost two kilometres, and made up of 253 arches, the tallest of which stands at 25 feet, Morelia's aqueduct is an impressive sight, especially when lit at night.

Pátzcuaro remains much smaller than Morelia, with roughly 80,000 inhabitants living at 7,000 feet. Bishop Quiroga had planned a grand cathedral with five naves, but only one was built, for he fell out of favour with the Spanish Crown. Nevertheless, the city maintained its religious character as a region dominated by Franciscan and Augustinian friars. Its fine crafts produced in the specialized villages are sold throughout the modern city, with emphasis on distinctive black pottery, copperware, musical instruments, straw baskets, and a wide selection of wool weavings, including rugs of many sizes. Gorgeous displays of flowers abound, especially begonias and the ubiquitous bougainvillea, lilies, and azaleas. Food specialties include local trout, cold corn drinks (*chichi*), and *tarasca* soup. Pátzcuaro's Museum of Popular Arts displays the wonderful crafts and costumes of Michoacán, including a large collection of fine lacquered items, which occupies another beautiful colonial building. Lake Pátzcuaro still has economic and cultural importance for the town, but its waters are now heavily polluted, and a project to clean up the basin of the lake is now underway. Tourists travelling by boat to visit the colourful islands that dot the lake can still see locals casting their distinctive butterfly nets, but most fish are raised in commercial ponds.

Excursions to the picturesque Indian villages in the Pátzcuaro region are well worth taking. Tzintzuntzan, "place of the pummingbird" in the Tarascan language (Purepechan), lies eighteen kilometres northeast of Pátzcuaro, overlooking a beautiful lake. Its crafts market is rich in local products, and the seventeenth-century Temple of San Francisco is another legacy of the highly accomplished Bishop Vasco de Quiroga. He planted olive trees in the front courtyard, and they still bear fruit. About a kilometre outside the village are the remains of a pre-Hispanic Tarascan town that served as the kingdom's religious and administrative capital. A visit south, some twenty-five kilometres to the copper centre of Santa Clara de Cobre, is also worthwhile. In this town, local artisans can be observed making copper vessels by the age-old method of hammering pieces out by hand. Their wares are available in the hundreds of shops in Santa Clara de Cobre.

CHAPTER 16

The Principal Volcanoes of the Mexican Highlands

DISTRIBUTION OF THE VOLCANOES

Any visitor to the Mexican highlands comes away with a powerful impression of their dominant volcanoes. From the westernmost Nevado de Colima to the easternmost Pico de Orizaba lie eight remarkable mountains, ordered from west to east in Table 16.1. Two of these are recently formed volcanoes, the product of eruptions well within historical memory. El Jorullo, lying in southern Michoacán, broke the Earth's surface in 1759, while Paricutín was born only in 1943. Conversely, the still active Popocatépetl is ancient, dating back roughly 30,000 years.

The Nahuatl names for the mountains are descriptive, but the symbolism in Indian, Mexican, and Spanish colonial culture is rich, varied, and, for the most part, contrasting. After a brief geographical introduction, this chapter will compare the contrasting European and Indigenous representations of these powerful markers, and it will end with a portrait of how various Mexican writers and artists have visualized these volcanoes.

The best way to picture the distribution of mountains in Mexico is to recognize that there are two ranges running roughly north to south and a volcanic range bisecting them, running east to west. The eastern chain, called the "Sierra Madre Oriental," is in low relief and lacks prominent peaks. The second, the "Sierra Madre Occidental," constitutes a land barrier between the Pacific and the interior; it is

TABLE 16.1
Principal volcanoes of the Mexican highlands

Name	Location in Relation to Mexico City	Altitude (feet)
Nevado de Colima	West	14,600
El Jorullo	West	4,365
Paricutín	West	9,210*
Nevado de Toluca (Xinantécatl, "The Naked Lord")	West	15,430
Popocatépetl (Smoking Mountain")	Southeast	17,800
Iztaccíhuatl ("White Woman")	Southeast	17,300
La Malinche	Northeast	14,600
Cofre de Perote (Nauhcampatépetl, "Four-Sided Mountain")	East	14,050
Pico de Orizaba (Citlatépetl, "Star Mountain")	East	18,850

*Above sea level. Paricutín is 1,345 feet above ground.

much more rugged, covers a larger, more arid area, and averages 10,000 feet in elevation. Lying between the two ranges are the central highlands, which include Mexico City and the major cities visited by Humboldt in 1803–04.

Mexico's volcanoes run roughly along the 19th parallel, on a line just south of Mexico City. The volcanoes are called the "Cordillera de Anáhuac," the "Sierra Volcánica Transversal," and the "Cordillera Neovolcánica." Humboldt never observed the westernmost peak, the Nevado de Colima, which straddles the border between the states of Colima and Jalisco and lies twelve kilometres south of Guadalajara, but he dedicated much effort to visiting, measuring, describing, and climbing most of the others. His 1803 trip to El Jorullo while it was still smouldering, forty-four years after its eruption, is a classic in the annals of volcanology. Paricutín's formation in 1943 has enabled contemporary documentation of how Mexican volcanoes are created. Humboldt climbed the Nevado de Toluca, a feat that need not be emulated today because it is the only one of Mexico's great volcanoes where a road enables today's visitor to reach its crater and lake by vehicle. Guarding the southeastern entrance to Mexico City are the snow-covered twin peaks of Popocatépetl and Iztaccíhuatl, both of which can be seen from the nation's capital on a clear morning. In the nearby state of Tlaxcala lies La Malinche, named after the controversial Indian woman who served as Cortés's translator and mistress. Two peaks dominate the eastern highlands, the Cofre de Perote and the Pico de Orizaba, Mexico's tallest mountain, situated only 110 kilometres from the Gulf of Mexico.

EUROPEAN REPRESENTATIONS

There is little question that, for Humboldt, volcanoes were one of Mexico's greatest attractions. Sixteenth-century Spanish descriptions of the mountains whetted his appetite, and his mountain climbing in the European Alps and the South American Andes lent him experience and skills. Lest there be any doubt that Humboldt was systematic in his approach to American mountains, he offered a formal statement in his book *Aspects of Nature* explaining why he was so compulsive about climbing and measuring the mountains of Mexico: *As it is an honorable object for the exertions of scientific societies to trace out perseveringly the cosmic variations of temperature, atmospheric pressure, and magnetic direction and intensity, so it is the duty of the geological traveler, in determining the inequalities of the earth's surface, to attend more particularly to the variable height of volcanoes.*

The Spanish conquerors were not intimidated by the volcanoes guarding the entrance to Tenochtitlán from the east. Some might have been daunted, however, in October 1519, when Cortés and his men arrived in Cholula, near the base of Popocatépetl, when it was in full eruption. His Indian informants told him that climbing at this time was impossible, but that word was not part of the conquistador's vocabulary. Cortés chose Diego de Ordaz and nine Spanish soldiers, accompanied by several Indians, to attempt the ascent. The men failed because of thick snow and wind blowing ash in their faces, but not before they had gotten very near the summit. Ordaz later became an enemy of Cortés, which might explain why Cortés did not want to give him credit for the near success. A few years later, other Spaniards, at great risk, scaled the mountain to replenish their supply of sulphur, used to produce gunpowder. Lowering themselves by pulleys into the still-smoking crater, they harvested some 140 kilograms of sulphur.

Mountain climbing had deep roots for Europeans, sometimes as a vocation and always as a challenge and an adventure. The mountaineering feats of Humboldt and his companions in the Americas were prodigious. Most spectacular was Humboldt and Bonpland's near ascent of Mount Chimborazo in 1802 in Ecuador; at 19,286 feet, they achieved an altitude record for Europeans that stood for over half a century. In Mexico, Humboldt climbed El Jorullo and the Nevado de Toluca while studying the vertical distribution of plants and animals. He also explored the lower reaches of the Cofre de Perote and the Pico de Orizaba but did not reach their summits. His busy schedule precluded other ascents, including the planned ascents of Popocatépetl and Iztaccíhuatl in the late spring of 1803, which had to be postponed because of the onset of the rainy season.

After Humboldt's visit in 1803–04, attempts to reach the various summits in Mexico became more frequent. A party of American marines climbed Popocatépetl during the war of 1847, and a certain Lieutenant William F. Reynolds led a party to the summit of the Pico de Orizaba. Reynolds left no formal record of the feat, but a lone Frenchman made it in 1851 only to find the year "1848" carved on the pole of a tattered American flag.

A bizarre tale surrounds the first recorded ascent of Iztaccíhuatl. Iztaccíhuatl is perhaps the most challenging of all the volcanic mountains, since glaciers on the western side of the mountain, the preferred route, produce large icefields that require the use of ice picks. In November 1889, H. Remsen Whitehouse, the British ambassador to Mexico, set out with his friend and colleague Baron von Zedwitz, the

German ambassador to Mexico. In two days, they established themselves in a cave near the terminus of the Ayoloco Glacier on the western side of the mountain. At 4 a.m. the next morning, up they went, cutting steps in ice, and at 9 a.m., they reached the summit only to discover a bottle with a calling card inside. James de Salis, a Swiss mountaineer who had been trying to conquer Iztaccíhuatl for two years, had beaten Whitehouse and von Zedwitz to the summit by five days.

Today, mountaineering has grown into a popular sport, and Americans as well as Mexicans are attracted to the challenge. The views are beautiful and the risks manageable if reasonable precautions are taken. Only Popocatépetl still gives evidence of its volcanic past when it occasionally gives off steam. Nevertheless, there was a major eruption of Popocatépetl in 1919, and seventeen people were killed in the municipality of Amecameca. Dense pine forests and meadows of bunch grass and lupines dot the landscape of the mountains. The boreal forest exists at heights from 9,500 to 11,800 feet. A few hardy animals can be found: coyotes, wolves (rarely), field mice, and ravens. As with mountain climbing in general, health risks materialize when simple precautions are not taken. For example, acute mountain sickness occurs if ascent to 5,000 or 6,000 feet is too rapid. Symptoms involve headache, dizziness, drowsiness, shortness of breath, nausea, and vomiting. Descent to a lower altitude usually cures this condition. A much more serious condition is high-altitude pulmonary edema, which can cause death in less than forty hours after a too rapid climb to 10,000 feet. Symptoms are a cough with bloody or foamy sputum, shortness of breath, and general weakness. Here too the treatment requires descent to a lower altitude and the administration of oxygen. A third condition, cerebral edema, is still worse, although rare. It usually presents at over 13,800 feet and produces severe headache, hallucinations, and staggering, and can lead to coma and death.

Mountaineers prefer climbing in the dry winter season between November and March. Temperatures are lower then, and Popocatépetl has sometimes been blanketed with about thirty centimetres of powder snow and covered by a continuous ice sheet. But climbers have the luxury of not facing summer rainstorms and rarely need ice axes, crampons, or ropes.

The following section shows what awaits those seeking to tread in Humboldt's footsteps on the volcanoes he held in such high regard.

El Jorullo and Paricutín, Michoacán

By far the more popular site to visit is the now dormant Paricutín volcano, close to the town of Angahuan, about thirty-four kilometres northwest of Uruapan. This volcano erupted on 20 February 1943, springing out of a cornfield owned by a local farmer, Dionisio Pulido, to rise some 1,700 feet above the surrounding valley. The volcano grew quickly, reaching five storeys in only a week, and could be seen from afar in a month. Much of the volcano's growth occurred during its first year, and though its activity slowed, eruptions did not end until 1952. Paricutín's eruption forced over 4,000 people to abandon their homes and move to an entirely new village. All that remains of their original village of San Juan Parangaricutiro is part of a church, now lying amidst boulders and lava fields. The volcanic cone and blackened surrounding lava fields can be reached by hiking or on horseback. The photos of this new mountain must be similar to what Humboldt had observed at El Jorullo in 1803.

Today, few people in Michoacán, including most tourist guides, have any historical recollection of the story of El Jorullo's eruption in 1759 or of Humboldt's detailed account of his visit there forty-four years later. To follow in Humboldt's footsteps, it is necessary to journey south into the tropical zone of Michoacán to the village of La Huacana, 100 kilometres south of Pátzcuaro. The trip by bus is very pleasant and takes visitors through a great variety of landscapes. South of Santa Clara del Cobre and heading towards Ario de Rosales, lush vegetation begins. Orange groves, coffee plantations, and especially avocado trees are clearly evident in the fertile farmlands surrounding the highway. Avocados are packaged here and in Uruapan for export to the United States and even Japan. Soon the temperatures rise and avocados are replaced by banana groves and cattle ranches. Gone are the pine woods, replaced now by palm groves. Like Mexican locales half a century ago, La Huacana is a ranching town, with two active bull rings, each owned by ranchers who could not get along.

The site of El Jorullo lies fifteen kilometres east of La Huacana. The route passes along an unmarked side road to small pueblos called *ranchos*, as in Rancho Barillo, Rancho San Pedro, and Rancho Mata de Plátano, where the road turns into black volcanic sand from the original eruption. Vehicles can easily become stuck in the dry season, but rains pack the sand down, allowing access halfway to the crater, where a hiking trail begins. The state of Michoacán, hoping to turn El Jorullo into a tourist attraction, built a small museum at Rancho Mata de Plátano (House of the Volcano) in 2007. But the museum is only open one day a year, for a fiesta on 27 September, when roughly 300 people, mostly locals and students, gather there. Teachers from the surrounding villages and towns bring their students to climb to the El Jorullo crater and learn about the behaviour of volcanoes. Clearly, large-scale tourism has never embraced this remote site, and El Paricutín is the much more accessible and informative locale.

Nevado de Toluca

This is the only Mexican volcano whose crater can be reached by automobile. Highway 130 south of Toluca eventually branches off to Sultepec, from which a seven-kilometre gravel road leads up to the peak. Located roughly eighty kilometres west of Mexico City, near the city of Toluca, the summit of this extinct volcano rises to over 15,000 feet. Two lakes sit in its crater. A road runs into the 1.5 kilometre-wide crater, which opens to the west, making the Nevado de Toluca the most accessible of Mexico's volcanoes. It is estimated that the last eruption took place around 1350 BCE, and deposits excavated there included mammoth bones and those of other mammals of Central Mexico.

Popocatépetl and Iztaccíhuatl

These two peaks form part of a national park roughly eighty kilometres from Mexico City in the state of Mexico. Climbers head for Amecameca and then proceed to Paseo de Cortés at 12,000 feet, the low point between Popocatépetl and Iztaccíhuatl and, as the name suggests, the route taken by Cortés when he first saw the city of Tenochtitlán in 1519. Amid spectacular views, a monument commemorates this event. Finally, a dirt road leads up to Tlamacas at 12,950 feet. The Mexican government has built two lodges for mountaineers to rest in overnight before accomplishing the ascent the next morning.

Puebla's Four Volcanoes

Surrounded on all sides by four great snow-capped peaks, the city of Puebla offers one of the world's most breathtaking views. Forty kilometres to the east are the Popocatépetl and Iztaccíhuatl volcanoes. To the north sits the dormant La Malinche, while on the eastern horizon rises the Pico de Orizaba, Mexico's highest mountain. The combination of altitude and closely grouped mountains has provided a temperate and reasonably wet rainy season so that Puebla's climate is comfortable by day all year-round, though nights can be chilly, even in summer. Access to three of the four peaks is best achieved through Mexico City or Veracruz, but La Malinche lies only twenty kilometres northeast of Puebla. Most ascents begin at the town of Huamantla, on the northeast side of the mountain, on Highway 136 past Tlaxcala, after taking Highway 117 to Apizaco.

Pico de Orizaba

Mexico's highest mountain is a favourite target of alpinists in North America. Either Puebla or Veracruz are practical starting points for a visit. The most popular climbing season is around Christmas, since good weather then makes it possible for the ascent and descent to be accomplished in one day. For an ascent from the south, drive to Acatzingo, then take Highway 140 to Ciudad Cerdan. For the north slope, take 140 north and turn right towards Tlachichuca. Proceed on to Piedra Grande.

MEXICAN REPRESENTATIONS

For the Indigenous people of Mexico, representations of their volcanic environment provide many contrasts with the European approach. The local population could not practise maize agriculture at the higher altitudes at which the volcanoes sit, and apart from the few who ventured up to glaciers to harvest ice and snow, no direct economic activity took place on the slopes. Instead, the high mountains were considered dangerous and hostile. Religious and cultural admonitions against venturing too high probably reflected empirical experiences of the disasters that could result from climbs by inexperienced individuals, but especially from the instability and unpredictability of seismic activity. Within collective memory, Popocatépetl, for example, has experienced at least twenty eruptions since a catastrophic one unfolded in 800 CE, with especially notable ones occurring in 1345–47, 1522, 1545, 1804 (witnessed by Humboldt from San Nicolás de los Ranchos, a good observation point even today), 1827, 1852, 1919, 1927, 1946, 1947, 1982, and 2016. The inhabitants of Mexico City frequently see fumaroles (volcanic areas from which smoke and gases escape) rising on Popocatépetl, but authorities do not feel there is need for evacuation of villagers in its potential path. The Nevado de Colima, on the other hand, offers a more serious threat. One of the most active volcanoes in Mexico, it has erupted more than forty times since 1576, the latest eruption occurring in February 2008 when an earthquake measuring 5.4 on the Richter scale also shook the region. About 300,000 people live within forty kilometres of the volcano's active cone, and evacuations are carried out according to the situation in this densely populated area. The largest eruption in several years took place on 24 May 2005. An ash cloud rose three kilometres over the volcano, and satellite monitoring indicated that the cloud spread over an area extending 200 kilometres west in the hours after the eruption. Authorities established an exclusion zone within 6.5 kilometres of the summit. A second eruption occurred on 8 June of the same year, with plumes reaching heights of 5 kilometres above the crater rim, prompting the evacuation of three neighbouring villages.

To mitigate the damage this fragile world might render, rituals have long served to propitiate the power of the volcanoes. One ancient Nahuatl ritual involved the imposition of feast days, where miniature mountains made of dough were placed in homes. People would throw four colours of corn – black, white, yellow, and mixed – in the four cardinal directions. Two young slave girls who were sisters would dance before being sacrificed. Apocalyptic visions were also involved. Some held that the end of a millennium, however calculated by the various calendars, would coincide with the imminent eruption of several volcanoes, which would expel fire and signal the end of the world. These ancient forms of mitigation of prophecy have been replaced in recent times by specialists in weather management. Around the mountains of Popocatépetl and Iztaccíhuatl, in Morelos, Puebla, and the state of Mexico, these specialists, known variously as *tiemperos* (weathermen), *graniceros* (hail specialists), or *pedidores de agua* (petitioners for water), are said to use magic to participate in weather management. They are individuals who have been struck by lightning and have survived after being treated by a village healer. It is assumed that they have established a special relationship with the heavens, which provide them with their power to interpret dreams forewarning them of volcanic activity. They stress the limitations of their skill and believe that it is God's will as to whether the outcome will be benign. They consider modern scientific measurements and predictions of seismic activity absurd.

Cultural representations of the Popocatépetl and Iztaccíhuatl volcanoes run deep in Mexican history. The two peaks are so dominant a part of the horizon of the Valley of Mexico that they have long been included in artistic depictions. The Aztec codices offer examples, as have artists and poets over the centuries, of how the mountains' eruptions have shaken the earth and the popular imagination. Margarita de Orellana puts it beautifully: "Their unmistakable silhouettes are inwardly reflected in the body and soul of Mexicans. We can draw their outline with our eyes closed. They continue to exist within us even when pollution shrouds them from sight."

For the seventeenth-century poet and philosopher Sor Juana Inés de la Cruz, who was born on the slopes of Popocatépetl in the town of Amecamcca, Iztaccíhuatl evokes the image of the Virgin Mary:

I would compare thee, my Lady,
To this snowcapped peak
Who, though smoke be near it,
Is ever white.

For the Mexican poet José Emilio Pacheco, the mountains show how ephemeral humans are in comparison to powerful giants, which were present

when we were unthinkable
and will be here tomorrow.

For the Chilean Nobel laureate poet Gabriela Mistral, who lived in exile near Orizaba, Iztaccíhuatl "with her human profile, sweetens the sky [and] refines the countryside." Other invocations are less gentle. Some see the volcanoes as dreadful forces that devour those who worship them most devoutly.

In art, representation tends towards the power of nature, not towards its sweetness. The tone was set by arguably the painter most associated with Mexican volcanoes, Gerardo Murillo, the Guadalajara-born artist and philosopher who took the Nahautl name of Dr Atl, or "Dr Water." Early in his career, he developed a fervour for volcanoes that would last his entire life. As an art student in Paris, he opened an exhibition in 1914 entitled the *Mountains of Mexico*, and while visiting Italy, he sketched Mount Etna and the Stromboli volcano. Married to his passion for volcanoes was a revolutionary anarchist's ardour that saw him inspire and encourage other young Mexican artists, including, later, muralists Diego Rivera and especially Juan O'Gorman. Dr Atl helped a twenty-year-old Rivera mount an exhibition in Mexico City to raise funds for a study trip to Europe

Figure 16.1
Gerardo Murillo (Dr Atl), *Popocatépetl*, 1908. (In ADM)

in 1905. Through Dr Atl's endorsement and contacts, the virtually unknown Rivera was able to sell all his paintings, travelling first to Spain and then to France. When the Paricutín volcano was born in 1943, Dr Atl hurried to the scene and withdrew from Mexican life to live as a recluse in a shack on the slopes of the volcano. Perhaps his signature painting emerged from this experience. Entitled *Eruption of Paricutín* and located in the National Museum of Art in Mexico City, this extraordinary painting shows a glowing trajectory of lava flowing down its side, light on naked trees, and plumes of black ash under the gaze of cold stars on a clear night. Dr Atl's many representations of Popocatépetl over the years show his continuing obsession with landscapes of fire and ice (see, for example, those of 1908, 1913, 1932, and 1934).

The Mexican volcanoes have provided a folkloric subject for artists. In 1900, the great popular artist José Guadaloupe Posada produced graphic caricatures of Iztaccíhuatl and Popocatépetl for the book cover of Heriberto Ferias's *Historia de los dos volcanes*; a white lady could be seen beside a male flaming with passion. At roughly the same time, Saturnino Herrán offered his vision of the peaks in a similarly romanticized and sensual manner. Thirty years later, Jesús de la Helguera, a calendar illustrator, evoked a stereotyped nationalism that remained ingrained in the minds of Mexicans throughout the mid-twentieth century. He used a triptych to illustrate how a white princess fell in love with an indigenous prince.

Not all renditions were gaudy and sentimental. The Mexican muralists invoked their didactic skills to show how peasants and proletarians served as symbols of a new social order against a violent volcanic horizon. Diego Rivera included Paricutín in a 1943 painting and the twin peaks guarding his *Great City of Tenochtitlán* in 1945. Juan O'Gorman proved a true disciple of Dr Atl's by depicting Popocatépetl as a fiery inferno in several canvases, especially in his dramatic *Mexico City* in 1949, showing that the urban skyline does not end at the city limits but merges with the mountainous rim and the volcanoes. The mural stands as a marker of the time when the exponential urban growth of Mexico City began to accelerate after the Second World War.

At the turn of the twenty-first century, it was clear that such Mexican artists as Vicente Rojo, Luis Nishizawa, Luis Covarrubias, and Froylan Ruiz have moved away from fire and brimstone in favour of gentler contemporary landscapes. Rojo's abstract was chosen as the cover for *Los dos volcanes*, while Nishizawa's *El Regreso* offers a beautiful luminous purple landscape, and his *Iztaccíhuatl* evokes his heritage to blend the mountain within a Japanese landscape. Covarrubias's *El valle de Tenochtitlán* presents a stylized historical vision, while Ruiz's "Viva Mexico" playfully inserts watermelons on the slopes of the two volcanoes.

Figure 16.2
Luis Nishizawa, *El Regresso*. (In ADM)

PART THREE

Homeward Bound, 30 January to 7 March 1804:
Demography, Disease, and Departure
from Veracruz

CHAPTER 17

Puebla: Churches, Libraries, and Beautiful Pottery

On 20 January 1804, after being in Mexico City since October, Humboldt and his companions were finally ready to make the long journey back to Europe. For some time they had been packing, filling their trunks not only with new botanical and geological specimens as had been the case in South America, but also with cultural objects such as the Indian codices and sculptures they had purchased. It is evident that Humboldt was anxious to reach Veracruz and then Europe because he uncharacteristically recorded very little about this part of his travels. His *Diario* is completely silent on the length of time he sojourned in Puebla, although the *Political Essay* does discuss aspects of Indian culture in nearby Cholula. Mexico's second metropolis at the time with a population of over 50,000 people, Puebla was nicknamed the "City of Tiles" because of the beautiful hand-painted ceramics that adorned so many buildings there.

The visitors did spend some time examining the ruins of the pyramid at Cholula no more than thirty kilometres from Puebla. It was once the largest Indian city in the Puebla valley and a major Indian ceremonial centre standing on the ruins of several older sites. Following a precedent repeated throughout the conquest era, Cortés destroyed the site in 1519, and his successors erected the Nuestra Señora de los Remedios Church atop the rubble of the great pyramid. In fact, archaeologists have revealed seven different structures, each constructed by a different culture.

Figure 17.1
Cholula pyramid, after a sketch by Alexander von Humboldt

Puebla, short for "La Puebla de los Ángeles," is named after a legend in which a group of angels appeared in a dream to the bishop of
Tlaxcala, Julián Garcés, in 1530. The dream instructed him to locate
a new Spanish settlement between Mexico City and the port of Veracruz. Puebla lies at 7,000 feet in the large valley called "Cuetlax-
coapán," through which run the San Francisco, Atoyaca, and Alseseca
Rivers. Initially, constant flooding in the rainy season created serious
problems for the townspeople, but in the long run, the availability of
water, as well as its strategic location, helped the city grow prosperous in the colonial period. Today's metropolitan population counts
well over 1.5 million people.

Colonial Puebla, still well preserved in the city's historic centre, is
replete with churches, monasteries, and private mansions, mostly
built in cream-colored *cantera* stone and red brick and decorated
with splendid multicoloured tiles. Called "the cradle of the Mexican

Baroque," its decorative arts and architecture and its conservative religious atmosphere became well known throughout Mexico, even if
the environment was not in keeping with Humboldt's tastes.

One of the city's wealthiest and most controversial residents was
Juan de Palafox y Mendoza, a Spanish ecclesiastic born in Navarre. He
served as bishop of Puebla from 1640 to 1655 and as acting archbishop
of Mexico from 1642 to 1643. As bishop, he worked hard to protect
Indians from abuse and forbade methods of conversion other than
persuasion. He contributed significantly to the building of church
institutions in Puebla, to the founding of the Dominican Convent of
Santa Inés, the colleges of San Pedro and San Pablo, and the girls'
school Purísima Concepción, and to the completion of the cathedral,
although it was not finished until two centuries later, in 1849.

Palafox was dedicated to the arts, and he made Puebla the musical
centre of New Spain. He sponsored Juan Gutiérrez de Padilla, the
most famous composer in seventeenth-century Mexico, and he encouraged the introduction of European music to Mexico. But his
greatest intellectual contribution was the library named after him, to
which he donated his own collection of 5,000 books of philosophy
and science. The Palafoxiana Library, opened in 1646, was the first
library in the Americas and the only one to survive to the present
day. Additions gave it a decidedly baroque flavour in the eighteenth
century. UNESCO has made the library part of its Memory of the
World Programme, and it has been declared a Historical Monument
of Mexico.

Palafox's political career was marked by his bitter rivalry with the
Jesuits, whom he placed under an interdict in 1647. The Vatican refused
to approve his censures but ordered the Jesuits to respect his episcopal
jurisdiction. He quarrelled with Viceroy Cabrera y Bobadilla, accusing
him of being in league with Portugal in opposition to the Spanish
Crown, and orchestrated Cabrera y Bobadilla's arrest and deportation
to Spain, where he was acquitted of the charges of treason.

Another fine space in the colonial core of Puebla is the building
that houses the Amparo Museum. It is dedicated to viceregal and
nineteenth-century art, and its eclectic holdings range from formal

sculptures and religious paintings to furniture for family use and special occasions. The building began as a sixteenth-century hospital, but it became a school for girls under a decree from Bishop Palafox around 1642. By the late nineteenth century, the site became the private property of the Yglesias family. It was willed to the public in 1991 as the Amparo Museum.

Puebla has a long association with fine ceramics, especially the style that has come to be known as Talavera pottery. The name derives from the town of Talavera de la Reina in Spain. One story has it that a potter from Talavera came to New Spain and introduced locals to European techniques. Between 1550 and 1570, artisans took advantage of the abundance of the high-quality clay in the region to learn how to use the potter's wheel and tin-glazing. Another theory has it that local potters adapted their style from imported blue and white Chinese porcelain. In fact, Puebla's Talavara pottery is unique and its origins suggest an interesting fusion rather than a single style. The ceramic reveals a multiplicity of cultures coming together in Puebla. Arab, Spanish, Chinese, and Mexican elements are subtly transformed by the technique and line of the material. Mixed with Native designs, the glazing technique was first used for tiles and then for pots, plates, jars, religious figures, and other items. Blue was confined to the most expensive products owing to the cost of the dye. A potters' guild helped ensure quality and solidarity among producers. After 1813, certain terms of the new constitution of Mexico eradicated the potters' guild, and the industry collapsed in the nineteenth century. A renaissance, however, began in 1897, with Enrique Luis Ventosa, a twenty-nine-year-old Catalan potter, quickly becoming the leading force in the revival of Talavera ware.

Talavera tiles and ceramic ware are among Mexico's most famous traditional art forms. Their decorative beauty can be seen in the façade and interior of homes, especially the kitchen. In a typical Puebla kitchen, tiles cover the walls, sometimes including the ceiling, and the Talavera food platters reflect the richly flavoured recipes associated with the city, such as *mole poblano*, a spicy brown sauce flavoured with chocolate in combination with at least twenty ingredients, and *chiles en nogada*, a sweet and spicy dish filled with pork, chicken, and sweetmeats in a walnut cream sauce. Another site for this special pottery is the traditional pharmacy, its shelves lined with Talavera containers of all shapes and sizes. The jars were often inscribed before firing with the name of the herb they would contain, or they might have emblazoned on them the emblem of a religious order.

Myth and tradition surround two iconic symbols of Puebla that resonate throughout Mexico and beyond. One is *mole poblano*. Although the first recipes emerged at the time of independence in 1810, its antecedents are much older. The term *mole* derives from the Nahuatl *milli*, or "sauce," and the presence of chocolate has led to a probably apocryphal story of Moctezuma serving the dish to Cortés at a banquet. No evidence that the Aztecs ever cooked with chocolate or served it to the Spaniards has ever surfaced in the voluminous Spanish writings about food and drink among their Indian hosts. Instead, chocolate was a beverage of the elite. The more common stories focus on a feast prepared in the seventeenth century either for the visiting archbishop or for Viceroy Palafox. Learning of the impending visit of this dignitary, the poor nuns at the Convent of Santa Rosa in Puebla prayed for inspiration as they chopped and roasted many ingredients, combining spices with chiles, day-old bread, nuts, and a little chocolate. They boiled the concoction for hours and reduced it to a thick, sweet, rich, and fragrant sauce. They killed an old turkey and doused it in the sauce, making their guest happy and saving face in the bargain. A variation has it that the feast for the archbishop was prepared by a monk, Fray Pascual. As the turkey was roasting in their pots, a gust of wind gathered up a concoction of spices and spilled the unlikely combination over the turkey. In any event, *mole poblano* has become Mexico's signature national dish. While Puebla remains its quintessential origin, two other towns have laid claims. In Southern Mexico, Oaxacans produce their own version, while the small town of San Pedro Atocpan, just south of Mexico City, is now the centre of thriving production on a mass scale and responsible for over half the *mole* consumed in Mexico. Families in Central Mexico have their own secret combinations of spices, but electric mills now toast and grind the large mass of ingredients needed for industrial quantities on festive occasions.

Puebla symbolism also surrounds a saintly woman and the dress she wore. La China Poblana, or the "Chinese Pueblan," a slave of South Asian origin, became an iconic figure of the seventeenth century. The term "Chinese" was used to designate anyone of Asian origin at the time. Born in Cochin, now Kochi, in southern India, this young woman, known as Mirra, converted to Catholicism and was given the name Catarina de San Juan before being captured and sold into slavery by Portuguese pirates. Escaping from their grasp, she was nevertheless sold as a slave in Manila and shipped aboard a galleon to Acapulco. Instead of delivering her to the viceroy of New Spain, her master sold her to Miguel de Sosa, a wealthy Puebla merchant. Moved by her simplicity and spirituality, de Sosa exempted her from chores and freed her upon his death. She married and became a *beata*, a devout woman who took personal religious vows without entering a convent.

By the time of her death at age eighty-two, she had become famous in Puebla as a revered and austere mystic, renowned for her visions of the Virgin Mary and the infant Jesus. Mixing a blend of Catholicism with her Indian beliefs and developing a large popular following, she alarmed the Church with her syncretism, and in 1691, the Inquisition banned devotion to her. She was laid to rest in the sacristy of the Temple of the Company of Jesus in Puebla in the so-called Tomb of the Chinese Pueblan, but authorities later moved her remains in order to discourage the cult that was forming around them.

La China Poblana also achieved fame for her clothing. Her dress, consisting of a white blouse with fringing and beaded embroidery work, had become the folkloric outfit for the city by the early nineteenth century. No longer the garb of a pious woman, it was the outfit of a "china" woman and was stereotypically associated with a low-born woman of loose morals, lusted after by men but disapproved of by respectable women. The dress was colourful and low-cut, allowing part of the neck and bosom to be seen. An attractive shawl sometimes accompanied the decorated blouse and colourful skirt cut so that the woman's legs could be seen. A version of the outfit became internationally symbolic in the twentieth century when it was adopted by the iconic painter Frida Kahlo.

Puebla has remained an important city culturally and economically. In the nineteenth century, its thriving textile industry attracted immigrants from Spain, Italy, Germany, and France. The architectural influence of France, especially iron-girded buildings designed by Eiffel, dates from this time, as does France's culinary influence on Puebla's leading restaurants. A German presence was even stronger. The Bavarian-style houses and the Alexander von Humboldt College, established in a suburb of the town named after the great explorer, were distinctive elements. Much later, in the 1960s, Puebla became the centre of modern German manufacturing in Mexico. Volkswagen de México built a two million square–foot plant in the western suburbs in 1965, and by 1980, over one million "beetles" or *vochos*, as the diminutive cars are called in Mexico, had rolled off the factory floors, many of them exported via Veracruz or Acapulco to Central and South America. Other German companies followed this lead. Siemens, which had begun activity in Mexico back in 1894 when it provided the first electric lighting for the Paseo de la Reforma, has also had a strong presence in Puebla.

Cholula today is virtually a suburb of Puebla, and the ruins of its remarkable pyramid attract visitors. Its pyramid encompasses an estimated 14,800 square feet, making it the largest in the world, though only a fraction has been excavated. A museum across the road from the pyramid contains pottery and artifacts found at the site as well as indications of the various underground tunnels built by archaeologists as they worked the sites. A winding stone trail leads to the church, 230 feet above ground level, where a splendid view of the Puebla valley can be obtained.

Ƒ

CHAPTER 18

Humboldt to the Fore Again: Water Issues and Mexican Demographic History

Chapter 8 examined Humboldt's view of Mexican ecological history contextually in the light of more recent scholarship. This chapter resumes the discussion by elaborating on Humboldt's views on water and on demography.

WATER ISSUES

Humboldt's interest was frequently drawn to water issues, and specifically to hydraulic engineering projects. He was impressed by the twenty-kilometre canal and tunnel system at Nochistongo, designed and built by Enrico Martínez in 1607 with an army of 15,000 Indian labourers to provide protection against flooding. The job was completed in only ten months, but at great human cost. Martínez, who was also a talented mathematician, originally designed the plan with a tunnel eleven feet wide and fourteen feet high, but the tunnel was inadequate and had to be extended and remodelled; the delay meant that it was not completed until 1767, at great expense and at the cost of 70,000 workers' lives. Humboldt was given fossilized mammoth bones that had been kept from the original excavations, but this did not prevent him from complaining about the quality of the engineering or the callous disregard for the lives of the Indian labourers.

Humboldt understood the importance of water in and around Mexico City. A chain of five major and several smaller lakes had surrounded the Aztec capital of Tenochtitlan and provided the basis for the *chinampa* system, which not only provided richly irrigated land recovered for agriculture, but also helped control salinization. The sweet water of lakes Chalco and Xochimilco permitted fish to thrive, thus providing a good source of food. Yet Humboldt was also well aware that Spanish decisions to cover over much of the lake system brought risks of flooding. Spanish planners relied essentially on canals and tunnels leading to the Pánuco River. Lake Texcoco, the lowest lying of all the lakes, occupied the minimum elevation in the Valley of Mexico so that water ultimately drained towards its location in the northeast corner of the city. During high-water periods after the May–October rainy season, the lakes could be joined as a single body of water, especially with flooding in the neighbourhoods in the northeast.

In modern times, the water issue in Mexico City has required increasing attention. In 1967, authorities developed the Deep Drainage System (Drenaje Profundo), a network of several hundred kilometres of tunnel at a depth between 100 and 800 feet, with a central tunnel 21 feet in diameter to carry rainwater out of the basin. The ecological consequences of this engineering feat have been enormous. Today, Lake Texcoco occupies a small area surrounded by salt marshes a few kilometres northeast of the city. Nearby is the small remnant of Lake Zumpango, while in the extreme south of the city, lakes Xochimilco and Chalco are much smaller versions of what the Aztecs had known. The water is so salty that a company has engaged in the commercial evaporation and marketing of this salt.

During his travels in the great plains in the northern part of the Valley of Mexico, Humboldt carefully examined the canals and water-drainage systems. At great expense, the colonial government had built two new canal and lock systems, one from Lake San Cristóbal and the other from Lake Zumpango, in 1796 and 1798 respectively. He described Lake Zumpango as being more like an inundated meadow than a lake. Overall, he believed the project was well conceived but poorly executed, and thus required structural changes. To overcome these water problems, Humboldt recommended that the colonial administration hire Dutch hydraulic engineers, whose particular experience of keeping sea water out of their irrigation systems would serve New Spain very well: *From every side there were highly unstable, almost perpendicular, earthen walls. Great piles of earth filled the canals so that it required 3 [sic] to 4,000 piastres each year to clean them. By means of a system of locks, a constant quantity of water was drawn from Lake Zunpango to irrigate the more distant fields. The Spaniards treat water like it were the enemy. It seems they believe that New Spain is as dry as the interior of their own ancient lands. This has become a moral as much as a physical vision.*

HUMBOLDT ON MEXICAN DEMOGRAPHY

Humboldt's appreciation of Mexico's demography reflected the better assumptions of contemporary experts. Like all who addressed the question of population decline or growth, he was aware that a significant decline had begun with the arrival of the Spaniards. The more modern consensus that the loss was catastrophic, from 70 to 90 per cent of the population, was beyond the imagination of early nineteenth-century scientists. Humboldt's optimism about Central Mexico's healthy environment led him to estimate the ratio of births to deaths to be two to one. In contrast, he assumed a huge mortality in the low tropical areas. He felt that the population of Mexico City was underestimated by local census takers, who put it at 112,000 and argued it to be greater than 135,000. He cited the 1793 tally for New Spain as a whole, made by the viceregal government of the Count of Revillagigedo, as 4.4 million. By 1803, Humboldt upgraded this figure to 5.8 million and thought it erred on the low side.

Humboldt's estimate remains within a consensus figure among historical demographers of our age. Arguing that Mexico had fertile land available for expansion, unlike France, he believed Mexico's population could double every thirty-six to forty years if it did not encounter any calamities. He noted that the central tableland stretching from Puebla to Mexico City and then on to Salamanca and Celaya was as densely covered with villages and hamlets as the most cultivated parts of Lombardy. But to the east and west of this narrow strip were tracts of uncultivated land where the population was thinly arranged. Like political economists of his time, Humboldt shared a linear view about the limits to population growth relative to food supply. Neither Humboldt nor, more to the point, leading economic theorists like Thomas Malthus could envision the impact that a global agricultural revolution and, later, reliable means of contraception would have on pessimistic assumptions. For example, the price of wheat in the United States has fallen by about two-thirds over the last 200 years.

A friend of fellow British thinkers like James Mill and David Ricardo, Thomas Robert Malthus was an economist and demographer who is best known for the doctrine named after him, Malthusianism, which holds that population growth will always tend to outrun the food supply and that improvement in human society could not occur without strict limits on reproduction. Malthus was an influential antidote to the idealists of the Enlightenment such as Jacques Rousseau and William Godwin. His economic pessimism was empirical but his statistical work was weak, even allowing for the age. His influence helped justify a theory of wages based on the wage earner's minimum cost of subsistence, and he discouraged traditional forms of charity.

Today's historical demographers argue that the pre-Columbian population was larger than an older generation had believed. At one end of the spectrum, Cook and Borah estimated the population of Central Mexico, from its frontier with Chichimecas to the Isthmus of Tehuantepec, to be 25 million in 1519. Only four years after the Spanish invasion, the population collapsed to 17 million Native Americans and, by 1548, to 6 million. Twenty years later, the same authors lowered the estimate to only 3 million in 1568, to about 2 million in 1580, and, in 1630, to scarcely 750,000, only 3 per cent of the population at conquest. William T. Sanders and Barbara J. Price, however, reduce the pre-Columbian population by about a half, to 12 million, but agree that the nadir of about 750,000 was reached around 1630, which represented a loss of 90 per cent.

The causes of such a steep decline were multiple and were felt unevenly in different regions. A contemporary eyewitness to Spanish excess of violence towards Indians, Bartolomé de Las Casas, attributed the catastrophe to the ferocity of the Spanish conquest and early rule. The litany of abuse is well known: plunder, rape, public and private exaction of tribute, enslavement, and cruel overworking in farming and mining operations. But the list did not factor in terrible losses to epidemic disease, negative changes in diet, and new methods of food production. Wild herds of horses and cattle destroyed crops, and wheat took over the best land to pay tributes and taxes, although this European crop gave lower yields than indigenous maize. Finally, psychological impacts were severe; they included demoralization, depression, suicide, and individual decisions to limit fertility through abortion and birth control, notwithstanding the fact, for example, that male infertility rose among survivors of smallpox.

Demographic recovery eventually occurred. Mortality rates remained high throughout the seventeenth and eighteenth centuries, but a decline in these rates began at the end of the eighteenth century, for reasons not easy to explain. One factor was improvement in hygiene, though this would have mostly benefited the urban population and the wealthier classes. In rural Mexico, people started marrying earlier, and it is estimated by some that there was a progressive increase in the fertility rate of 1 per cent per annum. Nevertheless, demographers caution that marriage rates are not a reliable indicator of population growth and that illegitimate births, always high, need to be estimated, however unreliable the data.

To summarize, in 1800, Spanish America had about 13.5 million inhabitants. Spain itself counted roughly 10 million, while New Spain, the largest colony, counted about 6 million people. About 90 per cent were concentrated in the centre and south, but the density was uneven. Prosperous Guanajuato had a high density of 36 inhabitants per square kilometre, while more remote regions in the north had much lower densities.

Xalapa: A Brief Stay in the City of Flowers

Humboldt, Bonpland, and Montúfar travelled from Puebla to Xalapa in early February 1804. They collected rocks and plants on the slopes of the Cofre de Perote on 7 February and the Pico de Orizaba soon after. From 10 to 15 February, they sojourned in Xalapa, but this part of their trip was never recorded. It is possible that they were accommodated at the Hacienda El Lencero, ten kilometres south of Xalapa and a favourite rest stop for large travelling parties coming up from, or going down to, Veracruz.

The visitors noted with considerable interest how Indians carried ice from the snowy fields of Orizaba all the way to the coast at Veracruz to supply sherbet makers there. Sherbet was said to have been at a premium during yellow fever epidemics. And like many before and after, Humboldt was awed by the floral beauty of Xalapa, dubbing it "the city of flowers." The party then began the treacherous descent to the coast and reached Veracruz on 19 February, hoping to embark quickly on a vessel to Cuba and then on to Europe.

Humboldt's diary provides extensive comments on the politics of trade and transport in the Xalapa and Veracruz region. All the coast from Coatzacoalcos to Pánuco, he argues, could produce even more cotton than the region of Colima, *but it is uninhabited and the government is doing nothing to boost the population. The result is a shortage of labour in one of the most fertile regions. Every one takes refuge in the highlands not because of the heat and insalubrity of the*

coast, but because the great landowners treat their tenants badly, ex-
pelling them when they wish because they prefer to draft them for the
navy and the militia. There is too large a militia for a region that is so
thinly populated.

As Humboldt and his party approached Xalapa before beginning
their abrupt descent to the coast, they encountered political tensions
arising from the competing interests of two factions. Humboldt had
strong opinions about the continuing political quarrel between Mexico City merchants and local Veracruz traders who had country
homes in Xalapa and resided in both places. The Mexico City merchants should recognize the needs of the locals, he argued, rather
than opt for such drastic solutions as abandoning Veracruz and keeping only the garrison at Ulúa.

Not only did Humboldt oppose the alternative of an Orizaba
route to Mexico City (which would bypass Xalapa), he had no sym-
pathy for the way the porters on the routes were viewed: *Mule drivers
and other labourers begin to die from fever when they descend lower
than Jalapa [Xalapa] and Encero, so black mule drivers living in Veracruz should take over from them. This is the much cheaper solution,
but cynics in Veracruz welcome yellow fever* [vómito negro] *as a bless-
ing in disguise because it makes the coast inhospitable to highlanders.*

Humboldt ended the Veracruz entry in his *Diario* with a return to
the political quarrels. He commented on the role of Spanish con-
sulates, which in his day were merchant guilds, not official diplomatic
bodies. He found the Spanish consul in Mexico City to be a distinguished man, but one who wished to see Veracruz destroyed because
he considered it *a nest of smugglers and revolutionaries. But the consulate at Veracruz is very active and the most illustrious in all the Americas.* He liked the consul there personally and found him to be a
younger, more liberal figure than the Spanish consul in Mexico City.
Humboldt expressed his pleasure at the decision of the town hall
early in 1804 not to close the port, then turned to what he considered
the major issue, the bad road running up from Veracruz: *The treasures
from Vera Cruz pass along a road which is frequently nothing but a narrow and crooked path and is one of the most difficult in all America.*
The viceregal government planned to construct and improve the road

to Veracruz, but disputes over the optimum route had delayed any progress. Mexico City merchants wanted a route via Orizaba, but Veracruz merchants, *who [as noted] have country houses at Jalapa, and who maintain numerous commercial relations with that town, insist that the new carriage road should go by Perote and Jalapa. After a discussion of several years, the viceroy declared himself in favor of the road via Jalapa as of the greatest utility.*

Humboldt noted that the construction of a new road had begun, and he found the plan magnificent, as it avoided rapid ascents and was wide enough for carriages. It was costly, estimated at over 15 million francs (600,000 pounds sterling), but necessary and would pay dividends by pushing down prices of imports and exports, both to the benefit of Mexican trade. Having given a reasoned opinion on the Veracruz route, Humboldt then shifted ground and offered a novel and unorthodox opinion: *The introduction of camels would be exceedingly useful in Mexico. The table-lands over which the great roads pass are not sufficiently elevated for the cold to be prejudicial to these animals; and they would suffer less than horses or mules from the aridity of the soil and the want of water and pasturage to which the beasts of burden are exposed.*

MODERN XALAPA

Modern Xalapa is a breath of fresh air to those travelling inland from the sweltering coast. The capital of the state of Veracruz, the city sits at roughly 5,000 feet beneath the black volcanic peaks of the Sierra Madre Oriental. Its 800,000 residents enjoy a wonderful view of the mountains, especially the snowy summit of Pico de Orizaba, Mexico's highest, measured at 18,400 feet. A light but persistent winter rain, called *chipichipi*, dominates owing to the quick rise in altitude from coast to highland. In summer, this climate produces evening mists. With an annual average rainfall of 1,500 millimetres, Xalapa is the wettest town in the Mexican highlands. Warmth and moisture produce a natural greenhouse effect, earning Xalapa its reputation as a floral wonder. Flowers play an important role in the metropolitan economy, as does coffee, which is grown in both small holdings and large estates in the surrounding hills. Tree-shaded Juárez Park across from the Municipal Palace is an example of the prevailing lushness.

Like Guanajuato, Xalapa is today a university town. Veracruzana University is the main public university in the state of Veracruz, while two smaller centres of higher learning are the University of Xalapa and the Universidad Anáhuac of Xalapa. The large population of students in the town contributes to the atmosphere found in the numerous cafes and bars. Young people are also attracted to the theatres, museums, and street art.

Dominating the city is Macuiltépetl Ecological Park, a fine green space astride the summit of the mountain on which Xalapa is built. The park is carefully maintained, and Xalapeño families and visitors to the city can enjoy the varied vegetation of a subalpine forest, a variety of birds, and dazzling views at the summit. Clear mornings provide a vista of both the Cofre de Perote and the Pico de Orizaba. To the east can be seen the last belt of mountains before the land begins its sharp descent to the coast.

The Museum of Anthropology in Xalapa is the second largest such museum in the country after that of Mexico City, and arguably its finest. Opened in 1986 by the state of Veracruz and dedicated largely to Gulf coast cultures, especially the Olmec and the Totonac, the building boasts architecture that is itself a work of art. Its layout descends gradually south to north, emulating the region, and vegetation is used to set off larger archaeological pieces, such as the colossal Olmec heads. Artefacts from major Veracruz sites, such as El Tajín and Zempoala, are featured. Zempoala lies astride the Actopan River, southeast of Xalapa, on the way to the Gulf of Mexico. The museum's collection makes it clear that Xalapa and its region supplied significant quantities of cotton in tribute to the Mexica conquerors in the late fifteenth century.

Hacienda El Lencero, at kilometre 10, southeast of Xalapa on Highway 140, replicates the trajectory of the old Camino Real. The hacienda dates back to 1525, when a soldier of Cortés, Juan Lencero, was granted the land. It changed hands several times and grew larger in colonial days when it became a ranch and stagecoach stop, supplying horses, donkeys, and mules for those travelling between Mexico City and Veracruz. Its name became corrupted to "El Encero" by the time of independence, when it became a large sugar estate. Such leading figures of the period as Agustín de Iturbide, Viceroy José de Iturrigaray, and Ignacio de Allende all sojourned here on their way to or from Veracruz. In 1842, General Antonio López de Santa Anna, a native of Veracruz and many times president of the republic, purchased the estate and held it for fourteen years as his rural retreat from disease-ridden and steamy Veracruz. The vegetation at the hacienda is a mixture of temperate and tropical, as the descent to the coast begins here. The museum is well maintained and offers a portrait of the luxurious hacienda life enjoyed by wealthy plantation owners in the nineteenth century. Especially attractive are the finely crafted Mexican rugs and the expensive imported furniture.

Visitors do well to take in the coffee plantations at Coatepec and Xico, eight and nineteen kilometres south of Xalapa. Each one sells locally grown and roasted coffee. Coatepec, restored to resemble a colonial town, specializes in the cultivation of orchids, while Xico remains an agricultural village where sacks of coffee beans are a common sight. A few kilometres beyond Xico, the Texolo Waterfall plunges into a gorge surrounded by lush greenery.

CHAPTER 20

The Ruins of Zempoala in the Gulf Lowlands

THREE ZEMPOALAS

Considerable confusion surrounds the place name Zempoala, some-times spelt Cempoala. Three very different Mexican locales bear this name: the lagoon system in the State of Morelos; the municipality in the State of Hidalgo; and the archaeological site close to the Gulf of Mexico in the state of Veracruz. Lake Zempoala, from the Nahuatl meaning "place of many waters," is one of seven lagoons only fifty kilometres southwest of Mexico City. Now a national park, it forms part of the biological corridor of Chichinautzin and sits at the high elevation of about 9,500 feet amidst abundant forests of oaks, cedars, pine, and fir. The town of Zempoala in the semi-arid plains of Hidalgo has a population of around 25,000, and its name derives from *cempoalla*, meaning twenty. Perhaps this refers to the market that was held every twenty days at this location after the town's founding by Toltecs in the period from 100 to 300 BCE, when groups migrated there from central Veracruz and from the Valley of Mexico. The third Zempoala, the one featured in this chapter, is derived from "Cem-poalatl," the "place of twenty waters" in Nahuatl. The name may reflect the presence in ancient times of the numerous aqueducts that were used to irrigate gardens in the surrounding fields.

Figure 20.1
Ruins of Zempoala. (In APV)

ONE OF HUMBOLDT'S OMISSIONS

Humboldt has been taken to task for his allegedly Eurocentric approach to Mexico, despite his admiration for pre-Hispanic cultures. Perhaps his most serious critic has been Mary Louise Pratt, who picks up on Edward Said's *Orientalism* in her influential 1992 publication *Imperial Eyes: Travel Writing and Transculturation*. Pratt accuses Humboldt of reinforcing the colonial myth that America was a pristine and primordial continent. She maintains that Humboldt, using the expression "New Continent" constantly, as if three centuries of European colonization had never occurred, turned a chauvinistic assumption into a scientific fact: that undeveloped and unproductive pre-colonial landscapes needed economic development that only progressive Europeans could provide. She argues that Humboldt's very authoritativeness reinforced attitudes towards the environment in the Americas in the early nineteenth century. Andrew Sluyter, however, finds Pratt's indictment overstated. While it is true that

Humboldt regarded the Gulf lowlands as "pristine," he clearly understood that the basin of Mexico had been productively developed before the Spanish arrived. Humboldt, Sluyter argues, neither ignored nor minimized the achievements of pre-Hispanic economic actors. He accepted that the basin was densely inhabited by Indigenous people who were technologically sophisticated managers of irrigation and other aspects of water management. Addressing this issue in the highlands, Humboldt expressed admiration for the Albarradón of Nezahuacóyotl, a ten-kilometre dike that prevented Lake Texcoco's saline water from penetrating the *chinampa* zone that partially ringed Tenochtitlán.

Although he travelled to the edge of the Gulf lowlands on his way from Xalapa to Veracruz, Humboldt did observe that this region too had experienced extensive pre-colonial settlement. Travelling in February in the depths of the dry season, Humboldt did not acknowledge what had been clearly documented in the writings of the conquest period to which he had access. Díaz del Castillo gave an account of the large city of Zempoala, as did Gómara in 1552, noting that Cortés had written that Zempoala was the first Mesoamerican city he visited and that it was "completely covered with gardens and freshness, and with fine irrigated gardens." The Spaniards took to calling Zempoala *Villaviciosa*, or "fertile town," because of the many festivals, vast orchards, and gardens found there. The humid Gulf zone permitted intensive wetland cultivation, and archaeological work has revealed that sloping field terracing, platforms, and canals for drainage were all used to grow maize, cotton, and agave. Indeed, when Cortés arrived in 1519, he saw a rich and potentially promising ally in the state of Totonac and in what the Spaniards called its "fat chief" Xicomecoatl. Inhabited mainly by Totonacs and Zapotecs, Zempoala may have had a population of 30,000 when Cortés passed through. Together, some fifty towns maintained a population of as many as 250,000 people in a state they called Totonacapán, a region stretching from northern Veracruz to the Zacatlán district of Puebla. Arguably the most important Totonac site in post-classical Mesoamerica, Zempoala was founded 1,500 years before the arrival of the Spaniards by Totonacs forced out of the Sierra Madre Oriental mountains.

Defeated by the Aztec emperor Moctezuma I in the mid-fifteenth century and burdened with a heavy tax in goods and prisoners for sacrifice, the Totonacs of Zempoala welcomed the arrival of Cortés in 1519. They were the first to rebel against Moctezuma and ally themselves with the Spaniards to throw off the Aztec yoke. Unfortunately, ridding themselves of one burden only brought a far greater one: epidemic disease. When a terrible smallpox epidemic struck Mesoamerica between 1575 and 1577, Zempoala was one of the most badly affected regions. The site was completely abandoned and a few survivors found their way up to Xalapa. Others in the former Totonac state were enslaved and worked to death on the new Spanish sugar plantations. Soon, slave labour from Africa replaced them on the narrow lowland plain. Yellow fever remained a scourge, especially for unseasoned new arrivals from the interior highlands.

The Spanish did not cultivate the Gulf wetlands and instead introduced tens of thousands of cattle to graze during the dry season, retreating with them to higher ground at the onset of the rains. People only began to reoccupy the coastal wetlands after the revolution of 1910, when some of the haciendas were broken up and the land redistributed.

Humboldt was pessimistic about the agricultural potential of the Gulf lowlands, regarding as serious impediments the threat of yellow fever and what he believed to be lassitude produced by the steamy tropical environment. The question is, why did Humboldt not acknowledge Zempoala's past or the lowland's future? Humboldt journeyed along the royal highway, but he left this route where it crossed the Antigua River, proceeding to Veracruz by way of the coast. Possibly, he did not even see the wetland fields, even though he was so close to them. Had he known about the ruins of Zempoala, his reading of the landscape might have been different. Zempoala was only a few kilometres directly inland from the spot where the watchtower at Point Zempoala guarded the coast during the eighteenth century. Had he inquired, locals may very well have directed him to the ruins. As it was, the site's location faded from the literature and was only rediscovered around 1880 by Estefania Salas de Broner, a Mexican archaeologist whose wife, a German researcher, had been alerted to the

site by local farmers. Her initial observations were enormously helpful to Hermann Strebel, a leading German archaeologist working on
the Veracruz coast who published the first study of the site in 1883.

It seems unfair to lay the crime of omission on Humboldt when
he saw so much that others did not. Humboldt was in a hurry to
reach Veracruz. When he was delayed there until 7 March, he occupied himself by exploring the port rather than the coastal lowlands.

THE ZEMPOALA AND TAJÍN SITES

Vincent H. Malmstrom, a geographer from Dartmouth College, has
provided a provocative and brilliant argument about the importance
of the two Toltec sites of El Tajín and Zempoala. His analysis is part
of the path-breaking reinterpretation of Mesoamerican astronomy
found in his *Cycles of the Sun, Mysteries of the Moon: The Calendar in
Mesoamerican Civilization.*

El Tajín at first glance is the more dramatic site. Located in the
hills of northern Veracruz, the settlement goes back as far as 1500
BCE, but its early stage of city growth came later, between 100 and
500 CE, within the Toltec sphere of expansion from the north. Strongly influenced by Teotihuacán, El Tajín may have been a commercial
outlier, supplying lowland tropical products to the great plateau
metropolis. Its greatest development occurred as Teotihuacán waned
and finally disappeared between 500 and 1100 CE. At its height, the
city counted no fewer than eleven ball courts, but the pyramid of
the niches was its crowning feature. On each of its four sides, this
spectacular pyramid contained decorated box-like niches. Attempts
have been made to interpret these as representing the counting of astronomical cycles, but Malmstrom strongly disagrees. El Tajín may
have commemorated astronomical cycles, but its location was ill-
suited to astronomical observation. It sits on the lower slopes of the
Sierra Madre Oriental and is dominated by overcast skies and light
drizzle through much of the year. Its very name commemorates the
storm god.

In contrast, Zempoala was the Totonac capital and ceremonial centre, situated in a far more open setting than El Tajín. As noted earlier, its name derives from the Nahuatl "Cempoalatl" (the place of twenty waters), possibly because there were numerous irrigation channels for the many farms and fields. El Tajín was one of the first ceremonial centres in the central Veracruz region to demonstrate a solstitial orientation, in this instance towards the Orizaba volcano and the winter solstice sunset, evidence it had been touched by Olmec influences from the south. Dense sugar cane fields surround the ruins, much of which have not been excavated. The impressive city lies on extensive mounds, built to provide protection against flooding. It contains a Templo Mayor, a Great Pyramid, and a Sun Temple resembling the one at Tenochtitlán. But its most intriguing aspect is the presence of three remarkable stone rings lying beneath the massive pyramid in the central plaza. The rings are surmounted by thirteen, twenty-eight, and forty step-like pillars, respectively, and were used by Totonac priests as counting devices to track the eclipse cycles of the moon. Each stone ring was fashioned of rounded beach cobbles cemented together to form a series of small stepped pillars. The idea was to move a marker or an idol from one stepped pillar to the next with each passing day. By calibrating the movements of the moon this closely, the intellectually curious priests could predict the next time it would be "devoured," that is, totally eclipsed.

Vincent Malmstrom's publications reveal an innovative thinker in the spirit of Humboldt. Despite the high quality of the journals in which his research has appeared, many of the specialists who have dominated Mesoamerican studies still consider him an amateur outsider. Nevertheless, his writings make him a legitimate contributor to the debate on Mesoamerican calendrics, especially the architectural and geographic alignments of ceremonial centres with their surrounding mountainous topography. His curiosity was first kindled by the so-called Mayan sacred calendar, which has only 260 days. His research led him to a new view of the birthplace of Mesoamerican culture and of the origin and diffusion of Mesoamerican calendrical systems. Malmstrom posits that the 260-day calendar marked the interval between passages of the sun at its zenith over Izapa, an ancient ceremonial centre in the Soconuso region of Mexico's Pacific coastal plain. Previous scholarship had pointed to Copán as the birthplace of the calendar. At Izapa, the beginning of the year was fixed by the rising of the sun over the highest mountain in all of Central America, the volcano Tajumulco, 13,842 feet, as seen from Izapa, a horizon-based event that takes place on the summer solstice of 22 June.

Malmstrom shows how, through the diffusion of calendrics in the course of their migrations, successive cultures, beginning with the Zoque at Izapa, laid out all Mesoamerican ceremonial centres to be oriented to the highest mountain within view. Examples Malmstrom gives include San Lorenzo mountain, 11,138 feet, at the winter solstice sunset; La Venta and the San Martín volcano; Laguna de los Cerros and the peak of Cerro Santa Martha at the summer solstice sunrise; and even the colossal Aztec city of Teotihuacán, the "Place of the Gods." Until work was done in 1993, it had not been realized that the entire city had been built on a meticulous grid oriented to the sunset position on 13 August. Like all Olmec-inspired ceremonial centres, Teotihuacán owes its precise location to the fact that it is solstitially oriented, but in this instance the mountain in question is not visible. A low ridge obscures the southeastern horizon, but the crest of this ridge is precisely on the azimuth of the winter solstice between Teotihuacán and the highest mountain in Mexico, the volcano Orizaba at 18,700 feet.

A series of articles in prestigious journals made Malmstrom's views widely known. These included *Science* in 1973, *Nature* in 1976, and the *Journal of the History of Astronomy* in 1978. He received positive feedback on his deductions, but also a hostile note from Sir John Eric Sydney Thompson, dean of British Mayanistas. One of Thompson's students said Malmstrom had been "anticipated" by earlier "discredited" researchers whom he had failed to acknowledge, perhaps deliberately. This vitriolic attack from such leading archaeologists came as a shock. A second reason for hostility towards Malmstrom was that his results affected the debate over whether the Maya or the Olmec had been the true founders of civilization in Mesoamerica.

Mexican researchers for the most part favoured the Olmec, while the old guard represented by Thompson and the American Sylvanus Morley remained intransigent Mayanistas.

Mostly preliterate, Mesoamerican societies were limited to travel on foot in a daunting landscape. Yet their priests developed the concept of zero, discovered the properties of magnetism and the celestial pole, worked out the length of the Venusian cycle, were able to predict eclipses, and successfully located the Tropic of Cancer. Vincent Malmstrom has helped illuminate these achievements, and his research deserves recognition.

The ruins of Zempoala, lying just north of the town of Cardel, are even more accessible than Tajín's more famous ruins, which lie to its north. Located only one kilometre from the Actopan River and six kilometres from the Gulf coast, Zempoala can be reached by buses that leave Veracruz every fifteen minutes to take visitors on an easy forty-kilometre drive along Highway 180 north.

CHAPTER 21

Veracruz: Journey's End

It took Humboldt and his companions three days to make the descent to Veracruz. Arriving in the port city on 19 February 1804, they anxiously cooled their heels until 7 March, no doubt near exhaustion after their arduous adventures. Perhaps this would explain why Humboldt uncharacteristically confined himself to Veracruz, not venturing along the Gulf lowlands and unaware that on his descent he had narrowly missed the extensive ruins of Zempoala.

Humboldt was struck by the way that weather conditions dictated port life in Veracruz: *No ship dares leave the port of Veracruz without consulting the harbormaster, Señor Orta, who is called "king of the winds." It can be said that his barometer has earned millions of piastres for the king. On 29 February we were supposed to take a short sail under a gentle breeze. Señor Orta said no because his barometer was dropping. Sure enough, on 1 March a furious northerly arose that would have placed us in grave danger. Several ships which set out the previous evening had to scuttle back to port … The heat and humidity of the coast is oppressive, even in the middle of the night, and even then, the mosquitoes are cruel. A storm can appear suddenly, within ten minutes.*

Called by a variety of names and in Mexico most commonly known as *vómito prieto* or "black vomit," yellow fever was an unpredictable but frequent caller at the port of Veracruz. It was sometimes called "yellow jack," after the quarantine flag that adorned suspect ships in the harbours of ports throughout the South Atlantic and the

Figure 21.1
The port of Veracruz in 1804. (Public domain)

Gulf of Mexico. Here are Humboldt's remarks: *The port of Veracruz is considered the principal seat of yellow fever. Thousands of Europeans landing in Mexico at the period of the great heat fall victim to this cruel epidemic. Some vessels prefer landing at Veracruz in the beginning of winter, when the tempests begin to rage, rather than exposing themselves in summer to the loss of the greater part of their crew from the effects of yellow fever, and to a long quarantine on their return to Europe.* When the fever season arrived, muleteers and merchants in the highlands refused to descend to the coast, thus inhibiting trade. When bad yellow fever outbreaks occurred in 1802 and 1803, the colonial government again discussed whether to compel all residents to move to Xalapa or some other point in the mountains. A debate prevailed in Mexico, one party seeking to abandon Veracruz, the other to ameliorate the situation there somehow. People believed the disease was imported from elsewhere, carried aboard crowded vessels with bad ventilation, or that it was the result of *the effects of an ardent and unhealthy climate on newly landed sailors.* People in the great ports in the Gulf of Mexico and the Caribbean, whether Havana, Veracruz, or New Orleans, accused one another of being the source of this scourge.

Veracruz, Humboldt continues, was overcrowded and unsanitary, but he refused to see the city only in negative terms: *The population*

of Vera Cruz is too great for the small extent of ground which the city oc-
cupies. Sixteen thousand inhabitants are confined within a space of half
a square kilometer. The streets are broad and straight, but as the town
is surrounded with a high wall, there is little or no circulation of air …
The strangers who frequent Vera Cruz have greatly exaggerated the dirt-
iness of the inhabitants. For some time the police have taken measures
for the salubrity of the air, and Vera Cruz is at present not so dirty as
many of the towns of the south of Europe. But as it is frequented by thou-
sands of Europeans not seasoned to the climate, and situated under a
burning sky, and surrounded by small marshes from whose emanations
the air is infected, the fatal effects of the epidemics will not diminish till
the police shall have continued to display their activity for a long suc-
cession of years.

It was widely held in Mexico that disease varied with temperature,
but Humboldt was not convinced: *I am far from considering extreme*
heat as the only and true cause of yellow fever, but how can it be denied
that there exists in places where the disease is endemic an intimate con-
nection between the state of the atmosphere and the progress of the dis-
ease? The disease was not contagious, Humboldt correctly stated, but
he did not understand the process of immunity acquired in childhood by seasoned populations, and instead erred in believing that
only strangers born in temperate climates were at risk: *As the* vómito
only attacks individuals born in cold countries, and never the natives, the
mortality of Vera Cruz is not so great as might be supposed. The great
epidemics have only carried off within the town about fifteen hundred
individuals per annum, but there are years when the number of deaths
within the town and in the environs amounts to eighteen hundred or
two thousand.

There was no secret cure for yellow fever, but Humboldt suggested
several sanitary measures that might be helpful: *if the authorities*
could but drain the marshes in the neighborhood of the town; if they
could supply the inhabitants with potable water; if the hospitals and
church-yards could be removed to a distance; if frequent fumigations of
oxygenated muriatic acid were made in the apartments of the patients,
in churches, and especially on board of vessels; and finally, if the walls of

the town, which force the population to be concentrated in a small space of ground, and prevent the circulation of air without preventing contraband trade, were to be thrown down.

Moving the location of the town would not solve the dangers for arriving seafarers. The proposal to shut the port during the dangerous months seemed sound, but that would mean confining activity to the winter, after the hurricane season ended. Humboldt wisely thought it best to attempt the cleanups first, *before having recourse to such extraordinary measures.*

While some of these proposals could not later be linked to the complexities of yellow fever and its insect vectors, they were progressive for the time and indicated that Humboldt anticipated the new sanitary reforms that were soon to spread throughout Western society. For example, Humboldt had always maintained an early sanitarian's concern for the quality of drinking water, though it was too early in the history of public health to know what constituted safe water. Nevertheless, he was not at a loss to suggest solutions: *People who are well off drink water from cisterns in Veracruz and the water consumed by the military at the Fort of Ulúa is very good. But the lower classes drink poor water from the Tenoya river or from a ditch that comes from Méganos. As well, every house has a well. Nevertheless, water has been a problem for over a century. A French engineer was sent out, but the cost of his proposed projects was considered prohibitive. Politics was also an issue. Why not capture the abundant rain water for consumption?*

In Humboldt's day, medical knowledge of yellow fever was virtually non-existent. Not only were breakthroughs in medicine based on the existence of tiny organisms within the body unknown, even the sanitarian reforms that predated germ theory in the early nineteenth century had not yet emerged. The very notion that biting insects could transmit infectious disease seemed totally absurd. Among the many erroneous theories circulating as late as the 1880s was the idea that yellow fever was a *virulent filth disease* brought to the New World in ships fouled by the excrement of African slaves. It was thought that ships' bilges had contaminated the harbours the vessels had called upon and also that yellow fever spread through fermentation in the new soil.

Perhaps the one area of emerging modern science where Humboldt fell short was scientific medicine. He was, of course, deeply interested in medical geography, or what Rupke calls "Humboldtian medicine." This movement had a modest following in nineteenth-century Germany and Britain, and Humboldt's isotherm mapping did anticipate the first global distribution maps of human diseases like malaria, for example. But Humboldt's stress on the importance of nature and the environment to the spread of disease tied him closely to explanations of disease based on temperature, humidity, and vegetation rather than on conditions of social deprivation. Like many others, he believed that malaria and yellow fever were caused by atmospheric phenomena called "miasmas." Such an approach missed the emergence of the new bacteriology pioneered by Louis Pasteur in France and Robert Koch in Germany. This approach led to the germ theory of infectious disease according to which social causation and public health became the dominant variables.

Despite the prevailing ignorance of the day about infectious disease throughout Europe and the Americas, Veracruz in particular was not a backward outpost of medical ideas and techniques. The College of Surgery in Cádiz was Spain's leading innovative institution, and at least one of its graduates practised medicine in Veracruz after 1799. This graduate was Florencio Pérez y Comoto, who actively translated European medical papers and had them published in the *Gazeta de México*, including one that Humboldt presented to a forum of learned medical people during his very brief visit to Veracruz in 1804.

Some empirical observations for yellow fever did hold true. Although no one could explain why, yellow fever attacked new arrivals to tropical and subtropical locales most severely. Racial notions of why some Indigenous people but not others were immune to the scourge never grasped the fact that the childhood exposure that Africans had had back home in West Africa had given them immunity as slaves in the New World.

False remedies ran a gamut of measures, many associated with efforts to rid the soil or air of its poisons. For yellow fever and a host of other epidemic diseases, miasmatists recommended burning pine tar to dispel poisons in the air. Meanwhile, the social impact of yellow fever was huge. Self-preservation led to the shunning of victims and flight from the contaminated zone by those with the means to travel. Ports suffered economic disaster as the corpses piled up, businesses and trading houses closed, and farms grew idle. Statistics on mortality from yellow fever in colonial Mexico were unreliable, since only non-immune new arrivals presented classic symptoms; mild cases, especially of children of all races, went unrecognized as mere fevers. With only severe cases recorded, the very high mortality of 70 per cent cannot be accepted, though the figures presented by Humboldt in the *Political Essay* are a reliable indicator of what was known.

One final subject needs mention. The danger posed by yellow fever among newly arrived Europeans or highland residents was recognized as potential protection against military intervention. The unmitigated disaster of Napoleon's attempt to defeat the uprising of black slaves in Haiti served as a cautionary tale. In Veracruz, military defence relied on local, and seasoned, troops. In 1799, however, fearing a British attempt to capture the port, the viceroy committed thousands of highlanders to defend the town, despite warnings from his military advisers. Over the course of the year, almost 1,000 of the 4,000 troops stationed there did not survive.

Attempts to time yellow fever outbreaks were hazardous. In the war with Mexico from 1846 to 1848, American general Winfield Scott planned to hit the coast between the winter storms and the onset of yellow fever season in the spring. But his landings were delayed by two whole months, and thus his troops attacked Veracruz in late March, just as the yellow fever season was beginning. By 29 March, Veracruz surrendered, and on 2 April, Scott moved out to Mexico City via the Sierra Madres and the fever-free zone. Few American troops acquired yellow fever but Scott had been very lucky.

MODERN VERACRUZ

Mexico's oldest and largest port, Veracruz – more formally, Villa Rica de Vera Cruz (Rich Town of the True Cross) – was so named by Cortés because he and his expedition landed there on Good Friday, 1519. Today, its population numbers roughly one million. At times during the colonial period, the city's merchants thrived and the mercantile class outstripped that of Mexico City. At other moments, pirates from the Gulf of Mexico and the West Indies, including the notorious English buccaneers John Hawkins and Francis Drake, found the city such an easy mark that the Crown built Fort San Juan de Ulúa on an island in the bay to protect the town. The city only came into its own in the middle of the seventeenth century when the Barlovento Armada was stationed there to further guard Veracruz against pirates.

French and American invaders of Mexico captured the port at various times during the nineteenth and early twentieth centuries. Even after the Spanish were obliged to recognize Mexican independence in 1821, they stubbornly held on to Fort San Juan de Ulúa and would occasionally bombard Mexican forces on land. Spain did not hand over the island and the fort until 1825, when a final treaty allowed ships to dock in the Veracruz port. Today, the modernized port moves tons of cargo and serves as the gateway for Mexico's automobile exports and imports. A new truck bypass leads directly from the highway to the port.

Its port status has helped make Veracruz somewhat unique among Mexican cities. It has more Afro-Cuban influences than can be found elsewhere in Mexico; its music and cuisine are good examples of this. Locals, known as *jarochos*, take part in colourful folk dances in the Plaza de Armas, the city's main square, and strolling musicians play such tunes as "La Bamba," which originated in Veracruz. Salsa is particularly popular, as is Afro-Cuban marimba music.

Tourism has been slower to develop. Veracruz can be a raucous port city, but it is much enjoyed by Mexicans attracted to its music, its colourful tropical birds and flowers, and its local cuisine. *Pescado a la verocruzana* tops the list, but a wide variety of other fish and seafood dishes are also available. In the south of the city and in the neighboring municipality of Boca del Río, modern hotels attract visitors to nearby Mocambo Beach and to the reasonably priced open-air restaurants.

The Fort of San Juan de Ulúa is located in the harbour on Gallega Island and can be reached by car or on foot over a toll-free causeway. In addition to its long history as a Spanish stronghold, the fort became a prison after independence, counting as its inmates such illustrious figures as Benito Juárez. The massive fort provides a fine view of the port, and its dungeons, ramparts, and barracks are open to the public.

ε

CHAPTER 22

The Impact of Smallpox and Yellow Fever on Mexico

SMALLPOX

Of all the infectious diseases challenging the health and well-being of Mexicans, the two greatest scourges were smallpox followed by yellow fever. Of these two viral threats, smallpox, called *huitzahuatl* in Nahuatl and translated into Spanish as "great leprosy" (measles was known as *lepra*, or "little leprosy"), caused by far the greatest physical and psychological damage, especially among Indians who had never acquired immunity to this imported disease. Yellow fever, on the other hand, a much more localized infection, caused more fear and alarm among new arrivals to the Mexican Gulf coast who were "unseasoned"; such individuals had never acquired childhood exposure when yellow fever infections were invariably mild and carried with them lifelong immunity.

Smallpox ravished New Spain beginning in 1519, returning every ten to twenty years thereafter and causing 25 to 50 per cent mortality among the infected. The deaths of Aztec leaders, including the emperor Cuitlahuac in 1520, led to huge demoralization, the collapse of political authority, and, often, the decision of non-Aztec peoples to ally with the Spanish. The most serious consequence of smallpox epidemics was population decline in many regions. Estimates of the demographic loss range as high as 90 per cent, though 75 per cent is now the consensus figure. The devastation was so great that water systems and food production were dramatically affected, and there is little doubt that an unknown number of deaths were indirectly the result of smallpox. Of course, depredations of the colonial regime also contributed to these losses. In the spiritual sphere, smallpox was seen as divine punishment. The Europeans blamed the sins of the Indigenous population, but Indian interpretation was more complicated and required the propitiation of two gods, one European, the other indigenous. In some parts of Spanish and Portuguese America, messianic movements sprang up in response to the terror, confusion, and despair resulting from a collapsing world view.

The deaths of perhaps one half the population of Tenochtitlán, with a population of roughly 250,000 in 1519, produced the horrors related by Indian informants to Bernardino de Sahagún, the scribe of Cortés, in 1521: "And before the Spaniards had risen against us, a pestilence first came to be prevalent: the smallpox … it spread over the people as great destruction. Some of it quite covered all parts – their faces, their heads, their breasts, etc. There was great havoc. Very many died of it. They could not walk; they only lay on their resting places and beds. They could not move; they could not stir; they could not change position, nor lie on one side, nor face down, nor on their backs. And if they stirred, much did they cry out. Great was the destruction."

ETIOLOGY AND TREATMENT

Caused by the *Variola virus*, the most virulent form of which is *Variola major*, smallpox has been a scourge of humans from antiquity to the middle of the twentieth century. Highly contagious and easily diagnosed owing to its characteristic rash, smallpox, unlike other viral threats such as yellow fever, counted on only one host in nature, human beings. Eventually, this enabled modern international public-health authorities to succeed in eradicating this scourge.

Incubation of smallpox ran about twelve days, followed by an abrupt and debilitating onset marked by high fever, headache, muscle and back pain, and, occasionally, vomiting and convulsions. Two to five days later a rash erupted, and in a few more days, pustules formed. In uncomplicated cases, just over a week after the first eruptions, the pustules began drying and forming scabs. By the third or fourth week after onset, the scabs fell off, and the victim was again well and in possession of lifelong immunity, although marked for life by a pock-marked or scarred face. Male survivors might also be afflicted by infertility, which added another dimension to the effects that smallpox had on population reproduction.

The mortality rate from smallpox can only be approximated because of the crude statistics of the day, but a 25 to 34 per cent die-off could be expected from *Variola major* outbreaks, the most common form of the disease. Fatal cases progressed rapidly and dramatically. Blood poisoning could lead to massive hemorrhaging into the skin and internal organs, followed by rapid death. Other cases developed pustules that appeared more densely on the face, the palms of the hand, or the soles of the feet than on the trunk.

Treatment of this virulent disease was limited. Good nursing could ease the patient's suffering somewhat. More significantly, some societies practised variolation, or inoculation, whereby smallpox matter was extracted from a diseased person and introduced into the body of a healthy person to cause a mild infection, induce immunity, and prevent a lethal case. Practised in parts of Africa and Asia, where it had been used as part of Chinese medicine since the thirteenth century, variolation had spread to Europe by the eighteenth century, when people of means took up the practice.

A dramatic breakthrough occurred at the end of the eighteenth century when cowpox matter replaced smallpox strains in inoculations. In 1799, an English country physician, Edward Jenner, published the results of his remarkable trial involving what he called "vaccination" (from the Latin *vacca*). Jenner had noticed that variolation produced no symptoms in people who had previously contracted cowpox and that milkmaids and others who contracted cowpox did not contract smallpox during smallpox epidemics. He used cowpox matter to inoculate his own children and himself. His published results earned an instant response. Only two years later, in 1801, more than 100,000 people in England had been vaccinated. The number would rise to millions across Europe by 1815, even though the Continent was at war for much of this time. In 1840, the British Parliament made variolation illegal and empowered local officials to use public funds to vaccinate the poor. Between 1853 and 1873, vaccination became compulsory in England, with civil fines levied for failure to comply. In Prussia, state intervention also occurred, and both countries had nearly eradicated the disease by 1900. Jenner's technique was based on a folk practice he could not explain even though he confirmed its efficacy experimentally. Virologists today know that the smallpox virus is genetically related to the cowpox virus, and the genetic resemblance allows each to produce a cross-defence against the other in the human body.

In Humboldt's time in Mexico, important advances in smallpox prevention occurred, although he reported bad outbreaks in 1763 and 1779, when the disease killed 9,000. More promising, however, was his report that an American living in Mexico, Thomas Murphy, had introduced the Jennerian vaccine to the country on several occasions and it had been well received by the populace. In Mexico City and Valladolid (now Morelia), up to 60,000 people had been inoculated successfully.

THE BALMIS VACCINATION EXPEDITION

Humboldt left Mexico only a few months before the unfolding of an extraordinary medical event in Mexico, the Balmis vaccination expedition. Because Humboldt made no mention of Balmis in his writings, it may safely be assumed that he was not informed of this event. Francisco Javier de Balmis was a Spanish physician who had once lived in New Spain and who became a physician to the Spanish court. Aware of Jenner's breakthrough, Balmis persuaded the reform-minded Bourbons to sponsor a vaccination campaign throughout the vast Spanish colonial empire. The difficulty in using the cowpox inoculation lay in maintaining its efficacy while transporting the virus over long distances. Balmis's solution to maintaining the virus was to keep it alive in the bodies of children who had been inoculated. Balmis sailed from the Spanish port of La Coruña with a large medical team and dozens of orphan boys selected from the orphan-age in the port city after it was verified that they had never been in-fected with smallpox previously. That way, Balmis could draw matter from their pustules with the confidence that it was cowpox that would later give the orphans immunity to smallpox, as it would the hundreds of thousands of colonial children and adults who would received vaccines from the various Spanish orphans who kept the vaccine alive. In fact, many other orphans had to be recruited – for example, in Acapulco – before the Balmis expedition sailed on to the Philippines. Balmis divided his expedition after touching down in the Canaries, Puerto Rico, and the northern coast of South America. While some physicians on his team vaccinated thousands from New Granada to Peru and Buenos Aires, Balmis himself led a team to Cuba and then the Yucatan before continuing on to Veracruz, Puebla, and Mexico City, with a foray via Zacatecas as far north as Durango.

In New Spain, the Balmis team performed over a 100,000 inocu-lations between July 1804 and January 1806, with priority given to im-munizing children. Cities were much better served than rural areas, as were people from high ranks, and the campaign left out an esti-mated 80 per cent of the number needing vaccinations. Nevertheless, among the public and the medical profession in the Spanish world, the Balmis voyage dramatically succeeded in spreading the knowl-edge that smallpox could be prevented.

YELLOW FEVER

Unfortunately, New Spain suffered from a second viral killer, yellow fever, and the etiology of this disease, as well as efforts to contain it, remained elusive until much later, at the beginning of the twentieth century. Caused by a flavivirus, yellow fever infects humans, all species of monkeys, and certain other small animals. The virus probably originated in West Africa among forest monkeys, and the disease first appeared among Europeans in conjunction with the Atlantic slave trade, beginning in the sixteenth century. It spread throughout the

Caribbean, the Gulf of Mexico, and the South Atlantic, but did not reach the Pacific. Similarly, in Africa, the disease slowly made its way to East Africa but never reached across the Indian Ocean to Asia. It remained primarily a disease of the tropics, but it did make its way as far north as Philadelphia, New York, and Boston, and as far away as port cities in Spain, Italy, France, and England.

Yellow fever is transmitted from animals to humans and among humans by several species of mosquito, the most efficient of which is *Aedes egypti*. Thriving in urban areas of heavy rainfall where small ponds and puddles essential to the insect's multiplication can form, the mosquito has a limited range and rarely ventures above 3,000 feet. A humid tropical port at sea level with little variation in temperature throughout the year, Veracruz was an ideal niche for the vector and the virus for centuries.

Yellow fever epidemics required the presence of a significant number of non-immune humans. This was because the virus was rarely lethal for children, who acquired lifelong immunity after a benign and often subclinical infection. Adult strangers from a non-endemic environment, however, provided an excellent opportunity for the vector and virus.

Seasonality was also an important variable in yellow fever outbreaks. In Veracruz, isolated cases could appear in any month, but the most dangerous time was after the summer rains began in late May, allowing a new generation of mosquitoes to breed. Their six-month life cycle meant peak morbidity and mortality until September or October. That was also the time when prevailing northern winds from the Caribbean, the *nortes*, helped drive off some of the mosquitoes. On the other hand, these winds coincided with the hurricane season. The result was that the safest period for ships to arrive in Acapulco was confined to the small window in winter from January to April. Humboldt was well advised of this situation, and this explains why he chose not to descend to Veracruz and sail home until that time of year.

ETIOLOGY AND CONTROL

The course of yellow fever is rapid. Incubation lasts several days from the time of an infected mosquito bite until the abrupt onset of symptoms after the virus has multiplied within the body. The patient suddenly experiences headache, backache, rapidly rising fever, nausea, and vomiting. An acute stage is reached in two or three days, after which recovery or decline occurs. Fatal cases present a deeper toxic state with high fever, a slow pulse rate, and the tell-tale vomiting of dark blood. Death occurs in one week from the onset of symptoms. Since the virus destroys liver cells, jaundice (the yellowing of the skin and eyes by deposition of bile pigment) is a common sign. Recovery can be prolonged, but it is complete and confers lifelong immunity. Mortality is variable, and some get only a mild infection that lasts a few days, for reasons still not understood.

There never has been an effective treatment for yellow fever beyond good nursing and supportive care. But the development of an effective vaccine in the 1930s now makes yellow fever completely preventable, and epidemics can be avoided through controlling or eliminating mosquito populations. The disease cannot be eradicated, since there remains a vast natural reservoir of the virus among forest monkeys.

Scientific understanding of yellow fever was slow to develop. In 1881, the Cuban physician Carlos Finley proposed that yellow fever was caused by an infectious agent transmitted by the *Aedes egypti* mosquito. Finley was unable to demonstrate his theory, but he inspired an American-Cuban team led by Major Walter Reed to do so in Havana in 1900. The research showed that yellow fever was not contagious and could only spread from human to human through the agency of a mosquito bite. Quickly, American military researchers realized that controlling the mosquito vector was the best path to the elimination of epidemics. Using vector control, the American surgeon William Crawford Gorgas eliminated yellow fever from Havana, and a few years later, he removed the threat of yellow fever to workers building the Panama Canal. Meanwhile, in 1903, Gorgas's success was repeated in Rio de Janeiro by the Brazilian physician Oswaldo

Cruz. Soon, French researchers from the Pasteur Institute travelled to Brazil to study Cruz's techniques and then applied these methods in colonial French West Africa. The last American outbreak of yellow fever occurred in New Orleans in 1905. The development of an effective vaccine took somewhat longer. The Pasteur Institute was able to develop a vaccine in West Africa and Madagascar, and to begin widespread injections in these colonies. Problems with the French vaccine persisted, however, and another vaccine came to replace it as the gold standard. The Rockefeller Institute had sponsored yellow fever research from the 1920s and was rewarded with the development of a safe attenuated vaccine, the so-called 17D virus strain. Max Theiler, a South African–born researcher who worked for the Rockefeller Institute in the United States, was awarded the Nobel Prize in 1951 for this great accomplishment. As a result of widespread preventive vaccinations, herd immunity has been achieved in most parts of the world and so-called urban or classical yellow fever has been virtually eliminated. Nevertheless, a distinct jungle transmission cycle from animal to animal and from animal to human was recognized in 1933 and remains a threat to isolated human communities in tropical settings.

CONCLUSION

Humboldt's Legacy

It is a task to summarize the achievements of such a multi-faceted luminary as Alexander von Humboldt. His impact was profound, and changing, both in his day and after. One useful approach on a much larger canvas – one showing how opinions have changed over time – is that of historian of science Nicolaas A. Rupke's "metabiography" of Humboldt. Rupke has organized the writing in German about Humboldt around six different personas. First came the subversive liberal democrat who hoped for the demise of the Prussian state he served. Then, after Humboldt's death, German nationalism in several varieties appropriated him. The German Empire, unified and seeking a global reach, saw Humboldt as an avatar. Third, in the wreckage of defeat in 1918, the fragile Weimar Republic continued to express pride in a German culture for which Humboldt was a central figure. Completely ignoring Humboldt's cosmopolitanism and rejection of racism, Nazi Germany appropriated Humboldt (and his brother Wilhelm) as pure Aryan exemplars. After total defeat in 1945, the divided Germanies split Humboldt in two. The Communist DDR took Humboldt's abolitionism and his concern for the condition of those who toiled as miners as proof of his proletarian tendencies. In Bonn meanwhile, West German interpretations were also self-serving. Humboldt's affinity for Americans, his approval of British mining capitalism, and his philo-Semitism were all endorsements of German rapprochement with other nations. Finally, various forms of postmodernism, environmentalism, feminism, even queer studies, could all make their claims to this extraordinary man.

In Mexico, expressions of appreciation of Humboldt have reflected the turbulent history of this land after 1804. Public honours have come, as we observed in this volume's introduction, from heroes and villains alike, whether the visionary liberal Benito Juárez or the self-serving opportunist Santa Anna. As Covarrubias and Souto have shown, nineteenth-century Mexican figures like Lucas Alamán, José Luis Mora, and Tadeo Ortiz de Ayala regarded Humboldt as a progressive follower of Adam Smith, and as someone who helped consolidate classical capitalist economic theory in the republic. Cities like Taxco, Guanajuato, and Cuernavaca have commemorated Humboldt with plaques, streets named after him, and statuary, whether or not his passage in 1803 was widely noted at the time.

Criticisms of Humboldt by Mexicans and others did emerge, and they can be reduced to five arguments, only the last two of which have merit. First, it is argued, he was an ambiguous apologist for Spanish colonial rule; second, he was an agent, willing or not, for British mining capitalists wishing to profit from Mexican independence; third, his admiration for the United States led him to serve its interests; fourth, he was an obsessive generalist prone to shoddy and erroneous research; and fifth, he was a European cultural annexationist.

An Apologist for Spain

Perhaps Humboldt's greatest critics are those Mexican nationalists who decided that Humboldt's loyalties lay with their opponents, whether Spanish, American, or British. José Iturriaga de la Fuente, for instance, argues that Humboldt's historical judgment was compromised because the Spanish Crown had been kind enough to allow him full access to Spanish America. Iturriaga also blames Humboldt for turning over confidential maps and other documents of New Spain to Jefferson and his cabinet, not realizing that this information provided a formidable instrument with which to further their imperialist designs. While blaming the conquest for its brutality,

Humboldt, it is argued, whitewashes three centuries of Spanish mis-rule and exploitation of Native Mexicans. Iturriaga uses Humboldt's own words as evidence: *Happy is that part of the globe that has en-joyed three centuries of peace, erasing from memory almost every vestige of the crimes committed by the insatiable avarice of the first conquerors.* Iturriaga's assumption is that Humboldt's aristocratic birth, wealth, and elite status in the upper echelons of society on both sides of the Atlantic made him a natural apologist for Spanish colonial rule.

An Agent for British Mining Capitalists

Clearly, Humboldt was the principal source for European knowledge about Mexico's silver mining. Whether he should be held responsible for how others exploited his information is another matter. It should be noted that his account of the mines preceded the War of Inde-pendence and could not anticipate that many mines would be delib-erately flooded by both sides in order to sabotage the plans of the other. The mines needed far more capital investment to make them productive than rosy company prospectives indicated. Angry inves-tors in England and the US naturally blamed him for the disastrous Mexican-mining stock bubble that resulted in the 1820s. Humboldt wrote his brother on several occasions, commenting on the latter's involvement in mining investment. He expressed his confidence in the integrity of his *intimate friend* Lucas Alamán and was pleased that his own name had helped raise investment funds in England for Alamán's venture. When he was attacked in the press for lending his name to mining investment, Alexander wrote Wilhelm that his con-science was untroubled and that he had avoided any hint of specula-tion or of collusion with capitalists. A related issue is whether his glowing reports of Mexico's potential had raised false expectations, giving Mexicans grandiose dreams of wealth and leading to an inevi-table souring of what was seen as his excessive optimism. What crit-ics ignored was Humboldt's pessimism over whether Mexico would be able to transform its social order and mitigate antagonism among classes and races so that its glorious potential could be realized. Lucas

Alamán offers a good example of how disappointments over the course of events after independence could be unfairly laid at Humboldt's feet. Although Alamán was a great admirer of Humboldt's in the 1820s, his bitterness permeated his major opus, *Historia de México*, published in 1849. Here, Alamán argues that Humboldt's economic statistics were incomplete and inaccurate and that he was too optimistic about the nation's economic potential.

An Agent for the Expansionist-Minded United States

Humboldt's more severe critics have focused on what they regard as his too comfortable relationship with Thomas Jefferson and the young American republic to the north. Ortega y Medina puts it most dramatically: "With Humboldt's map, the U.S. expansionists acquired a formidable instrument with which to further their imperialist plans. The poor draftsmen and students of mining who aided Humboldt in preparing these documents must never have realized for whom they really had been working and, what is worse, without pay. Humboldt's *Essay* as well as his *Atlas* of New Spain were documents which, during the first half of the nineteenth century, were considered of strategic importance by U.S. military intelligence. Our traveller was well aware of the pretensions which Mexico's northern neighbor harbored."

Ortega y Medina is too harsh in assuming Humboldt's awareness of American expansionist intentions. Though he inadvertently abetted the Americans, the explanation lies in his deep admiration for Jefferson. He regarded him as a kindred spirit, an enlightened natural philosopher who, as president, would apply the great principles of the US Constitution to daily life. In this as with other assumptions, Humboldt was naïve. He overlooked the contradiction in Jefferson being a slave-owning member of the privileged American landowning class as well as someone open to the idea of US territorial expansion westward. In 1803, Jefferson negotiated the Louisiana Purchase with Napoleon for $15 million, gaining territory that not only included French lands in Louisiana and the Mississippi Basin but also Spanish Crown lands in Florida and on the north shore of the Gulf

of Mexico. With regard to Jefferson's request for information pertinent to this recently acquired territory, Humboldt could not do
enough to satisfy the American president. He even agreed to lend, for
several days, his newly produced maps of northern Mexico and beyond, which he and his assistants had compiled in Mexico City based
in part on confidential information provided by the Spanish colonial government. Zebulon Pike is said to have copied Humboldt's
maps as they lay open on the desk of US secretary of the treasury Albert Gallatin.

Humboldt believed in Jefferson's integrity not only as president
of the republic but also in his continuing duties as president of the
American Philosophical Society. Like Humboldt, Jefferson had expressed respect for Indigenous peoples, had not thought of the West
as a blank, unoccupied space ready for the taking, and had instructed
government explorers like Lewis and Clark to collect data on the cus-
toms and languages of Indigenous peoples. Of course, later presidents,
beginning with Andrew Jackson, did not share these Enlightenment
perspectives, and Humboldt in later life must have regretted that information he had unwittingly provided in his maps and publications
was put to crass purposes. He could hardly have rejoiced at the 1830
Indian removal bills aimed mainly at the Cherokee, which the expansionists in Congress finally succeeded in passing.

A more moderate voice than Ortega y Medina's is that of Mexican
historian Enrique Krauze, who has dismissed as unsustainable the
charge that Humboldt was an advocate, complicit or not, of American expansionism. Krauze does acknowledge that Humboldt's meet-
ings with Jefferson and Gallatin in Washington in 1804 provided the
Americans with what would now be called secret intelligence about
the territories of northern Mexico, but he never endorsed the "manifest destiny" of the northern republic to take control of Mexican
lands. Given his concern to show North Americans and Europeans
that Mexico had great artistic and scientific worth, Humboldt was
instead "a scientific evangelist" bent on dispelling the myth of the
congenital degradation of America, one who sought "to implant
definitively the idea of a promising and respectable Mexico." Humboldt saw clearly the good and the bad in Mexican cultural history,

the Indian love of beauty and colour, but also the cruelty and violence of both Aztec and Spanish despotism. For Krauze, Humboldt
was a well-intentioned paternalist, treating Indians as minors. But he
did understand that Indians would only be truly free if they had the
freedom to travel and relocate where they wished. Krauze argues that,
with the exception of Chiapas, Mexico had gradually moved to greater
ethnic tolerance and freedom by the end of the twentieth century
and that this way forward was Humboldt's way.

A Generalist Prone to Shoddy Research

A recurring criticism of Humboldt was that he was an obsessive
generalist, unable to penetrate the surface of nature to observe more
fundamental theoretical principles. A secondary critique, sometimes
linked to the first, was that his research was uneven and sometimes
shoddy. Occasionally, some could stoop to petty and entirely unfair
levels of accusation. Iturriaga, for example, has read Humboldt on
Mexico with an eye to exposing every inaccuracy or exaggeration he
could find. Humboldt was prone to use hearsay as evidence for areas
like Sonora, which he never visited, and wrote that in the Pimeria
Alta region, *every ravine and even the rolling plains have gold scattered
everywhere, especially in dry river beds and runoff areas. One can find
pure gold nuggets of up to three kilograms in weight.* As well, he put
forward entirely impractical ideas, ranging from the use of camels to
reduce transportation costs to the construction of a navigation canal
from Mexico City to Tampico by using the Tula and Pánuco Rivers,
regardless of the cost of such an ambitious project. Ortega y Medina
adds that Humboldt's estimates of the population of regions he had
never observed, such as Léon and Guadalajara, were seriously flawed.
Even an analyst much more supportive of Humboldt like Rayfred
Lionel Stevens-Middleton, systematically points out Humboldt's
errors in measurement by modern standards.

Of course, Humboldt was not infallible, but it is grossly unfair to
chastise him for errors based on yesterday's obsolete scientific equipment or to hold him responsible for the sometimes dubious quality
of the sources he was able to access. What is remarkable is just the

opposite of a failure – how conscientious and successful Humboldt was in bringing forward information of a scientific and popular nature on Mexico. When he reached Xalapa in February 1804, fatigue together with his anxiousness to reach Veracruz and sail home caused him to write very little in his diaries about this colourful city. Yet his concern for accuracy led him to write a long letter from Xalapa, on 16 February 1804, to Manuel Ruiz de Texada at the Colegio de Minería in Mexico City, providing final corrections to his maps.

A more serious charge holds that Humboldt was a compulsive empiricist and compiler whose obsession with measurement buried his analysis in detail. Humboldt's seeming aversion to theoretical analysis and his own doubts about the quality of his research, especially in his early writings, have led to such conclusions as those reached by Ortega y Medina, who writes: "This great traveler and geographer was not without his own glow of inspiration, although he was by no means a blinding luminary ... Humboldt's strong point was that he had an insatiable appetite for information ... and his greatest fault was that he was incapable of digging to the roots of a phenomenon, but rather tended to stay on its surface." Even more-balanced critics find Humboldt wanting when held to the highest standards in the history of science and philosophy. José Miranda argues that Humboldt was not an original thinker like Isaac Newton, Immanuel Kant, or Adam Smith, and instead made his mark by applying the original ideas of other Enlightenment figures.

Our earlier discussion has already addressed the issue of Humboldt's standing in the history of science. Perhaps those who seem constantly to dwell on the German traveller's preoccupation with measurement have failed to grasp the irony so brilliantly evoked by Lord Byron's satirical description of Humboldt in *Don Juan* (Canto 4, verse 112 [1821]):

> Humboldt, "the first of travellers," but not
>   The last, if late accounts be accurate.
> Invented, by some name I have forgot,
>   As well as the sublime discovery's date,
> An airy instrument, with which he sought

> To ascertain the atmospheric state,
> By measuring "the *intensity of blue*;"
> Oh! Lady Daphne! let me measure you!

A European Cultural Annexationist

The most influential criticism of Humboldt comes from the pen of Mary Louise Pratt in her *Imperial Eyes: Travel Writing and Transculturation*. Following closely Edward Said's pioneering post-colonial attack on "orientalism" as a doctrine masking European cultural chauvinism, Pratt argues that nineteenth-century European travel writers served as cultural annexationists and as "advance scouts for European capital." *Imperial Eyes* includes an entire chapter on Humboldt, demonstrating how he imposed a Western rationalist model on Indigenous American peoples and cultures that deprived them of their originality and autonomy. Pratt's sophisticated accusation can be supported by several examples. Humboldt had an affinity for large Indian polities, for example, but was less enamoured of stateless Indians living in technologically primitive conditions. It is no doubt the case that Humboldt spent far more time in the company of creole intellectuals than he did with Indigenous Mexicans. His contact with Mexican cuisine must have been very limited, for he wrote that *the Indians … have given up the age-old custom of seasoning their dishes with chile* [sic] *instead of salt.* Perhaps his association with Creoles led Humboldt occasionally to share their contempt for the "indolent" Native, and his cultural preference for the Greco-Roman aesthetic did cause him to patronize indigenous cultural forms: *It would be very interesting to place these monuments, fashioned by the semi-barbaric inhabitants of the Mexican Andes*[!] *beside the beautiful forms sculpted under the skies of Greece and Italy.*

A deeper reading of Humboldt's assessment of indigenous American culture counters Pratt's charges. Humboldt detested the social and physical damage wrought by colonialism, and his writing on the subject was one of the early nineteenth century's most powerful attacks against an economic system that combined forced labour with plantation agriculture. Humboldt's works of cultural description tacitly acknowledged the limits and risks of imposing a European view on others: witness his severe criticism of Buffon and other racists who sought *to colonize all other sensibilities with their own.* There is, finally, an attractiveness to Humboldt's balanced thinking on Indian issues. He rejects the dual and opposing mythologies of the black legend and the noble savage.

Among Humboldt's defenders against the charge of cultural chauvinism are two distinguished Mexican scholars. Elías Trabulse, arguably the leading historian of science at the Colegio de México, praised Humboldt for his diligence and for bringing to light documents and texts from the colonial archives that might well have been lost otherwise. Miguel León-Portilla, an authoritative expert on Mesoamerican Mexico, acknowledges Humboldt's determined search for documentation on codices and states that naming a fragment of the Otomi codex of Huamantla after him is "a fitting tribute to a savant whose knowledge extended to so many fields during his long and fecund life."

Reflecting one last time on Humboldt's American adventure, one can fairly say that he was extremely fortunate. Not only did he enjoy good health in the face of daunting challenges, but the very fact that he visited the Americas, and not Egypt or Australia, was serendipitous. Indeed, in his *Political Essay,* he reminded readers several times that he still hoped to connect with Baudin and sail on to the Philippines. Much later, however, a more reflective Humboldt had time to recast his research purposes in a less unstructured manner: *I endeavored to employ the time spent in Mexico not merely in scientific investigation, but in acquiring an accurate knowledge of the political condition of this extensive and remarkable country. The civilization of New Spain presented a striking contrast to the limited amount of culture, both moral and physical, visible in those countries I had recently visited. I carefully compared all that I had seen ... The result of this comparison was to incite me to investigate the causes, as yet but partially developed, which have proved so favorable for the increase of population and of national industry in this country.*

The circumstances in which I was placed were highly advantageous for the prosecution of this object, since in the collection of materials in which no published book could be of any avail, various manuscripts were placed at my disposal, and I was allowed free access to the public archives.

Humboldt's contributions to knowledge were formidable. He discovered the magnetic equator. He experimented with electric eels, measuring their lethal power while suffering violent shocks. He invented a new type of respirator and a better safety lamp for miners. He invented isotherm mapping, connecting regions that shared the same average temperature and atmospheric pressure. He discovered and identified 2,000 new plant species and contributed 60,000 botanical specimens to the Jardin des Plantes in Paris. These he classified by climate zones, not taxonomy, on the basis of altitude, temperature, and location. While he was not responsible for a single overriding and enduring theory, he hinted at many, including Darwin's concept of natural selection. Most importantly, he gave us a modern conception of nature as an integrated ecosystem. Andrea Wulf skilfully summarizes his legacy this way: "Unlike Christopher Columbus or Isaac Newton, Humboldt did not discover a continent or a new law of physics, Humboldt was not known for a single fact or discovery but for his world view. His vision of nature has passed into our consciousness as if by osmosis. It is almost as though his ideas have become so manifest that the man behind them has disappeared." Wulf argues persuasively that Humboldt recognized the dangers of environmental degradation and destructive climate change brought about by uncontrolled human actions. For example, Humboldt recognized that deforestation and irresponsible irrigation practices could become catastrophic if humans continued to disturb the world so *brutally*. In Russia during a year-long expedition in 1829, he addressed the Imperial Academy of Sciences at St Petersburg and called for international collaboration among scientists in the collection of data on deforestation. One hundred and fifty years later, such an initiative would become a model for the study of the deleterious impact of climate change.

While it may be a stretch to turn Humboldt into a full-blown spokesperson for environmentalism, he is clearly finding new favour today. His integrated and non-specialized view of the planet is enjoying a revival as older scientific prejudice about generalists and universal thinkers is wearing thin. Interdisciplinary approaches such as he pioneered, even his enthusiasm for what is now called "networking," appeal to environmentally sensitive contemporary observers, who admire Humboldt's ecologically friendly and holistic approach to nature. As for his contribution to Mexico, awe-inspiring is what can best be said of his 190 days of research in Mexico City and his 157 days of travelling throughout the heartlands.

A Guide to Publications on or about Alexander von Humboldt in Mexico

ATG *Atlas geográfico y físico del Reino de la Nueva España*, edited by Charles Minguet and Jaime Labastida. Mexico City: Siglo XXI, 2003. Introduction by Elías Trabulse.

COR "Correspondencia Mexicana, 1803–1854," 127–212, in TAB below. Includes letters to or from Alamàn, Bolívar, Santa Anna, and others.

DIA "Diario de viaje (de Acapulco a Veracruz)," 215–311, in TAB below. Introduction by Elías Trabulse, 11–22. Faak, Margot, ed. *Alexander von Humboldt: Reise auf dem Río Magdalena, durch die Anden und Mexico. Part I: Texte. Aus seinen Reisetagebüchern*. Berlin: Akademie Verlag, 1986 (Beiträge zur Alexander-von-Humboldt-Forschung, 8).

DJ *Die Jugendbriefe Alexander von Humboldt 1787–1799*, edited by Ilse Jahn and Fritz G. Lange. Berlin: Akademie Verlag, 1973.

KOS *Kosmos, Entwurf einer physischen Weltbesschreibung.* 5 vols. Stuttgart: Cotta, 1845–62. Published in English as *Kosmos: A General Survey of Physical Phenomena of the Universe*, translated by E.C. Otté. New York: Harper Brothers, 1858–59.

PE *Political Essay on the Kingdom of New Spain*. John Black Translation [of 1811, abridged], edited and with an introduction by Mary Maples Dunn. New York: Alfred A. Knopf, 1972. First published as *Essai politique sur le royaume de la Nouvelle-Espagne*. Paris: Schoell, 1811.

PN Wilson, Jason. "Introduction." In *Alexander von Humboldt: Personal Narrative of a Journey to the Equinoctial Regions of the New Continent*, abridged and translated by Jason Wilson. London: Penguin Books, 1995. First published 1814–25 as *Relation historique du voyage aux régions équinoxiales du nouveau continent*.

TAB *Tablas geográficas políticas del reyno de Nueva España*, edited
by Charles Minguet and Jaime Labastida. Mexico City: Siglo
XXI, n.d. (2003?).

TGB *Tagebucher*. Field notebooks/Diaries. Published 1986–90 in
German. Excerpts also published as "Diario de viaje (de
Acapulco a Veracruz)," 215–311, in TAB above. Introduction
by Elías Trabulse, 11–22.
Leitner, Ulrike. *Alexander von Humboldt: Von Mexiko-Stadt
nach Veracruz, Tagebuch*. Berlin: Akademie Verlag, 2005.

VC *Vues des Cordillères et monuments des peuples indigènes de
l'Amerique*. Paris: Schoell, 1810. Republished in 1814 in English; newest version is Vera M. Kutzinski and Ottmar Ette,
eds, *Views of the Cordilleras and Monuments of the Indigenous
Peoples of the Americas: A Critical Edition*. Chicago and
London: University of Chicago Press, 2012.

Alexander von Humboldt left an enormous corpus of primary material dealing with his scientific career and a bewildering array of editions and translations in many European languages. Well known as
well as obscure editions are scattered in libraries and research centres
stretching from Mexico to Poland, and including the United States,
Germany, and the Vatican. New fragments of interest to Humboldt
experts seem to appear yearly, though the corpus has long since been
established. By the time of his death, says Mary Dunn, to whom we
are eternally grateful for her erudite single-volume edition of the *Political Essay* (PE), which Knopf made widely available in its popular
Everyman's Library edition in 1972, Humboldt had published sixty-
nine works of varying importance on his American journey alone.
First editions usually appeared in French, the pre-eminent scientific
language of his day, but sometimes in English or in German. Not all
of this material was translated, and works in Spanish were sometimes
slow to appear. Humboldt tried to supervise the translations, but they
were uneven and today they are antiquated.

Nevertheless, less confusion among the texts has resulted from a
recent burst of studies on Humboldt. There has been a decade-long
effort, 1997–2006, to catch the bicentennial of his American travels,

which took place from 1799 to 1804, marked by exhibits, conferences, and workshops in Mexico, Cuba, Venezuela, Germany, Colombia, Ecuador, Peru, Spain, England, and Austria. In 2011 and 2012, the University of Chicago Press acknowledged awareness of Humboldt's importance by offering several Humboldt works in English, with new and improved translations edited by Vera M. Kutzinski and others. Ottmar Ette's view that Humboldt was a contributor to globalization suggests a new perspective.

Of special note have been the efforts of German scholars Ulrike Leitner and Margot Faak to edit Humboldt's confidential diaries and notebooks, the *Tagebücher* (TGB). The diaries belong to the von Heinz family, descendants of elder brother Wilhelm, and can be found in the manuscript department of the Berlin State Library at Schloss Tegel. Because they record Humboldt's voluminous scientific observations and measurements, they run to over nine volumes, but they also note his personal views on a variety of political and social issues. Their use is mandatory to bolster his analysis, but they also contain his sometimes angry criticism of Spanish colonialism, which he did not want to appear in his formal published works, lest he offend his royal host Charles IV.

A Guide to Readings on Humboldt

No shortage of biographies on Humboldt can be found, but a number could be considered the most definitive. Karl Bruns edited a joint biography in two volumes, published and translated into English in 1873 to commemorate the centenary of the scientist's birth. Almost a century later, from 1959 to 1961, Hanno Beck produced two volumes in German. In 2005, Nicolaas Rupke's *Metabiography* constituted a brilliant example of how Humboldt has been received by different German political regimes since Bismarck's day. In English, a good number of biographies have appeared, including Helmut De Terra in 1955, Lotte Kellner in 1963, Douglas Botting in 1973, and Gerard Helferich in 2004. Andrea Wulf in 2015 wrote the most recent and best biography of Humboldt. Charles Minguet offered an excellent biography in French for Maspero in 1969. In 1997, Suzanne Zantop explored the impact of Humboldt's ideas on Germany. In 2009, Laura Dassaw Walls provided insights on Humboldt's importance for North America, and David Blackbourn gave readers of the *London Review of Books* a balanced portrait of the "Great Man" in 2011.

Biographers were not alone as Humboldteans. A formidable number of editors and translators have been hard at work in several languages, including Mary Maples Dunn, Margot Faak, Frank Holl, Vera M. Kutzinski, Jaime Labastida, Ulrike Leitner, and Jason Wilson.

Several close associates of Humboldt's also make for interesting reading. His brother William left his two volumes of collected love letters, *Briefe an eine Freundin*, and William's biographers Paul R. Sweet and John P. Roberts published studies in 1978 and 2009, respectively. Alexander's loyal companion Aimé Bonpland, moreover, has benefited from a definitive biography by Stephen Bell, which appeared in 2010.

For accounts of Humboldt's interest in Spanish science and history, including mining, see the Bibliography for the following: Bakewell, 1984; Brading, 1971 and 1991; Chambers, 1996; Engstrand, 1981;

Gibson, 1984; Liss, 1983; Tutino, 1986, and Whitaker, 1958. The physicist Michael Dettelbach has a major article on Humboldt's contribution to physics, published in 1996; and in Environmental Studies, Humboldt is discussed at length in Stephen Jay Gould, 1989; J.R. McNeill, 2000; Arij Ouweneel, 1996; and John F. Richards, 2003. Aaron Sachs in 2006 provided the best account of Humboldt's links to environmentalism.

Humboldt's insatiable curiosity about medicine, demography, and geography can be pursued but never satisfied in the following: Bowen, 1981; Cook and Borah, 1963; Cooper, 1965; Knaut, 1997; Mathewson, 1986; McEvedy and Jones, 1978; Rupke, 1996; Sánchez-Albornoz, 1984; and Sanders and Price, 1968. Alexander's passion for volcanoes is reflected in a classic study by Landívar published in 1782, and in a much more modern one by Secor in 1981.

An extensive bibliography provides background in the social sciences and the humanities. Classical studies range from Adam Smith's *The Wealth of Nations*, 1776, through William Robertson's three volumes, 1777, to William Prescott's three volumes, 1844. In 2012, José Enrique Covarrubias and Matilde Souto Mantecón edited a collection devoted largely to Humboldt's economic thought.

Several modern writers have engaged in lively debate over Humboldt's views. See Foner, 1983; and Miranda, 1962. Two of the most influential post-modernist critics of Humboldt have been Said, 1978; and Pratt, 1992. Ortega y Medina, 1960, has been an intelligent Mexican critic, but the list of defenders is much longer and includes Krauze, 1994; Sachs, 2003 and 2006; and Sluyter, 2006.

Humboldt's importance for the Humanities, especially the study of Mesoamerica, has attracted such distinguished specialists as Antonio León y Gama, 1792; Miguel León-Portilla, 2003; and Eloise Quiñones Keber, 1996. For literature and identity, see Baron, 2005; Carpentier, 1970; García Márquez, 1967 and 1989; Ochoa, 2004; and Sarmiento, 1868.

Citations

All Humboldt quotes are from his PE unless otherwise identified.

PREFACE

"the first modern description," Vivó Escoto, ed., *Ensayos sobre Humboldt*, 1962: 11–12.

"was named in honour," McIntyre, "Humboldt's Way," 318.

INTRODUCTION

"a mid-wife," Krauze, "Humboldt y México," 22.

"overwhelming excellence," Brading, *Miners and Merchants*, 129.

"disinclination for public affairs," Alexander to Wilhelm von Humboldt, 4 June 1823, COR, 187.

"Benefactor," Juarez, in Rupke, *Alexander von Humboldt*, 120.

"the entire nation," Alamán to Humboldt, Mexico, 21 July 1824, COR, 189.

"equinox, equinox, equinox," García Márquez, *One Hundred Years*, 78.

"portrayed," Sarmiento, in Wilson, "Introduction," xxxiv.

"The celebrity which," in Macgillivray, *The Travels and Researches*, 5.

"the mind is a chaos," Darwin, in Wilson, "Introduction," xxxvii.

PROLOGUE

"The damaged state," Alexander von Humboldt to National Institute of France, June 1803, COR, 137.

"only giving up," Alexander von Humboldt to Jean Baptiste Joseph Delambre, 21 July 1803, COR, 145.

"I have never," Alexander von Humboldt in Helferich, *Humboldt's Cosmos*, 332.

"exhilaration," Alexander von Humboldt to Johann Karl Freiesleben, August 1804, PN, liv.

"Alexander von Humboldt has been with me," Goethe, PN, xxxvii.

"Science was a male world," PN, xliv.
"shameless pederasty," García Márquez, *The General in His Labyrinth*, 88.
"That motherfucker," García Márquez, *The General in His Labyrinth*, 88.
"Humboldt and His Friends," Aldrich, *Colonialism and Homosexuality*, 24–9.
"convinced that the man," Alexander von Humboldt, in Botting, *Humboldt and the Cosmos,"* 116.
"I work a lot," Alexander von Humboldt to Karl Ludwig Wildenow, 29 April 1803, COR, 138–9.
"I have a big plan," Alexander to Wilhelm von Humboldt, 4 June 1822, COR, 187.

CHAPTER 2
"the secret of my best work," Rivera, *My Art*, 31.

CHAPTER 3
"I will collect," Humboldt to David Friedländer, 11 April 1799, DJ, 143.
"medium human development," UN Human Development Index (2006), www.undp.org/mx

CHAPTER 4
"Like many another liberal imperialist," Brading, *Church and State*, 228.
"In maintaining," Humboldt, in Foner, "Alexander von Humboldt on Slavery in America," 342.
"I am half American," Humboldt, in Foner, "Alexander von Humboldt on Slavery in America," 335.

CHAPTER 6
"my friend the American," Rivera, *My Art*, 101.
"with satisfaction," Morrill, *Silver Masters*, 10.
"same clay, same Indian," Rivera, *My Art*, 133.

CHAPTER 7

"the streets and lanes," Lowry, *Under the Volcano*, 9.

CHAPTER 10

"prodigious contribution," Quiñones Keber, "Humboldt and Aztec Art," 297.
"unintelligible daubings," *Quarterly Review*, 1816: 453.

CHAPTER 12

"We had the very difficult task," Buchan, "diary."
"The scenery," Calderón de la Barca, *Life in Mexico*, 171–2.

CHAPTER 13

"This pillage was," Alamán, *Historia de México*, vol. 1, 43–4, 1942 edition, translated in Meyer and Sherman, *The Course of Mexican History*, 289.

CHAPTER 14

"Over three centuries," Richards, *The Unending Frontier*, 366.
"Without my work," Alexander to Wilhelm von Humboldt, 15 October 1824, COR, 190.
"the 'ingenious' Humboldt," *Quarterly Review*.

CHAPTER 16

"Their unmistakable silhouettes," Margarita de Orellana, in "Los Dos Volcanes," 66.
"I would compare thee," Sor Juana Inés de la Cruz, in "Los Dos Volcanes," 67.
"when we were unthinkable," José Emilio Pacheco, in "Los Dos Volcanes," 67.
"with her human profile," Gabriela Mistral, in "Los Dos Volcanes," 80.

CHAPTER 20

"completely covered," Diaz del Castillo, *Historia veradera* (1552), 97.

CHAPTER 22

"and before the Spaniards," Sahagún, *Florentine Codex* (1585), 81.

CONCLUSION

"intimate friend," Alexander to Wilhelm von Humboldt, 4 June 1822, COR, 187.

"With Humboldt's map," Ortega y Medina, in Iturriaga de la Fuente, "Alexander von Humboldt," 20.

"a scientific evangelist," Krauze, "Humboldt y México," 22.

"This great traveler," Ortega y Medina, in Iturriaga de la Fuente, "Alexander von Humboldt," 21.

"advance scouts for European capital," Pratt, *Imperial Eyes*, 146.

"a fitting tribute to a savant," León-Portilla, "Humboldt y los Códices," 128.

"I endeavored to employ," Humboldt in Bruhns, *Life of Alexander von Humboldt*, vol. 1, 329.

"Unlike Christopher Columbus," Wulf, *The Invention of Nature*, 335.

"brutally," Wulf, *The Invention of Nature*, 59.

Bibliography

Ackerknecht, Erwin H. "George Forster, Alexander von Humboldt, and Ethnology." *Isis* 46 (1955): 83–95

A Guided Tour of the Xalapa Museum of Anthropology. Xalapa: Gobierno del Estado de Veracruz and Universidad Veracruzana 2004

Alamán, Lucas. *Historia de México*. 5 vols (1848–52). Editorial Jus 1942

Aldrich, Robert. *Colonialism and Homosexuality*. New York: Routledge 2003

Almanza Carrillo, Ricardo. "La contribución de Alejandro de Humboldt a la geología guanajuayense." In *Bicentenario de Humboldt en Guanajuato (1803–2003)*, edited by José Luis Valdés, 77–89. Guanajuato: Ediciones La Rana 2003

Bakewell, Peter J. *Silver Mining and Society in Colonial Mexico: Zacatecas, 1546–1700*. Cambridge: Cambridge University Press 1971

– "Mining in Colonial Spanish America." In *The Cambridge History of Latin America: Colonial Latin America*, vol. 2, edited by Leslie Bethell, 105–51. Cambridge: Cambridge University Press 1984

Baron, Frank. "From Alexander von Humboldt to Frederic Edwin Church: Voyages of Scientific Exploration and Artistic Creativity." *Humboldt Digital Library* 6, no. 10 (2005): 1–5

Beck, Hanno. *Alexander von Humboldt*. 2 vols. Wiesbaden: Steiner, 195–61

Bell, Stephen. *A Life in Shadow: Aimé Bonpland in Southern South America, 1817–1858*. Stanford: Stanford University Press 2010

Bernal, Ignacio. "Humboldt y la Arqueología Mexicana." In *Ensayos sobre Humboldt*, edited by Jorge A. Vivó Escoto, 121–32. Mexico City: UNAM 1962

Bernier, Olivier. *The World in 1800*. New York: John Wiley & Sons 2000

Blackbourn, David. "Great Man." *London Review of Books*, 16 June 2011, 32–3

Botting, Douglas *Humboldt and the Cosmos*. New York: Harper & Row 1973

Bowen, Margarita. *Empiricism and Geographical Thought: From Francis Bacon to Alexander von Humboldt*. Cambridge: Cambridge University Press 1981

Brading, D.A. *Miners and Merchants in Bourbon Mexico, 1763–1810*. Cambridge: Cambridge University Press 1971

– *The First America: The Spanish Monarchy, Creole Patriots, and the Liberal State, 1492–1867*. Cambridge: Cambridge University Press 1991

– *Church and State in Bourbon Mexico: The Diocese of Michoacán*. Cambridge: Cambridge University Press 1994

Bruhns, Karl, ed. *Life of Alexander von Humboldt, Compiled in Commemoration of the Centenary of His Birth by J. Lowenberg, Robert Ave-Lallemant, and*

Alfred Dove, translated by Jane and Caroline Lassell. 2 vols. London: Longmans, Green 1873

Buchan, "Diary." In *The Cornish Miner in Mexico*, www.poldarkmine.org.uk

Byron, Lord. *Don Juan*, Canto 4, verse 112 [1821], edited by T.G. Steffan, E. Steffan, and W.W. Pratt. London: Yale University Press 1982

Calderón de la Barca, Frances. *Life in Mexico* (1843). Berkeley: University of California Press 1982

Carpentier, Alejo. *Tientos y diferencias*. Montevideo: Arca 1970

Chambers, David Wade. "Centre Looks at Periphery: Alexander von Humboldt's Account of Mexican Science and Technology." *Journal of Iberian and Latin American Studies* 2 (1996): 94–113

Clavigero, Francisco S. *Historia Antigua de México* (1780). Mexico: Ed. Porrua 1958–59

Clement, Jennifer. *Prayers for the Stolen*. New York: Hogarth 2014

Cook, Sherburne F., and Woodrow Borah. *The Indian Population of Central Mexico, 1531–1610*. Berkeley: University of California Press 1960

– *The Aboriginal Population of Central Mexico on the Eve of the Spanish Conquest*. Berkeley: University of California Press 1963

Covarrubias, José E. *Visión extranjera de México, 1840–1867*. Serie Historia moderna y contemporánea de México 31. Mexico: UNAM 1998

– "La recepción de la figura y obra de Humboldt en México 1821–2000." *HiN-Internationale Zeitschrift für Humboldt-Studien* 10, no. 19 (2009): 92–104. http://www.uni-potsdam.de/romanistik/hin/hin19/covarrubias.htm

Covarrubias, José E., and Matilde Souto Mantecón, eds. *Economía, ciencia y política: Estudios sobre Alexander von Humboldt a 200 años del Ensayo político sobre el reino de la Nueva España*. Mexico: UNAM 2012

Covarrubias, José, and Richard Weiner, "Political Economy, Alexander von Humboldt, and Mexico's 1810 and 1910 Revolutions." *Rupkatha Journal on Interdisciplinary Studies in* Humanities 2, no. 3 (2010): 220–46

Craven, David. *Diego Rivera as Epic Modernist*. New York: G.K. Hall & Co. 1997

De La Cruz, Sor Juana Inéz. "Los dos volcanes, Popocatépetl e Iztaccíhuatl." *Artes de Mexico*, no. 73 (2005): 67.

De Terra, Helmut. *Humboldt: The Life and Times of Alexander von Humboldt, 1769–1859*. New York: Alfred A. Knopf 1955

Dettelbach, Michael. "Global Physics and Aesthetic Empire: Humboldt's Physical Portrait of the Tropics." In *Visions of Empire: Voyages, Botany, and Representations of Nature*, edited by David Philip Miller and Peter Hanns Reill, 258–92. Cambridge: Cambridge University Press 1996

Díaz del Castillo, Bernal. *Historia verdadera de la conquista de la Nueva España* (1552 edn). 2 vols. Madrid: Alianza Editorial 1989

Dunn, Mary Maples, ed. *Alexander von Humboldt, Political Essay on the Kingdom of New Spain*. John Black Translation of 1811, abridged. New York: Alfred A. Knopf 1972

Echegoyén, G. René. "Reflexiones sobre el impulso que dio Humboldt a la formación académica del ingeniero minero, con base en la experiencia que tuvo en las minas de Guanajuato." In *Bicentenario de Humboldt en Guanajuato (1803–2003)*, edited by José Luis Lara Valdés, 93–101. Guanajuato: Ediciones La Rana 2003

Engstrand, H.W. *Spanish Scientists in the New World: The Eighteenth Century Expeditions*. Seattle: University of Washington Press 1981

Ette, Ottmar. "Everything Is Interrelated, Even the Errors in the System: Alexander von Humboldt and Globalization." In *Alexander von Humboldt's Transatlantic Personae*, translated and edited by Vera M. Kutzinski, 15–28. New York: Routledge 2012

Faak, Margot, ed. *Alexander von Humboldt: Reise auf dem Río Magdalena, durch die Anden und Mexico. Part I: Texte. Aus seinen Reistagebüchern.* Berlin: Akademie Verlag 1986

Foner, Philip S. "Alexander von Humboldt on Slavery in America." *Science and Society* 47 (1983): 330–42

Forster, George. *A Voyage Round the World* [English edn, 1777], vol. 1, edited by Nicholas Thomas and Oliver Berghof. Honolulu: University of Honolulu Press 2000

García Márquez, Gabriel. *One Hundred Years of Solitude*, translated from the original Spanish *Cien años de soledad* by Gregory Rabassa. New York: Harper and Row 1967

– *The General in His Labyrinth*, translated and introduced by Edith Grossman. New York: Knopf, 1990. From the original Spanish *El general en su laberinto*. Madrid: Mondadori Espana 1989

Gibson, Charles. "Indian Societies under Spanish Rule." In *The Cambridge History of Latin America: Colonial Latin America*, vol. 2, edited by Leslie Bethell, 381–419. Cambridge: Cambridge University Press 1984

Gould, Stephen Jay. "Church, Humboldt, and Darwin: The Tension and Harmony of Art and Science." In *Frederic Edwin Church*, edited by Franklin Kelly et al., 94–107. Washington: Smithsonian Institution Press 1989

Helferich, Gerard. *Humboldt's Cosmos: Alexander von Humboldt and the Latin American Journey That Changed the Way We See the World*. New York: Gotham Books 2004

Holl, Frank, ed. *Los viajes de Humboldt: Una nueva visión del mundo, Antiguo Colegio de San Ildefonso, 25 Sept., 2003–25 Jan., 2004*. Mexico 2003–04

Horwitz, Tony. *Blue Latitudes: Boldly Going Where Captain Cook Has Gone Before*. New York: Henry Holt and Co. 2002

Humboldt, William von. *Briefe an eine Freundin*. 2 vols. Leipzig: 1847

Iturriaga de la Fuente, José. "Alexander von Humboldt." *México Desconocido* 140 (October 1988): 18–22

Jacobs, Michael. *Andes*. London: Granta 2010

Kellner, Lotte. *Alexander von Humboldt*. New York: Oxford University Press 1963

Kettenmann, Andrea. *Rivera*. Cologne: Taschen 2006

Klencke, Herman. *Alexander von Humboldt's leben und wirken, reisen und wissen*. Leipzig: Verlag von Otto Spamer 1870

Knaut, Andrew L. "Yellow Fever and the Late Colonial Public Health Response in the Port of Veracruz." *Hispanic American Historical Review* 77 (1997): 619–44

Krauze, Enrique. "Humboldt y México: Un amor correspondido." *Vuelta* 212 (July 1994): 21–4.

Kutzinski, Vera M. "Editorial Note." In *Views of the Cordilleras and Monuments of the Indigenous Peoples of the Americas: A Critical Edition*, edited with an introduction by Vera M. Kutzinski and Ottmar Ette; translated by J. Ryan Poynter; annotations by Giorleny D. Altamirano Rayo and Tobias Kraft, 551–7. Chicago and London: University of Chicago Press 2012

Labastida, Jaime, ed. *Humboldt, ciudadano universal*. Mexico City: Siglo XXI 1999

– "Humboldt: Su Concepto del Mundo." In *Alejandro de Humboldt: Una nueva visión del mundo*, 39–45. Mexico City: Exposición en el Antiguo Colegio de San Ildefonso, 25 de septiembre 2003–25 de enero 2004, UNAM 2003

Lafaye, Jacques. "Literature and Intellectual Life in Colonial Spanish America." In *The Cambridge History of Latin America*, vol. 2, edited by Leslie Bethell, 663–704. Cambridge: Cambridge University Press 1984

Landívar, Rafael. *Rusticatio Mexicana*. Mexico: Ed. Altera Bononiae 1782

Lara Valdés, José Luis, ed. *Bicentenario de Humboldt en Guanajuato (1803–2003)*. Guanajuato: Ediciones La Rana 2003

Leitner, Ulrike. *Alexander von Humboldt: Von Mexiko-Stadt nach Veracruz, Tagebuch*. Berlin: Akademie Verlag 2005

– "Los diarios de Alexander von Humboldt: Un mosaico de su conocimiento científico." In *Alexander von Humboldt: Estancia en España y viaje americano*, edited by Mariano Cuesta Domingo and Sandra Rebok, 163–76. Madrid: Real Sociedad Geográfica, CSIC 2008

León-Portilla, Miguel. "Humboldt y los Códices Mesoamericanos." In *Alejandro de Humboldt: Una nueva visión del mundo*, 123–9. Mexico City: Exposición en el Antiguo Colegio de San Ildefonso, 25 de septiembre 2003–25 de enero 2004, UNAM 2003

León y Gama, Antonio. *Descripción histórica y cronológica de las dos piedras.* Mexico: Impr. de Don F. de Zúñiega y Ontiveros 1792

Liss, Peggy K. *Atlantic Empires: The Network of Trade and Revolution 1713– 1826.* Baltimore: Johns Hopkins University Press 1983

Littleton, Taylor D., *The Color of Silver: William Spratling, His Life and Art.* Baton Rouge: Louisiana State University Press 2000

López González, Valentín. "Alexander von Humboldt, su Estancia en Cuernavaca." *Cuadernos históricos Morelenses*, 1–20. Cuernavaca, Morelos: 2003

"Los dos volcanes, Popocatépetl e Iztaccíhuatl." *Artes de México*, no. 73 (2005): 66–80

Lowry, Malcolm. *Under the Volcano.* New York: Penguin 1967 [1947]

McCrory, Donald. *Nature's Interpreter: The Life and Times of Alexander von Humboldt.* London: Lutterworth 2010

McEvedy, Colin, and Richard Jones. *Atlas of World Population History.* New York: Penguin 1978

Macgillivray, William. *The Travels and Researches of Alexander von Humboldt.* Edinburgh: Oliver and Boyd 1832 [reprinted, Lexington, KY: Ulan Press, 2012]

McIntyre, Loren. "Humboldt's Way: Pioneer of Modern Geography." *National Geographic* 168 (September 1985): 318–51

McNeill, J.R. *Something New under the Sun: An Environmental History of the Twentieth-Century World.* New York: Norton 2000

Malmstrom, Vincent H. *Cycles of the Sun, Mysteries of the Moon: The Calendar in Mesoamerican Civilization*: Austin: University of Texas Press 1997

Mark, Joan. *The Silver Gringo: William Spratling and Taxco:* Albuquerque: University of New Mexico Press 2000

Mathewson, Kent. "Alexander von Humboldt and the Origins of Landscape Archaeology." *Journal of Geography* 85 (1986): 50–6

Meyer, Michael C., and William L. Sherman. *The Course of Mexican History*, 2nd edn. New York: Oxford University Press 1983

Minguet, Charles. *Alexandre de Humboldt: Historien et géographe de l'Amérique Espagnol (1799–1804).* Paris: Maspero 1969

Miranda, José. *Humboldt y México.* Mexico City: UNAM 1962

– "Ensayo politico sobre el reino de la Nueva España: Razón, entidad, trascendencia." In *Humboldt en México*, edited by Leopoldo Zea and Carlos Magallón, 53–66. UNAM 1999

Mistral, Gabriela. "Los dos volcanes, Popocatépetl e Iztaccíhuatl." *Artes de México*, no. 73 (2005): 80

Morrill, Penny. *Silver Masters of Mexico: Héctor Aguilar and the Taller Borda.* New York: Schiffer 1997

Ochoa, John. *The Uses of Failure in Mexican Literature and Identity*, 81–109. Austin: University of Texas Press 2004

Orellana, Margarita de, ed. "Painting with Lava." *Artes de México*, no. 73 (2005)
– "Los dos volcanes, Popocatépetl e Iztaccíhuatl," *Artes de México*, no. 73
   (2005): 66
Ortega y Medina, Juan A. *Humboldt desde México*. Mexico City: UNAM 1960
– "Humboldt visto por los mexicanos." In *Ensayos sobre Humboldt*, edited by
   Jorge A. Vivó Escoto, 237–58. Mexico City: UNAM 1962
– "Otra vez Humboldt, ese controvertido personaje." *Colmex: Centro de
   estudios historicos* 25, no. 3 (January–March 1976): 423–54
Ouweneel, Arij. *Shadows over Anáhuac: An Ecological Interpretation of Crisis
   and Development in Central Mexico, 1730–1800*. Albuquerque: University of
   New Mexico Press 1996
Pacheco, José Emilio. "Los dos volcanes, Popocatépetl e Iztaccíhuatl."*Artes de
   Mexico*, no. 73 (2005): 67
Pratt, Mary Louise. *Imperial Eyes: Travel Writing and Transculturation*.
   London: Routledge 1992
Prescott, William H. *History of the Conquest of Mexico*. 3 vols. New York:
   Harper and Brothers 1844
Quarterly Review 15 (1816): 453
Quiñones Keber, Eloise. "Humboldt and Aztec Art." *Colonial Latin American
   Review* 5 (1996): 277–97
Randall, Robert W. *Real del Monte: A British Mining Venture in Mexico*.
   Austin: University of Texas Press 1977
Rebok, Sandra. "Two Exponents of the Enlightenment: Transatlantic
   Communication by Thomas Jefferson and Alexander von Humboldt."
   Southern Quarterly 43 (2005–06): 126–52
– "Alexander von Humboldt's Perceptions of Colonial Spanish America."
   Dynamis 29 (2009): 29–48
Richards, John F. *The Unending Frontier: An Environmental History of the
   Early Modern World*. Berkeley: University of California Press 2003
Rippy, J. Fred, and E.R. Brann. "Alexander von Humboldt and Simón Bolívar."
   American Historical Review 54 (1947): 697–703
Rivera, Diego, with Gladys March. *My Art, My Life: An Autobiography*. New
   York: Dover 1960
Roberts, John P. *Wilhelm von Humboldt and German Liberalism: A
   Reassessment*. Oakville, ON: Mosaic Press 2009
Robertson, William S. *The History of America*. 3 vols. London: Whitestone
   1777
Rochfort, Desmond. *Mexican Muralists: Orozco, Rivera, Siqueiros*. San
   Francisco: Chronicle Books 1993
Rupke, Nicolaas. "Humboldtian Medicine." *Medical History* 40 (1996): 293–
   310
– "A Geography of Enlightenment: The Critical Reception of Alexander von

Humboldt's Mexico Work." In *Geography and Enlightenment*, edited by David N. Livingstone and Charles W.J. Withers, 319–39. Chicago: University of Chicago Press 1999

– *Alexander von Humboldt: A Metabiography*. Frankfort am Main: Peter Lang 2005

Sachs, Aaron. "The Ultimate 'Other': Post-Colonialism and Alexander von Humboldt's Ecological Relationship with Nature." *History and Theory* 42 (December 2003): 111–35

– *The Humboldt Current: Nineteenth-Century Exploration and the Roots of American Environmentalism*. New York: Viking Penguin 2006

Sáenz de la Calzada, Carlos, et al. "Homenaje a Alejandro de Humboldt a los 200 años de su nacimiento," 11–116. In *Anuario de geografía*. Mexico City: UNAM, Año IX 1969

Sahagún, Bernardino de. *Florentine Codex: General History of the Things of New Spain, Book 12: The Conquest of Mexico* [1585], translated by Arthur J.O. Anderson and Charles E. Dibble. Salt Lake City: University of Utah Press 1955

Said, Edward. *Orientalism*. New York: Pantheon 1978

Salas, Guillermo P. "Estudios mineros y mineralógicos: Alejandro de Humboldt en México." In *Humboldt en México*, edited by Leopoldo Zea and Carlos Magallón, 121–32. UNAM 1999

Sánchez-Albornoz, Nicolás. "The Population of Colonial Spanish America." In *The Cambridge History of Latin America: Colonial Latin America*, vol. 2, edited by Leslie Bethell, 3–35. Cambridge: Cambridge University Press 1984

Sanders, William T., and Barbara J. Price. *Mesoamerica: The Evolution of a Civilization*. New York: Random House 1968

Sarmiento, Domingo F. *Civilization and Barbarism*. New York: Collier 1961 [original Spanish, 1868]

Secor, R.J. *Mexico's Volcanoes: A Climbing Guide*. Seattle: The Mountaineers 1981

Sluyter, Andrew. "Humboldt's Mexican Texts and Landscapes." *Geographical Review* 96 (2006): 361–81

Smith, Adam. *The Wealth of Nations*. London: 1776

Stevens-Middleton, Rayfred Lionel. "La obra de Alexander von Humboldt en México: Fundamento de la geografía moderna." *Boletin de la Sociedad Mexicana de Geografía y Estadística* 81, no. 2 (March–April 1956)

Strebel, Hermann. *Die Ruinen von Cempoallan im Staate Veracruz, Mexiko*. Hamburg: 1883.

Sweet, Paul R. *Wilhelm von Humboldt: A Biography*. Vol. 1: *1767–1808*; and vol. 2: *1808–1835*. Columbus: Ohio State University Press 1978 and 1980

Todd, A.C. *The Search for Silver: Cornish Miners in Mexico, 1824–1947*. Padstow, Cornwall: Lodenek Press 1977

Trabulse, Elías. "El destino de un manuscrito." In Alejandro de Humboldt, *Las tablas geográficas políticas del reino de Nueva España*, edited by Charles Minguet and Jaime Labastida, 11–22. Mexico City: Siglo XXI, n.d. (2003?)

– "Introducción." In Alejandro de Humboldt, *Atlas geográfico y físico del reino de la Nueva España*, edited by Charles Minguet and Jaime Labastida, 9–25. Mexico City: Siglo XXI 2003

Tutino, John. *From Insurrection to Revolution in Mexico: Social Bases of Agrarian Violence, 1750–1940*. Princeton: Princeton University Press 1986

Urquijo Torres, Pedro Sergio. *Humboldt y el Jorullo: Historia de una exploración*. Mexico City: UNAM 2010

Villalobos Velazquez, Rosario. *British Immigrants in the Mining Districts of Real del Monte and Pachuca, 1827–1947: An Approach to Daily Life*. Pachuca: Archivo Historico y Museo de Minería, n.d.

Vivó Escoto, Jorge A., ed. *Ensayos sobre Humboldt*. Mexico City: UNAM 1962

Walls, Laura Dassaw. "The Napoleon of Science: Alexander von Humboldt in Antebellum America. *Nineteenth-Century Contexts* 14 (1990): 71–98. Reprinted in *Nineteenth Century Literature Criticism*, vol. 170, edited by Russel Whitaker, 145–56. Oklahoma City: Thomson Gale 2006

– *The Passage to Cosmos: Alexander von Humboldt and the Shaping of America*. Chicago: University of Chicago Press 2009

Whitaker, Arthur P., ed. *Latin America and the Enlightenment*. Ithaca: Cornell University Press 1958

– "Alexander von Humboldt and Spanish America." *Proceedings of the American Philosophical Society* 104 (15 June 1964): 317–22

Wilson, Jason. "Introduction." In *Alexander von Humboldt: Personal Narrative of a Journey to the Equinoctial Regions of the New Continent*, abridged and translated by Jason Wilson. London: Penguin Books 1995 [first published 1814–25 as *Relation historique du voyage aux régions équinoxiales du nouveau continent*]

Wolfe, Bertram. *Diego Rivera: His Life and Times*. New York: Knopf 1939

Wulf, Andrea. *The Invention of Nature: Alexander von Humboldt's New World*. New York: Knopf 2015

Zantop, Susanne. *Colonial Fantasies: Conquest, Family, and Nation in Precolonial Germany, 1770–1870*. Durham: Duke University Press 1997

Index

Abad y Queipo, Manuel, 26
Acapantzingo, 58
Acapulco: and Manila Galleon trade, 4–6; in pre-Columbian days, 6–7; modern-day transformation in, 7–10; piracy in, 7
Actopan valley, 105
acute mountain sickness, 106
ADM (*Artes de México*), vvii
African Association, xxxiv
Agassiz, Louis, xlvi, 33
agriculture, 27, 29, 56, 62, 65–8
Aguilar, Héctor, 47–50
AH. *See* Humboldt, Alexander von
AKR (Andrea Kettenmann, *Rivera*), vii
Alamán, Lucas, xxix, 26–8, 109, 113, 121, 133–4, 200–1
Alaska, xlii, 26, 50
alcalde, 102, 104
Aldrich, Robert, *Colonialism and Homosexuality*, xlvii, 43
Alhóndiga de Granaditas, 120
Alzate y Ramírez, José Antonio de, 54, 91
America, xlii, xlv, 15, 27, 33, 37, 39 41, 44, 46, 51, 59, 80, 109, 145, 149, 187, 193, 196, 199–202. *See also* Latin America; United States of America
American Philosophical Society, 202
Amparo Museum, Puebla, 160
Anáhuac, 62, 64, 67
Anahuacalli Museum, Coyoacán, 17–18
Anderson, Elizabeth, and Sherwood Anderson, 40, 43

Anthropology Museum, Mexico City, 83, 93
Anthropology Museum, Xalapa, 172
APV (*Atlas del Patrimonio Natural*), vii
Arago, François, xlvi–xlix
Archive, Mexican National, 27, 81
Art Academy of San Carlos, Mexico City, xliii, 49, 78
Asia, 4–5, 29, 77
Aspects of Nature, 144
ATG (*Atlas geográfico y físico del Reino de la Nueva España*), vii, 209
Australia, xxxvii–xxxix, 110, 206
Aztecs, 6, 25, 56, 80, 87–8, 161, 165

Bacon, Francis, 20, 96
Balmis, Dr Francisco Javier de, 31, 193–4
Baroque Mexico, 36–7, 73, 79–80, 87, 122, 159
basalt formations, 103, 112–13
Basich, Antonio Castellanos, 83
Baudin, Captain Nicolas, xxxvi–xxxix, 4, 206
Berlin, xlvi, xlix, 74
Berlin State Library, 211
black legend, xli, 206
Bodega y Quadra, Juan Francisco, xxiv, 91
Bogotá, xliii, 74
Bolívar, Simón, xxx, xxxv, xlvii
Bonaparte, Josephine, xxxv
Bonaparte, Napoleon, xxxv–xxxvii, 26, 31
Bonpland, Aimé: ascends almost to

summit of Mt Chimborazo with
AH, 145; ascends El Jorullo volcano
with AH, 137; biography of, 213;
collects and tabulates plants, xxvii;
French botanist, xxxv; faithful
travelling companion of AH, xxi,
xliii
Borda, José de la (*also called* Joseph
de Laborde), 34–6, 40–1, 57
Borda y Verduga, Manuel de la, 57
Bourbons, Spanish: AH's ambiguous
attitude to their reforms, 26, 28, 30,
72; economic reforms in New
Spain, 62–3, 65; mining reforms,
126, 131; motivation for sponsoring
AH's travels, xxxix; sponsor small-
pox vaccination campaign in their
colonies, 193
Brading, David, xxv, 26
Brady, Robert, 59
Brazil, 26, 77, 196–7
British navy, xxxvii, xxxix
Buchan, John, 110–12
Buffon, Georges-Louis Leclerc,
Comte de, xxxviii, 206
Bustamante, Anastasio, 27
Bustamante, Carlos María de, 28
Bustamante, José Alejandro, 101
Byron, Lord: *Don Juan*, 204–5

Cabrera, Miguel, 37
Cádiz, xliii, 27, 30–1, 72, 78, 133, 186
Calderón de la Barca, Frances (Fan-
ny), *Life in Mexico*, 112–13
Calles, Plutarco Elías, 42
Camborne, 110, 114
camels, 171, 203
Campe, Joachim Heinrich, xxxii
Capuchins, 136
Caracas, 5, 32
Cárdenas, Lázaro, 81, 106

Carpentier, Alejo, *Tientos y diferen-
cias*, xxx
Cartwright, Lois (Aguilar), 47
Castillo, Antonio, and Reveriano
Castillo, 48–9
Cayetano, El, Church, 121–2
CEH (Fundación Carlos Slim, *Centro
Histórico, 10 Años de Revital-
ización*), vii
ceramics, 160–1
Cervantes Festival, 122
Chapultepec Castle, 80–1
Chapultepec Hill, 75
Charles III, xli, 30, 95, 131
Charles IV, xvi, xxxviii, xli–xlii, 7,
30–1, 75, 78, 95, 131, 199
Chilpancingo, 19–20, 22
Chimborazo, Mount, xxx–xxxi, vlix,
145
China, 5
chinampas system, 65, 165, 176
China Poblana, La, 162
Cholula pyramid, 157, 163
Chomsky, Noam, xlviii
Church, Frederic Edwin, xxxi
Churriguera, Don José de, 37
Clavigero, Francisco S., *Historia
Antigua de México*, 91–2
Clement, Jennifer, 24
climate, 53, 63, 106, 149, 171, 183, 207
Coatlicue ("Serpent Skirt"), 90, 92
codices, 90–2
Cofre de Perote Volcano (Nauhcam-
patépetl), "Four-Sided Mountain,"
143–5, 169, 172
colonialism, xvii, 62, 105
Condamine, Charles-Marie de la, xli
Conservative Party in Mexico, 27
Cook, Sherburne F., and Woodrow
Borah, 167
Cordry, Donald, 43

Cornwall, 110, 112, 114
Cortés, Hernán, 7, 27, 54, 56
Cosmos (also called *Kosmos*), xxviii, l, 33
Counts of Regla. *See* Romero de T errenos, Pedro
"Court of Labor," 12–13
Covarrubias, Miguel, 40–1, 48
Covarrubias, Rosa, 48
Coyoacán, 11, 17–18
Cruz, Sor Juana Inés de la, 152
cultural representations of mountains, 151–4
curare, xxviii
Cutter, Elizabeth Reeve (Morrow), 42

Darwin, Charles, xxx–xxxi, 207
Deep Drainage System (Drenaje Profundo), 165
demography, 62, 164–8
Detroit Art Institute, 16
devil's hand tree (*Chiranthodendron pentadactylon*), 139
Drake, Sir Francis, 7, 188
drug cartels, 8, 24
Dubuque, Iowa, li
Dunn, Mary, 210

East Germany (DDR), 198
Echevarría, Atanasio, xliii
ecology, 61–2
economics, 65–6
education, higher, 84, 94–7
Elhuyar, Fausto de, xliii
Encero Hacienda (originally El Lencero), 111, 169, 172–3
Enlightenment, xxxiv, xli, 26, 65–6, 87, 167, 202
Epelde, Ramón, 137

Faak, Margot, xvi, 211

Faulkner, William, 40
Ferdinand VII, 31
Fine Arts Academy of, Mexico City, 75, 94
Finley, Dr Carlos, 196
Florida Hacienda, La, 44
Ford, Edsel, and Henry Ford, 16
Forrell, Baron Philippe de, xxxviii
Forster, George, and Reinhold Forster, xxxii, xxxiv
France, xxxvi–xxxix, xlv, 14, 30, 34, 65, 153, 163, 166, 186, 195
Franklin, Benjamin, xxxv
Fraustros mine, 117
Franz Mayer Museum, Mexico City, 51
Frederick William III, xlvi
Frederick William IV, xlix
Free Royal Mining School at Steben, xxv, 123
Freiberg mining academy, xxxiv, xliii, 78, 95, 117, 125
Freiesleben, Karl, xlv

Gaceta de literatura, 54
Gallatin, Albert, 202
García Márquez, Gabriel, xxx, xlvii
Gay-Lussac, Joseph Louis, xlvi
Gazeta de México, 186
Germany, xvii, xxv, xxxiv–xxxv, xlv, xlvi–xlix, 12, 123–4, 163, 186, 198–9
Godoy, Manuel, xli, 30–1
Goethe, Johann Wolfgang von, xxxv, xlvi
Gorgas, Dr William Crawford, 196
Göttingen University, xxxiv
Greece, 40, 87, 205
Grutas de Cacahuamilpa National Park, 38
Guanajuato, 70, 109, 116–22
Guanajuato University, 120

guano, xxviii, xlvi
Guerrero, State of, 19–24
Guerrero, Xavier, 13
Gulf of Mexico Lowlands, 172, 175–8

Haiti, 187
Havana, 196
HCU (Jaime Labastida, ed., *Humboldt, ciudadano universal*), vii
Herz, Henriette (*née* de Lemos), and Marcus Herz, xxxv
Hidalgo, Father Miguel, 23, 25, 27
Hidalgo, State of, 106–7, 174
Hildebrandt, Charlotte, xlviii
Hollywood, 8, 51
hornos, 137
Huacana, La, 147
Huasca de Ocampo, 107, 112
Huasca River valley, 107
Huguenots, xxxiii
Humboldt, Alexander Georg von, xxxiii
Humboldt, Alexander von: admirers and detractors of, xxviii–xxxi; agriculture and, 177; alternative destinations for, xxxvi–xxxviii; arts and culture and, 84–90; botany, on, xxvii, xxviii; calendrics and astronomy, on, 92–3; clergy, on, 70–1; colonial rule in New Spain, on, 25–9; crafts and manufacturing, on, 71–3; critique of Catholicism, 36; death of, l–li; demography, on, 166–8; early years of, xxxiii–xxxv; ecology, on, 61–5; economic history, on, 65–6; Europocentric views of, 175–6; health and medicine, on, 182–7; higher learning, on, 94–7; humanities, on the, xxiii; indigenous peoples' love of colour, 22, 74–5; labour conditions in the mines, on, 127–31; Latin America

and, xxii–xxiii, 33; legacy of, 198–9, 206–8; life in Berlin, xlix–l; life in Paris, xlv–xlvi; magnetism, on, xxvi; mining, on, 103, 117–19, 123–7; mountain climbing, and, 136–9, 144–5; negotiations with Spanish Crown, xxxviii–xl; population density, on, 104; poverty, on, 76; pre-Columbian history, and, 91–2; preparations for travel, xxxv–xxxvi; privacy and sexuality of, xlvii–xlix; publication of *Cosmos*, l; scientific goals of, 20; scientific instruments and, 20–1; scientific precursors of, xl–xliv; slavery, on, 32; transportation, on, 21, 104, 170–1; travels in South America, xliv–xlv; travels in the Russian Empire, 1; United States, and, 32–3; urban architecture, on, 74–5; value of Mexican mines, on, 131–4; water issues, on, 164–6
Humboldt, South Dakota, xvii
Humboldt, Wilhelm, xxxiii, xlvii–xlix
Humboldt House, Taxco, 36
Humboldtian Medicine, 186
Humboldt University, xxxiii
Hume, David, 66
Hutton, Barbara, 59–60

Iberia, xxiii, xxxix, xli, l, 25–6, 28, 77
Iguala, 24
ilustrados, 26
immigration to Mexico, 29, 110
INAH (National Institute of Anthropology and History), 55, 58
India, xxxvii, 162
Indian Ocean, xxxviii, 4, 195
Indian Removal Bills of 1830, 202
indigenismo, 12
indigo, 137

isobars, xxvi, 20
isotherms, xxvi, 20
Italy, xxix, xlix, 40, 152, 163, 195, 205
Iturriaga de la Fuente, José, xxix,
    199–200
Iturrigaray, José de, 30–1, 173
Iztaccíhuatl Volcano ("White Wom-
    an"), 103, 143–6, 148–9, 151–3

Jackson, Andrew, 202
Jardin des Plantes, Paris, 207
Jefferson, Thomas, xx, 201–2
Jenner, Edward, 192–3
Jenson, George, 46
Jesuits, 79–80, 91, 102, 118, 120, 137, 159
jewellery, 5, 37, 39, 43–4, 47–51
Jews, xxxiv–xxxv
Jorullo, El, Volcano, 135–8, 142–3, 147
Juárez, Benito, xxix, 189, 199
Jussieu, Antoine-Laurent, xxxvii

Kahlo, Frida, 17–18, 59, 163
Kant, Immanuel, xxxv, 204
Koch, Robert, 186
Krauze, Enrique, xxiii, xxix, 202–3
Kutzinski, Vera M., 211

Landívar, Rafael, 137
Las Casas, Bartolomé de, 168
Latin America, xvii, xxii, xxx, xlix, 29,
    33
Ledesma, Enrique, 49–50
Leitner, Ulrike, 211
León-Portilla, Miguel, 206
León y Gama, Antonio, 92–3
Lessing, Gotthold Ephraim, xxxv
Liebig, Justus von, xlvi
Lindbergh, Anne Morrow, and
    Charles A. Lindbergh, 42
Lino Guerra, Manuel, 105
London, 91–2, 115, 133–4
Lowry, Malcolm, 58

Lyell, Sir Charles, xxx

Macgillivray, William, xxx
Machete, El, 14
Macintosh, Charles Rennie, 52
Macuiltépetl Ecological Park, 172
Madrid, xxxviii, xlii–xliii, 31, 78, 130
Magdalena River valley, xliii
magnetism, xxii, xxvi, 21, 181, 207
maize, 22, 69–70
Malaspina, Alejandro, xlii, 91
Malinche, La, Volcano, 144, 149
Malmstrom, Vincent H., xiii, 178–81
Malthus, Thomas Robert, 167
Manila Galleon, xxi, 47, 162
manufacturing, 29, 71–2, 163
Martínez, Enrico, 164
mathematics, 88, 95–6
Maximilian, Emperor, 58, 80
Mayas, 179–80
Mendelssohn, Felix, and Moses
    Mendelssohn, xxxv
mercantilism, 65
Mérida (also called Valladolid), 135–
    6, 139–40
merchants, 44, 74, 170–1, 183, 188
Mesoamerican culture, xiii, xxii,
    54–5, 87–8, 135, 176–80, 206
Metropolitan Museum of Art, New
    York, 41
Mexican-American War of 1846, 27,
    187
Mexican Communist Party (MCPP),
    13–14
Mexican Revolution of 1910, 23, 58,
    114
Mexico: governance of, 28; Hum-
    boldt's admiration for, xvi; Hum-
    boldt's plans to retire to Mexico, l;
    Humboldt's suggestions for reform
    in Mexico, xxiii; mining in Mexico's
    future, xxiv, xxix

Mexico City: appearance of, 74–8; as
  "City of Palaces," xxii; Manila
  Galleon and, 6; modernity and,
  77–8
Mezcala River, 21–2
Michoacán, xxvi, 26, 49, 63, 109, 135–
  6, 140, 142, 147
Minguet, Charles, 18, 26
Miranda, José, 204
militia, 118, 170
mining school. *See* Free Royal Min-
  ing School at Steben
Mocambo, 111, 189
Moctezuma (*also called* Montezu-
  ma), 75–6, 80, 177
mole poblano, 160–2
Montúfar, Carlos de, xxi, xliv, 3, 169
Mora, José Luis, 199
Morelos, State of, 23, 41, 56, 58, 151,
  174
Morelos y Pavón, José María, 7, 23,
  56, 59, 139
Moreno, Mario (*also called* Cantin-
  flas), 59
Morley, Sylvanus, 181
Morrill, Penny, 46–7
Morrow, Dwight, 41–2, 59
mosquitoes, xxviii, xlviii, 22, 182,
  195–6
Moziño, José Mariano, xlii–xliii
Muñoz, Juan Bautista, xxxix
Murillo, Gerardo ("Dr Atl"), 152–3
Mutis, José Celestino, xliii

Nahuatl, 3, 18, 54, 56, 142, 151, 161, 174,
  179, 190
Napoleonic invasion, xli
National Institute of France, xxxix
Natural History, Museum of, Mexico
  City, 27
Natural Science, Museum of,
  Madrid, xli

natural selection, 207
Navarrete, Artemio, 43
Nazi Germany, 198
Nevado de Colima Volcano, 142–3,
  150
Nevado de Toluca Volcano (Xinanté-
  catl, "The Naked Lord"), 64, 138,
  143, 148
New Spain, xxvii, xlii–xliii, 6–7, 19,
  21, 25, 28, 30–2, 35, 37, 62–3, 68, 70,
  72, 75, 77, 95–6, 103, 120, 125, 127, 131,
  159, 165–6, 168, 190, 193–4, 201, 206.
  See also Mexico
New York Times, 33
Niños Héroes, 80
Nishizawa, Luis, 154
Nootka Sound, xxiv, 91
Nuestra Señora de los Remedios
  Church, 157

Obregón y Alcocer, Antonio de,
  Count of Valenciana, 117–18
O'Gorman, Juan, 17, 154
O'Keeffe, Georgia, 48
Olmecs, 50, 54, 172, 179–81
Olmedo Patiño, Dolores, 8–9, 17, 49
Ordaz, Diego de, 145
Orellana, Margarita de, 151
Oroszco, José, 11, 17
Ortega y Medina, Juan A., xxix,
  201–4
Ortiz de Ayala, Tadeo, 199
Otero, Pedro Luciano de, 117–18
Ouweneel, Arij, 61–4
Owen, Robert, 123

Pachuca, xxiv, 34, 101–3, 105–10, 112,
  114–15, 124
Pacific Ocean, xxxviii–xxxix, xlv, 3–4,
  7–8, 21, 135, 142, 180, 195
Padilla, Juan Gutiérrez de, 159
Palacio de Cortés, 56, 59

Palacio de Minería, 78 81
Palafox y Mendoza, Juan de, 159–61
Palifoxiana Library, 159
Panama Canal, 196
Pánuco River, 165, 203
Paraguay, xxxv
Paricutín Volcano, 142–3, 147–8,
    153–4
Paris, xxvi, xxxv–xxxvii, xlv–xlvii, 74,
    133
Pasteur, Louis, 186
pasties (*pastes*), 115
Pátzcuaro, 136, 140, 147
Pátzcuaro Lake, 135, 140
Pavón, José Antonio, xlii
PE. See *Political Essay on the King-
    dom of New Spain*
Pérez y Comoto, Florencio, 186
Peru, xvii, xxxix, xlv, 35, 104, 127, 194
Pestalozzi, Johann Heinrich, 123
Philadelphia, xvii, 195
Philippines, xl, 4–7, 194, 206
physiocrats, 65–7
Pichardo, José Antonio, 92
Pico de Orizaba Volcano (Cit-
    laltépetl, "Star Mountain"), 142,
    144–5, 149, 152, 169–72, 179
Pineda y Ramírez, Antonio, 57
piracy, 7, 188
Poldark mine, 110
political economy, xxii–xxiii, xxxiv,
    62
*Political Essay on the Kingdom of
    New Spain*, xv–xvi, xxv, xliii, 26, 28,
    31, 66, 123, 131–2, 157, 187, 206
pollution, 62, 77–8, 128, 130
Popocatépetl Volcano ("Smoking
    Mountain"), 103, 142–4
Popular Arts Museum, Pátzcuaro, 140
population density, 62, 65
Portugal, 30, 77, 159
Pratt, Mary Louise, xxviii, 175, 205

pre Hispanic art and culture, xxi,
    xxiii, 14, 84–90
Prescott, William H., xxiii
Privada Humboldt, 57
Privada Rufino Tamayo, 57
professional soccer, 115
Prussia, xxv, xxxiii, xxxvi, xlvi, xlix,
    26, 123, 193, 198
Puebla (de los Angeles), 149, 151,
    157–63, 169
pueblo mágico, 114
Puente de Ixtla, 53–4
pulque, 106–7
pyramids, 157, 163, 178–9

Quarterly Review, 91
Querétaro, 6, 69, 71, 75, 101, 140
Quetzalcóatl, 55
Quiñones Keber, Eloise, 88, 93
Quiroga, Vasco de, 136, 140–1
Quito, xli, xliv

Real del Monte, 101–3, 107, 110, 112–15
Real del Monte Company, 109, 114
Reed, Walter, 196
restaurants, 42, 115, 163, 189
"Reveri," 49
Revillagigedo, Count of, xlii, 74, 93,
    166
Richards, John, 61, 130
Río, Andrés del, xliii, 78
Rivera, Diego: comparisons with AH,
    11; innovation and science, 16–17;
    legacy of, 17–18; love of pre-His-
    panic art, 14–15, revolutionary ide-
    ology of, 12–14
Robertson, William S., 92
Rockefeller, John D., and Nelson
    Rockefeller, 16–17
Romanticism, xxxiv, 66
Romero de Terrenos, Pedro (Count
    of Regla), 101–2

Rousseau, Jean-Jacques, 167
Royal Botanical Garden, Madrid, xli–xliii
Royal Botanical Garden, Mexico, xlii
royal mint in Mexico City, 72, 75
Royal Scientific Expedition for New Spain (RSE), xliii
Ruiz, Froylan, 154
Ruiz, Hipólito, xlii
Ruiz de Texada, Manuel, 204
Ruiz Saucedo, Rafael, 49
Rul, Diego, 117–18
Rule, Francis, 113–14
Rupke, Nicolaas A., 186, 198
Russia, l

Sáenz, Moisés, 42
Sahagún, Bernardino de, 191
Said, Edward, 205
Salamanca University, 101
Salas de Broner, Estefania, 177
Sanders, William T., and Barbara J. Price, 167
San Diego Church, 122
San Diego Fort, 7
San Felipe Neri Church (also called La Profesa, "the professed house"), 79, 92
San Gabriel de Barrera Hacienda, 119
San Juan Bautista Hacienda, 34, 38
San Juan de Ulúa Fort, 188–9
San Miguel Regla, 102, 104, 107–8
San Ramón mine, 119
Santa Anna, Antonio López de, xxix, 173, 199
Santa Clara Dairy, 107
Santa Clara del Cobre, 141
Santa María Regla Hacienda, 102, 108
Santa Prisca Cathedral, 35, 37, 51
Sarmiento, Domingo F., xxx
Schiller, Friedrich, xxxiv
Schoell, F., xvi

School of Mines, Mexico City, 26, 72, 75, 78, 94–5, 97, 120, 127, 133
science, xxvi, xxxiv, xxxvii–xliii, xlvii, xlix, 66, 95, 97
Scott, Winfield, 187
Scribner's Magazine, 40
Sessé, Martin de, xlii
Siemens, 163
Sierra de Chichinautzin, 53, 174
Sierra de Santa Rosa, 116
Sierra Madre del Sur, 19–20
Sierra Madre Occidental, 142
Sierra Madre Oriental, 142, 171, 176, 178
silver mining, xxi, xxiv, xxxv, 5, 34–7, 67, 101, 103, 107, 109–10, 114, 116, 118–21
Siqueiros, David, 11–12, 14, 41–2
slavery, 16, 29–30, 33, 162
Sluyter, Andrew, 170–1
smallpox (Variola major), 190–4
Smith, Adam, 26, 66, 199, 204
South America, xxvii, xxxiii, xxxv, xli–xlii, xlviii, 6, 8, 19, 21–2, 110 144, 157, 163, 194. See also Latin America
Spain, xxxviii, xli, xlii, 4–6, 14, 29–31, 34–5, 78, 101, 117–18, 159–60, 186
Spanish consul, 170
Spratling, William: as architect and writer, 39–40; commercial setbacks, 45–6; as cultural broker between Mexicans and Americans, 41–3; early years, 39; first visits Mexico, 40; later years, 50–2; sexual orientation of, 43; and silver jewellery, 41, 43–5
Stalin, Joseph, 14
Stevens-Middleton, Rayfred Lionel, 203
St Petersburg, 207
Strebel, Hermann, 178
Sucesores de William Spratling, 51

Sun Stone (*also called* Aztec Calendar), 89, 92–3

Tajín, El, xii, 172, 178–9, 181
Talavera pottery, 160–1
Taller Borda, 47–50
Taller de las Delicias, 43–4
Tamayo, Rufino, 50, 57, 59
Tarascan Indians (*also called* Purépecha), xxvi, 135–6, 140–1
Taxco, 23, 34–52, 55, 57, 103, 124, 199
Taylor, John, 109–10
Teatro Juárez, 122
Tegel, xvi, xxxiii, l
Teotihuacán, 54–5, 87, 178, 180
Texcoco Lake, 64, 75, 165, 176
Theiler, Max, 197
Thompson, Sir John Eric Sydney, 180
Tlaxcala, 72, 106, 144, 149, 158
Tolsá, Manuel, 75, 78–9
Toltecs, 54, 87–8, 135, 178
Totonacs, 172, 176–9
Trabulse, Elías, 206
Trans-Mexican Volcanic Belt, xxvii, 105–6
Trevithick, Richard, 110
Tzintzuntzan, 140

Ulloa, Antonio de, xli
Ulrich, Alberto, Consuelo, and Violante, 51
UNAM (Universidad Nacional Autónoma de México), xxix, 12, 37, 78
United Nations Human Development Index, 24
United States of America, xxix, 8, 24, 27, 33, 39, 42–4, 70, 94, 107, 147, 167, 197, 199–202
United States Smelting, Refining and Mining Company, 114
University of Berlin, xlix
UNV (Frank Holl, ed., *Los viajes de Humboldt: Una nueva visión del mundo*), vii
Urals, 1
Uruapan, 147

vaccination, 30, 190–4, 197
Valdés, José Luis Lara, 119
Valenciana, La, 30, 63, 116–18, 121–2, 128–9
Valley of Mexico, 30, 54, 64–5, 87, 151, 165, 174
Vasconcelos, José, 12
VDC (AH, *Vues des Cordillères et monuments des peuples Indigènes de l'Amérique*), vii, xxxi, 54, 84, 87–8
Velásquez de Léon, Joaquín Luciano, 96
Veracruz, 106, 111, 149, 157–8, 163, 169–70, 176–8, 181–9
Veracruz, State of, 171–2
Veracruzana University, 172
Veta Vizcaína, 101
Vidaurreta, Valentín, 47, 49
Virgin Mary, 152, 162
Vivó Escoto, Jorge A., ed., *Ensayos sobre Humboldt*, xvi
volcanoes of Mexico, 142–5, 150–4
Volkswagen de México, 163

Washington, DC, xvii, 202
water issues, 164–6
Weimar Republic, 198
Werner, Abraham Gottlieb, xxxiv
Wildenow, Karl Ludwig, xlvviii
Wilson, Jason, xlvii
Wright, Frank Lloyd, 18
Wulf, Andrea, *The Invention of Nature: Alexander von Humboldt's New World*, xv, 207

Xalapa, xxvii, xxviii, 31, 63, 111, 169–73, 176, 183

Xalapa University, 172
Ximeno y Planes, Rafael, 81
Xochicalco, 54–6, 87, 91
Xochimilco, 65, 165

yellow fever, 111, 169–70, 177, 182–7,
   190, 194–7

Zapata, Emiliano, 23, 58–9
Zavala, Lorenzo de, 28
Zempoala (*also called* Cempoala),
   172, 174–81
Zempoala Lake, 174
Zúñiga, Juana de, 56